EUROPEAN EMPLOYMENT
AND
INDUSTRIAL RELATIONS GLOSSARY:
SPAIN

EUROPEAN FOUNDATION
FOR THE IMPROVEMENT OF LIVING AND
WORKING CONDITIONS

EUROPEAN EMPLOYMENT AND INDUSTRIAL RELATIONS GLOSSARY: SPAIN

BY

ANTONIO MARTIN VALVERDE

SWEET AND MAXWELL
OFFICE FOR OFFICIAL PUBLICATIONS OF
THE EUROPEAN COMMUNITIES
1991

Published in 1991 by
Sweet and Maxwell Limited of
South Quay Plaza, 183 Marsh Wall, London E14
and
Office for Official Publications of the European Community
2 rue Mercier, L-2985 Luxembourg

Typeset by Printset and Design Ltd., Dublin
Printed in Great Britain by
BPCC Hazell Books Ltd.,
Aylesbury, Bucks.
Member of BPCC Ltd.

British Cataloguing in Publication Data

A catalogue record for this book is
available from the British Library

Sweet and Maxwell, South Quay Plaza, London E14
ISBN 0421-44840-7

Office for Official Publications of the European Communities,
2 rue Mercier, L-2985 Luxembourg
ISBN 92-826-2602-4
Catalogue Number SY-70-91-003-EN-C

Publication No. EF/91/10/EN of the European Foundation for the
Improvement of Living and Working Conditions,
Loughlinstown House, Shankill, Co. Dublin, Ireland.

General Editor of the European Employment and Industrial
Relations Glossary Series

TIZIANO TREU
Professor of Labour Law
Catholic University of Milan

Revising Editor for the English language volumes

MICHAEL TERRY
Senior Lecturer in Industrial Relations
University of Warwick

Project Manager

HUBERT KRIEGER
Research Manager
European Foundation for the Improvement of Living
and Working Conditions, Dublin

The present volume is an edited translation of an original Spanish
text prepared for the European Foundation for the Improvement
of Living and Working Conditions, Dublin

under the editorship of

ANTONIO MARTIN VALVERDE
Professor of Labour Law
University of Seville

Advisory Committee

**MANUEL ALCAIDE
CASTRO**
Professor of Industrial
Economics
University of Seville

FEDERICO DURAN LOPEZ
Professor of Labour Law
University of Cordoba

**SALVADOR DEL REY
GUANTER**
Professor of Labour Law
University of Seville

FERMIN RODRIGUEZ-SANUDO
Professor of Labour Law
University of Seville

with contributions from

JOAQUIN GARCIA MURCIA
Professor of Labour Law
University of Oviedo

STRUCTURE OF THE WORK

There are companion volumes of the Glossary (both national and international editions) already published for:

Country	National Team Leader
United Kingdom	Michael Terry, Warwick University
Italy	Tiziano Treu, Fondazione Regionale Pietro Seveso, Milan

Further volumes to appear will be:

France	Antoine Lyon-Caen
Germany	Manfred Weiss
Belgium	Roger Blanpain
Greece	Yota Kravaritou-Manitakis
Portugal	Mario Pinto
Ireland	
Denmark	
Holland	
Luxembourg	

TABLE OF CONTENTS

USER'S GUIDE

This Guide is designed to help readers use the Glossary by providing an explanation of the contents and some of the conventions adopted.

This volume of the Glossary contains the following sections:

1. *List of Abbreviations*

This list comprises all the principal abbreviations used in the text.

2. *Foreword*

Written by the Director and Deputy Director of the European Foundation, the Foreword sets out the Foundation's aims in publishing this series of Glossaries.

3. *Preface*

A Preface to the series has been prepared by Professor Tiziano Treu in his capacity as Co-ordinating Editor. It serves as a background introduction to the Glossaries, explaining the origination of the material and the method of compilation and translation.

4. *List of Entries*

For cross-referencing purposes, the entries have been listed alphabetically in both Spanish and English, with their relevant number in the text.

5. *Introduction*

The introduction provides a commentary and analysis of national characteristics, and highlights particular features giving an historical perspective to the background information.

6. *Glossary*

All the main entries are numbered and appear in **BOLD** upper case. They are listed alphabetically in Spanish with appropriate English translations.

Cross-references are indicated in the text by *e.g.* ''see'', ''see also'', etc., and also appear in **bold** upper and lower case.

Each letter of the alphabet starts on a new page. The running heads refer to the first and last main entry to appear on each double page.

7. *Tables*

A selection of tables is included showing employment trends and other statistical factors.

8. *Bibliography*

A selective Bibliography of suggested further reading and source material has been compiled by the editorial team for each volume. The titles of all references appear in Spanish, but other details have been translated where appropriate.

9. *Index*

The Index comprises two parts; an alphabetical index in English, followed by an alphabetical index in Spanish.

All Index entries refer to the numbers of the definitions in the Glossary text.

LIST OF ABBREVIATIONS

ABI	National Multi-Industry Basic Agreement (1979)
AEB	Spanish Banking Association
AES	Economic and Social Agreement (1984)
AFE	Spanish Footballers' Association
AMI	National Multi-Industry Framework Agreement (1980/1981)
ANE	National Employment Agreement (1981)
CC.OO.	Trade-Union Confederation of Workers' Commissions
CEIM	Madrid Confederation of Industrial Enterprises
CEOE	Spanish Confederation of Employers' Organizations
CEPYME	Spanish Confederation of Small and Medium-Sized Enterprises
CES	European Trade-Union Confederation (ETUC)
CGT	General Confederation of Labour
CIOSL	International Confederation of Free Trade Unions (ICFTU)
CISC	International Federation of Christian Trade Unions (IFCTU)
CMT	World Confederation of Labour (WCL)
CNT	National Confederation of Labour
CONFEMETAL	Spanish Confederation of Metalworking Employers' Organizations
CSE	European Social Charter
CSIF	Independent Trade Union Confederation of Public Servants
DLRT	Labour Relations Decree-Law (1977)
ELA-STV	Basque Workers' Solidarity
EPA	Survey of the Working Population (quarterly INE survey)
ET	Workers' Statute (1980)
FAI	Iberian Anarchist Federation
FOGASA	Wages Guarantee Fund
FSE	European Social Fund (ESF)
FSM	World Federation of Trade Unions (WFTU)
FTN	Promotion of National Labour (Catalonian employers' confederation)
ILE	local employment schemes
ILT	temporary incapacity for work/sickness absence
INE	National Institute of Statistics
INEM	National Institute of Employment
INP	National Institute of Social Insurance
INSALUD	National Institute of Health
INSERSO	National Institute of Social Services
INSS	National Institute of Social Security

INTG	Galician Trade Union Confederation
LAS	Trade Union Activity Act (1977)
LCT	Contracts of Employment Act (1931 & 1944)
LGSS	General Social Security Act (1974)
LISOC	Labour Offences and Sanctions Act (1988)
LOLS	Trade Union Freedom Act (1985)
LORF	Representation of Public Servants Act (1987)
LPL	Labour Procedure Act (1990)
LRL	Labour Relations Act (1976)
MLR	Recorded Movement of Labour (monthly INEM survey)
OGSH	General Ordinance on Health and Safety at Work (1971)
PCE	Communist Party of Spain
PER	Rural Employment Plan
PIB	gross domestic product (GDP)
PLAN FIP	Employment Training and Integration Plan
PSOE	Spanish Socialist Workers' Party
PYME	small and medium-sized enterprises (SMEs)
SMI	national minimum wage
UGT	General Workers' Confederation
USO	Workers' Trade Unionist Confederation

FOREWORD

The Foundation believes that social dialogue at international level should provide, for all those taking part in it, a better understanding of the different contexts — for example, legal frameworks and traditions — in which dialogue about employment and industrial relations takes place. An essential prerequisite for such improved understanding is an awareness of the precise meaning of the terms used to describe the features of industrial relations systems in each Member State of the Community. This series of glossaries sets out to provide clear explanations of terms and the context in which they are used.

The Foundation hopes that the series will be of value to a wide spectrum of users. Novices in the field of employment and industrial relations will welcome a guide to the working of the system in their own country, whilst experts will seek the distinguishing characteristics of systems operating in Member States other than their own. By providing both a national glossary for each Member State and also an "international" edition, the Foundation believes it is providing an important aid to international understanding in the complex field of employment and industrial relations.

Clive Purkiss   Eric Verborgh
Director   Deputy Director

European Foundation for the Improvement of Living and Working Conditions, Dublin

PREFACE TO THE SERIES

The idea to write a series of glossaries dealing with the industrial relations, labour markets and employment laws of the 12 EC Member States emerged gradually, out of the experience of expert academics and practitioners aware of the need to systematize and codify experiences in this important area. The development of a social dialogue, and the ever-increasing need for debate and discussion between the Member States, employers and unions, spurred by the prospect of full European economic integration in 1992, have given a fresh impetus to the need for clarity and mutual understanding in this vital subject. But these glossaries are not intended only as resources for such formal settings. Throughout Europe there are thousands of potential users of the glossaries: national and international administrators, academics and researchers, trade unionists and managers, and specialized journalists, among others. All these groups will increasingly need to communicate across borders in different languages, about a whole range of industrial relations-related topics. For them too, the need for greater understanding and clarity has become more urgent. The glossaries should become the standard tools for persons involved in meetings, formal and informal, of a whole range of interested economic and social actors.

The European Foundation for the Improvement of Living and Working Conditions immediately recognized the importance and usefulness of the proposal to compile a series of glossaries, and provided the funding for the first three: those dealing with Italy, Spain and the United Kingdom. Later, it was to agree to provide additional funding for the remaining nine states, with Belgium, the Federal Republic of Germany and France being the next three. It was agreed that the Foundation should provide resources for the translation of all the glossaries into English, for publication as a uniform series. It is now proposed to make the glossaries also available in electronic database form, which will greatly enhance the speed and flexibility with which they may be used. The glossaries for all countries are also available in their original languages, published domestically. In some cases these "domestic" glossaries are larger and longer than the English translations, since they have been designed as domestic as well as international sources of reference, and may contain material of little immediate relevance to the foreign reader.

Professor Tiziano Treu was appointed international co-ordinator, and he, in turn, worked to set up teams of experts in the first three countries, consisting of experts in all the disciplines involved in industrial relations, each team under its own co-ordinator. These teams were under instructions to provide comparable glossaries, covering the same range of topics. The intention was to produce volumes that would provide both definitions of several hundred terms of particular importance, and an insight into the relevance to the country concerned. The combined experience of all those involved in the project (academics, practitioners and others) was that simple translations of terms were insufficient, since they fail fully to communicate the substantive importance of the institutions and processes described. The products are designed to be of direct use both to the practitioner and to the academic student of the subject, so the glossaries have to be both technically correct and informed by relevant policy debate. The glossaries are intended to serve the practical needs of a diverse readership, of varying levels of knowledge and need, and to serve as an immediate reference or translation source or a starting-point for in-depth research. The audience will be a broad and diverse one; our researches have confirmed that the glossaries will be of interest to national, European and other international readers, given the worldwide interest currently expressed in European industrial relations.

Inevitably, we have had to be selective in our choice of terms. It was not the intention to produce an encyclopedia, but rather an annotated guide to key issues and concepts. In order to achieve this we sought both a degree of commonality in the terms to be covered (in order to ensure above all that the key concepts were dealt with in all the volumes) and a degree of differentiation, reflecting the national idiosyncrasies that remain important aspects of the European scene. Our descriptions have had to be less than encyclopedic; the entries do not provide all the detail with regard to specific pieces of legislation, for example. Readers who need further precision will be able to make use of the reference works cited in the concluding bibliographies.

The glossaries all share the same format. An introductory essay covers the key features of the national system: the political-economic environment, the key actors, the role of law, and the current state of labour relations. This is meant to help the average user of the glossary (it is not particularly designed for a specialist audience) and it has been written in such a way as to be understandable to an international audience, and therefore to be as clear and "candid" as possible. The main body of entries follows, and the volumes conclude with sets of tables showing trends in labour markets, collective bargaining coverage, unionization and industrial conflict, with a brief guide to further reading. Those texts which have been translated into English also contain an additional index in the original language.

Certain conventions have been adopted in the translation Wherever possible we have used English translations whose meaning is clear and which involve no specialist "jargon". But there are two other cases. First, where no English term in common usage exists and we have created our own translation. Here we have put the English term into double inverted commas, to indicate that it is not common English usage, but is simply an accurate translation. Second, in a few cases we have been unable to find a translation of less than a sentence for particular terms. Here we have left the term in the original language, and readers in English will need to read the entry to discover its meaning.

The process of writing and translating these glossaries has convinced the participants of the usefulness of the exercise. The European

Foundation has, in its usual way, sought the views of the social partners in the countries concerned, and their response has also been enthusiastic. The exercise has also revealed that beneath the superficial similarities of some terms there may lie significant differences of meaning and interpretation, but that, deeper still, lie important patterns of similarity and convergence and, above all, a keen interest in the consequences of an increasingly integrated and united Europe. We are confident that we have produced an instrument that will help forge a clearer understanding and, in its turn, a greater co-operation, in this vital area of social activity.

Acknowledgements

Many people have co-operated closely in the preparation of this series. This co-operation has been under the general direction of Hubert Krieger, the Foundation's manager for the project, and Tiziano Treu, the "rapporteur", who has acted as general editor.

The series is based on the dedicated efforts of the national teams, who have had the task of reducing formidable amounts of material to manageable proportions.

The task of editing the international (English-language) version has been particularly onerous. It is only fitting to acknowledge the exceptional contributions of Rita Inston, the reviser (of Cave Translations Ltd.), and of Michael Terry (Warwick University), who, in addition to having the main responsibility for the United Kingdom volume, has given invaluable advice on explanations in English of concepts peculiar to individual Member States. Anthony Ferner (Warwick University) made an essential contribution to the editing of the volume for Spain.

With regard to general aspects of publication, the Foundation is grateful for the co-operation of the publishers and for advice from the Office for Official Publications of the European Communities, for the services of the Commission and those of Solon Consultants (UK).

Throughout the project there has been close co-operation between the research, information and translation services of the Foundation.

Professor Tiziano Treu

NUMBERED ALPHABETICAL LIST OF ENTRIES IN SPANISH

SPANISH

ENGLISH

1. ABANDONO DE SERVICIO — "ABANDONO DE SERVICIO"
2. ABANDONO DE TRABAJO — QUITTING THE JOB
3. ABANICO SALARIAL — WAGE SPREAD
4. ABI — ABI
5. ABOGADO LABORALISTA — LABOUR LAWYER
6. ABSENTISMO — ABSENTEEISM
7. ABSORCION DE SUBIDAS SALARIALES — "ABSORPTION" OF PAY INCREASES
8. ACCESO A LOS CENTROS DE TRABAJO — ACCESS TO WORKPLACES
9. ACCIDENTE DE TRABAJO — ACCIDENT AT WORK/INDUSTRIAL ACCIDENT
10. ACCION ASISTENCIAL — SOCIAL WELFARE ACTION
11. ACCION POSITIVA — POSITIVE ACTION
12. ACCIONARIADO OBRERO — EMPLOYEE SHARE OWNERSHIP
13. ACOSO SEXUAL EN EL TRABAJO — SEXUAL HARASSMENT AT WORK
14. ACTIVIDAD SINDICAL — TRADE UNION ACTIVITY
15. ACTIVISTA SINDICAL — UNION ACTIVIST
16. ACUERDO BASICO INTERCONFEDERAL DE 1979 (ABI) — NATIONAL MULTI-INDUSTRY BASIC AGREEMENT OF 1979
17. ACUERDO ECONOMICO Y SOCIAL DE 1984 (AES) — ECONOMIC AND SOCIAL AGREEMENT OF 1984
18. ACUERDO INTERPROFESIONAL — GENERAL MULTI-INDUSTRY AGREEMENT
19. ACUERDO MARCO — FRAMEWORK AGREEMENT
20. ACUERDO MARCO INTERCONFEDERAL DE 1980 (AMI) — NATIONAL MULTI-INDUSTRY FRAMEWORK AGREEMENT OF 1980
21. ACUERDO NACIONAL DE EMPLEO DE 1981 (ANE) — NATIONAL EMPLOYMENT AGREEMENT OF 1981
22. ACUERDO SOBRE PARTICIPACION EN LA EMPRESA PUBLICA DE 1986 — AGREEMENT ON WORKERS' PARTICIPATION IN PUBLIC ENTERPRISES OF 1986
23. ACUERDOS/PACTOS EN LA FUNCION PUBLICA — PUBLIC SERVICE AGREEMENTS AND "PACTS"
24. ADHESION A UN CONVENIO COLECTIVO — ADOPTION OF A COLLECTIVE AGREEMENT
25. ADMINISTRACION DE TRABAJO — LABOUR ADMINSTRATION
26. ADMINISTRATIVO — OFFICE STAFF
27. AES — AES
28. AFILIACION SINDICAL — TRADE UNION MEMBERSHIP OR AFFILIATION
29. AGENCIA DE COLOCACION — PLACEMENT AGENCY
30. AGENTES SOCIALES — SOCIAL ACTORS
31. AJUSTE DE PLANTILLAS — STAFFING ADJUSTMENT
32. ALARGAMIENTO DEL TRABAJO — JOB ENLARGEMENT
33. AMBIENTE DE TRABAJO — WORK ENVIRONMENT
34. AMI — AMI
35. ANARCOSINDICALISMO — ANARCHO-SYNDICALISM
36. ANE — ANE
37. ANTICIPO DE SALARIOS — ADVANCE
38. ANTIGUEDAD — SENIORITY/LENGTH OF SERVICE
39. APOYO SALARIAL — WAGE SUPPORT
40. APRENDIZAJE — APPRENTICESHIP
41. ARBITRAJE — ARBITRATION
42. ARBITRAJE OBLIGATORIO — COMPULSORY ARBITRATION
43. ARRENDAMIENTO DE SERVICIOS — CONTRACT FOR SERVICES
44. ASAMBLEA — MASS MEETING
45. ASAMBLEA GENERAL — GENERAL MEETING
46. ASCENSO — PROMOTION
47. ASEDIO SEXUAL — SEXUAL HARASSMENT

211.	DESTAJO	PIECEWORK
212.	DIALOGO SOCIAL	SOCIAL DIALOGUE
213.	DIETAS	SUBSISTENCE AND TRAVEL ALLOWANCES
214.	DIRECCION DE LA EMPRESA	MANAGEMENT
215.	DIRECTOR DE PERSONAL	PERSONNEL MANAGER
216.	DISCIPLINA SINDICAL	UNION DISCIPLINE
217.	DISCRIMINACION	DISCRIMINATION
218.	DISCRIMINACION FAVORABLE O POSITIVA	POSITIVE (REVERSE) DISCRIMINATION
219.	DISCRIMINACION INDIRECTA	INDIRECT DISCRIMINATION
220.	DISMINUCION DEL RENDIMIENTO	GO-SLOW
221.	DIVISION INTERNACIONAL DEL TRABAJO	INTERNATIONAL DIVISION OF LABOUR
222.	DLRT	DLRT
223.	DUMPING SOCIAL	SOCIAL DUMPING
224.	ECONOMIA INFORMAL	INFORMAL ECONOMY
225.	ECONOMIA IRREGULAR	IRREGULAR ECONOMY
226.	ECONOMIA OCULTA	CONCEALED ECONOMY
227.	ECONOMIA SUMERGIDA	HIDDEN ECONOMY
228.	EDAD DE JUBILACION	PENSIONABLE AGE
229.	ELA-STV	ELA-STV
230.	ELECCIONES SINDICALES	UNION ELECTIONS
231.	EMIGRACION	EMIGRATION AND INTERNAL MIGRATION
232.	EMPLEADO	NON-MANUAL WORKER
233.	EMPLEADOR	EMPLOYER
234.	EMPLEO	EMPLOYMENT
235.	EMPLEO COMUNITARIO	COMMUNITY EMPLOYMENT PROGRAMME
236.	EMPLEO JUVENIL	YOUTH EMPLOYMENT
237.	EMPLEO SELECTIVO	SELECTIVE EMPLOYMENT
238.	EMPRESA	ENTERPRISE
239.	EMPRESA AUXILIAR	AUXILIARY ENTERPRISE
240.	EMPRESA DE SELECCION DE PERSONAL	PERSONNEL SELECTION AGENCY
241.	EMPRESA DE TRABAJO TEMPORAL	TEMPORARY EMPLOYMENT AGENCY
242.	EMPRESA IDEOLOGICA	IDEOLOGICALLY ORIENTED ENTERPRISE
243.	EMPRESA MEDIANA/PEQUEÑA	SMALL AND MEDIUM-SIZED ENTERPRISES
244.	EMPRESA MULTINACIONAL	MULTINATIONAL CORPORATION
245.	EMPRESA PUBLICA	PUBLIC ENTERPRISE
246.	EMPRESARIO	ENTREPRENEUR/OWNER OF AN ENTERPRISE
247.	ENCUESTA DE POBLACION ACTIVA (EPA)	SURVEY OF THE WORKING POPULATION (EPA)
248.	ENFERMEDAD PROFESIONAL	OCCUPATIONAL ILLNESS/INDUSTRIAL DISEASE
249.	ENLACES SINDICALES	OFFICIAL WORKPLACE REPRESENTATIVES
250.	ENRIQUECIMIENTO DEL TRABAJO	JOB ENRICHMENT
251.	ENTREVISTA DE SELECCION	SELECTION INTERVIEW
252.	ENTRISMO	INFILTRATION STRATEGY
253.	ERGONOMIA	ERGONOMICS
254.	ESCALA MOVIL DE SALARIOS	SLIDING PAY SCALE
255.	ESCALA SALARIAL	PAY SCALE
256.	ESCALAFON	EMPLOYEE RANKING
257.	ESQUIROL	SCAB/BLACKLEG
258.	ESTABILIDAD EN EL EMPLEO	JOB SECURITY
259.	ESTATUTO DE LOS TRABAJADORES (ET)	WORKERS' STATUTE
260.	ESTATUTO SINDICAL	UNION RULE-BOOK
261.	ESTRUCTURA DE LA NEGOCIACION COLECTIVA	COLLECTIVE BARGAINING STRUCTURE
262.	ESTRUCTURA ORGANICA DEL SINDICATO	UNION STRUCTURE
263.	ESTRUCTURA PRODUCTIVA	STRUCTURE OF PRODUCTION
264.	ESTRUCTURA SALARIAL	WAGE/PAY STRUCTURE
265.	EXCEDENCIA	LEAVE OF ABSENCE
266.	EXPEDIENTE DE CRISIS	CRISIS PROCEDURE
267.	EXPEDIENTE DE REGULACION DE EMPLEO	REDUNDANCY PROCEDURE

434.	PARTES PROPORCIONALES	END-OF-SERVICE PRO RATA ENTITLEMENTS
435.	PARTES SOCIALES	SOCIAL PARTNERS
436.	PARTICIPACION EN BENEFICIOS	PROFIT-SHARING
437.	PARTICIPACION EN LA EMPRESA	WORKERS' PARTICIPATION
438.	PARTICIPACION INSTITUCIONAL	REPRESENTATION ON PUBLIC BODIES
439.	PATRIMONIO SINDICAL	UNION ASSETS
440.	PATRONAL	"PATRONAL"
441.	PATRONO	"PATRONO"
442.	PAUSA EN EL TRABAJO	BREAK
443.	PAZ LABORAL	INDUSTRIAL PEACE
444.	PENSIONES	PENSIONS
445.	PENSIONES ASISTENCIALES	WELFARE BENEFITS
446.	PENSIONISTA	PENSIONER
447.	PEON	UNSKILLED WORKER.LABOURER
448.	PEON ESPECIALIZADO	SEMI-SKILLED WORKER
449.	PEONADA	UNSKILLED LABOUR
450.	PERFIL PROFESIONAL	PROFESSIONAL/OCCUPATIONAL JOB PROFILE
451.	PERIODO DE PRUEBA	PROBATIONARY PERIOD
452.	PERMISO DE TRABAJO	WORK PERMIT
453.	PERMISOS	TIME OFF
454.	PERSONAL	PERSONNEL
455.	PERSONAL DE ALTA DIRECCION	SENIOR MANAGEMENT
456.	PERSONAL ESTATUTARIO	PERSONNEL COVERED BY SPECIAL STATUTES
457.	PERSONAL FUERA DE CONVENIO	PERSONNEL EXCLUDED FROM A COLLECTIVE AGREEMENT
458.	PIQUETE	PICKET
459.	PLAN DE FORMACION E INSERCION PROFESIONAL (PLAN FIP)	EMPLOYMENT TRAINING AND INTEGRATION PLAN (PLAN FIP)
460.	PLAN DE FUTURO	ENTERPRISE PLAN
461.	PLAN FIP	PLAN FIP
462.	PLANES DE PENSIONES	PENSION SCHEMES
463.	PLANIFICACION DE RECURSOS HUMANOS	HUMAN RESOURCE PLANNING/HUMAN RESOURCE MANAGEMENT
464.	PLANTE	PROTEST
465.	PLANTILLA	STAFFING LEVEL/STAFF COMPLEMENT/WORKFORCE
466.	PLATAFORMA REIVINDICATIVA	LIST OF CLAIMS OR BARGAINING PROPOSALS/"PLATFORM"
467.	PLENO EMPLEO	FULL EMPLOYMENT
468.	PLURALIDAD SINDICAL	TRADE UNION PLURALISM
469.	PLURALISMO SINDICAL	TRADE UNION PLURALISM
470.	PLURIEMPLEO	MULTIPLE JOBHOLDING/MOON-LIGHTING
471.	PLUSES SALARIALES	ADDITIONAL PAYMENTS
472.	PODER DE DIRECCION	EMPLOYER'S MANAGERIAL AUTHORITY/MANAGERIAL PREROGATIVE
473.	POLITICA DE EMPLEO	EMPLOYMENT POLICY
474.	POLITICA DE RENTAS	INCOMES POLICY
475.	POLIVALENCIA	MULTI-SKILLING/POLYVALENCE
476.	PRACTICAS DE FORMACION	WORK EXPERIENCE
477.	PREACUERDO	DRAFT AGREEMENT
478.	PREAVISO	NOTICE
479.	PREAVISO DE HUELGA	NOTICE OF STRIKE
480.	PREFERENCIA DE EMPLEO	PREFERENTIAL EMPLOYMENT
481.	PREJUBILACION	PRE-RETIREMENT
482.	PRESCRIPCION	LIMITATION (OF ACTION)
483.	PRESTAMISMO	"PRESTAMISMO"
484.	PREVISION SOCIAL	SOCIAL WELFARE
485.	PRIMAS	INCENTIVE BONUS PAYMENTS

541.	SALARIO EN ESPECIE	PAYMENT IN KIND
542.	SALARIO EN MANO	TAKE HOME PAY
543.	SALARIO GLOBAL	AGGREGATE PAY
544.	SALARIO HORA	HOURLY PAY
545.	SALARIO INDIRECTO	INDIRECT PAY
546.	SALARIO LIQUIDO	NET PAY
547.	SALARIO MINIMO INTERPROFESIONAL (SMI)	NATIONAL MINIMUM WAGE
548.	SALARIO POR TAREA	JOB-AND-FINISH
549.	SALARIO SOCIAL	SOCIAL WAGE
550.	SALARIOS DE TRAMITACION	BACK PAY AWARDED AFTER DISMISSAL APPEAL HEARINGS
551.	SECCION SINDICAL DE EMPRESA	WORKPLACE BRANCH
552.	SECRETO PROFESIONAL	PROFESSIONAL SECRECY
553.	SECTOR PUBLICO	PUBLIC SECTOR
554.	SEGURIDAD E HIGIENE	HEALTH AND SAFETY
555.	SEGURIDAD SOCIAL	SOCIAL SECURITY
556.	SEGURIDAD SOCIAL DE LOS TRABAJADORES MIGRANTES	SOCIAL SECURITY FOR MIGRANT WORKERS
557.	SEGUROS SOCIALES	SOCIAL INSURANCE
558.	SELECCION DE PERSONAL	PERSONNEL SELECTION
559.	SERVICIO DOMESTICO	DOMESTIC WORK
560.	SERVICIOS DE EMPLEO	EMPLOYMENT SERVICES
561.	SERVICIOS DE SEGURIDAD Y MANTENIMIENTO	SAFETY AND MAINTENANCE SERVICES
562.	SERVICIOS ESENCIALES DE LA COMUNIDAD	ESSENTIAL PUBLIC SERVICES
563.	SERVICIOS MINIMOS	MINIMUM SERVICES
564.	SERVICIOS SOCIALES	SOCIAL SERVICES
565.	SERVICIOS SOCIALES EN LA EMPRESA	COMPANY WELFARE SERVICES
566.	SIGILO PROFESIONAL	PROFESSIONAL CONFIDENTIALITY
567.	SINDICALISMO	TRADE UNIONISM
568.	SINDICALISMO DE CLASE	CLASS TRADE UNIONISM
569.	SINDICALISMO INDEPENDIENTE	AUTONOMOUS TRADE UNIONISM
570.	SINDICALISMO LIBRE	FREE TRADE UNIONISM
571.	SINDICALISMO PROFESIONAL	OCCUPATIONAL TRADE UNIONISM
572.	SINDICALISTA	TRADE UNIONIST
573.	SINDICALIZACION	UNIONIZATION/UNION DENSITY
574.	SINDICATO	TRADE UNION
575.	SINDICATO AMARILLO	COMPANY UNION/ "YELLOW" UNION
576.	SINDICATO DE EMPRESA	ENTERPRISE UNION
577.	SINDICATO DE FUNCIONARIOS	PUBLIC SERVICE UNION
578.	SINDICATO DE OFICIO	CRAFT UNION
579.	SINDICATO MAS REPRESENTATIVO	MOST REPRESENTATIVE UNION
580.	SINDICATO SUFICIENTEMENTE REPRESENTATIVO	SUFFICIENTLY REPRESENTATIVE UNION
581.	SINDICATO VERTICAL	VERTICAL UNION
582.	SMI	SMI
583.	SOCIEDAD ANONIMA LABORAL	WORKERS' LIMITED COMPANY
584.	SOLIDARIDAD DE TRABAJADORES VASCOS	BASQUE WORKERS' SOLIDARITY (ELA-STV)
585.	SUBALTERNO	ANCILLARY EMPLOYEE
586.	SUBCONTRATACION	SUB-CONTRACTING
587.	SUBSIDIO DE DESEMPLEO AGRICOLA	AGRICULTURAL UNEMPLOYMENT BENEFIT
588.	SUELDO	MONTHLY SALARY
589.	SUPERVISOR	SUPERVISOR
590.	SUPLIDOS	EXPENSES
591.	SUSPENSION DE EMPLEO Y SUELDO	SUSPENSION OF EMPLOYMENT AND PAY
592.	SUSPENSION DEL CONTRATO DE TRABAJO	SUSPENSION OF THE CONTRACT OF EMPLOYMENT
593.	SUSTITUCION DE HUELGUISTAS	REPLACEMENT OF STRIKERS
594.	TABLA SALARIAL	PAY SCALE TARIFF
595.	TANTO ALZADO	LUMP SUM
596.	TARIFAS SALARIALES	WAGE TARIFFS

597.	TASA DE ACTIVIDAD	PARTICIPATION RATE/ ACTIVITY RATE
598.	TASA DE AFILIACION	UNION DENSITY
599.	TASA DE SINDICALIZACION	UNION DENSITY
600.	TECNICO	TECHNICAL PERSONNEL
601.	TELETRABAJO	TELEWORK
602.	TIEMPO DE TRABAJO	WORKING TIME
603.	TRABAJADOR	EMPLOYEE
604.	TRABAJADORES A TIEMPO PARCIAL	PART-TIME WORKERS
605.	TRABAJADORES DE EDAD MADURA	OLDER WORKERS
606.	TRABAJADORES ESTACIONALES	SEASONAL WORKERS
607.	TRABAJADORES EXTRANJEROS	FOREIGN WORKERS
608.	TRABAJADORES EVENTUALES	CASUAL WORKERS
609.	TRABAJADORES INTERINOS	RELIEF WORKERS
610.	TRABAJADORES MENORES	UNDER-AGE WORKERS/MINORS
611.	TRABAJADORES MINUSVALIDOS	DISABLED WORKERS
612.	TRABAJADORES SUSTITUTOS	SUBSTITUTE WORKERS
613.	TRABAJADORES TEMPOREROS	SEASONAL WORKERS
614.	TRABAJO	WORK
615.	TRABAJO A DOMICILIO	HOMEWORKING/OUT-WORK
616.	TRABAJO A REGLAMENTO	WORK-TO-RULE
617.	TRABAJO ASALARIADO	WORK UNDER AN EMPLOYMENT CONTRACT
618.	TRABAJO ATIPICO	ATYPICAL WORK
619.	TRABAJO AUTONOMO	SELF-EMPLOYMENT
620.	TRABAJO BENEVOLO	UNPAID WORK/VOLUNTARY WORK
621.	TRABAJO CLANDESTINO	CLANDESTINE EMPLOYMENT
622.	TRABAJO COMPARTIDO	JOB-SHARING
623.	TRABAJO DE COLABORACION SOCIAL	COMMUNITY WORK
624.	TRABAJO DE TEMPORADA	SEASONAL WORK
625.	TRABAJO EN CADENA	PRODUCTION-LINE WORK
626.	TRABAJO EN COMUN	JOINT WORK
627.	TRABAJO FAMILIAR	WORK PERFORMED WITHIN THE FAMILY
628.	TRABAJO FEMENINO	FEMALE EMPLOYMENT/ EMPLOYMENT OF WOMEN
629.	TRABAJO INTERINO	RELIEF WORK
630.	TRABAJO IRREGULAR	IRREGULAR EMPLOYMENT
631.	TRABAJO LENTO	SLOW-DOWN
632.	TRABAJO NEGRO	UNDECLARED EMPLOYMENT
633.	TRABAJO OCULTO	CONCEALED EMPLOYMENT
634.	TRABAJO SOMERGIDO	HIDDEN EMPLOYMENT
635.	TRAFICO DE MANO DE OBRA	ILLEGAL TRAFFIC IN LABOUR
636.	TRANSMISION DE LA EMPRESA	TRANSFER OF UNDERTAKING
637.	TRASLADO	TRANSFER
638.	TRIBUNALES DE TRABAJO	LABOUR COURTS
639.	TURNOS DE TRABAJO	SHIFTWORK
640.	UGT	UGT
641.	UNIDAD DE NEGOCIACION	BARGAINING UNIT
642.	UNIDAD SINDICAL	UNION UNITY
643.	UNION GENERAL DE TRABAJADORES (UGT)	GENERAL WORKERS' CONFEDERATION (UGT)
644.	UNION SINDICAL OBRERA (USO)	WORKERS' TRADE UNIONIST CONFEDERATION (USO)
645.	UNIONES TERRITORIALES	TERRITORIAL FEDERATIONS
646.	USO	USO
647.	VACACIONES	ANNUAL HOLIDAY
648.	VALORACION DE PERSONAL	STAFF APPRAISAL
649.	VALORACION DE PUESTOS DE TRABAJO	JOB EVALUATION
650.	VERIFICACION DE ENFERMEDAD	VERIFICATION OF ILLNESS
651.	VIDA ACTIVA	WORKING LIFE
652.	VIDA PRIVADA DEL TRABAJADOR	PRIVATE LIFE OF THE EMPLOYEE
653.	VIGILANTE DE SEGURIDAD	SAFETY OFFICER

NUMBERED ALPHABETICAL LIST OF ENTRIES
IN ENGLISH

ENGLISH

SPANISH

INTRODUCTION

1. The economic context of industrial relations

1.1 The development of Spain's economy in the early stages of the process of industrialization was characterized by various closely inter-related features. One of these features was protectionism, which enabled industries to become established and expand in the domestic market. A second feature was strong intervention by the authorities, normally with the aim of selectively promoting economic activities of certain kinds and occasionally (as in the early years of the Second Republic) with the idea of responding to popular demands. Another salient characteristic of Spain's economy in this period was the very marked influence of political factors or events, such as the instability of government institutions, the succession of different regimes each intent on emphasizing its differences from its predecessors, and the necessity of coping with episodes of war and the resultant need for reconstruction.

1.2 The outcome of this combination of factors was an economic system of "corporatist capitalism", not at all conducive to innovation and growth, in which the various actors clung stubbornly to their ideological positions and to the protection of their particular interests. All this largely accounts for the delay in industrialization in Spain compared with most other West European countries, a delay that can be illustrated by a single figure: as recently as 1950, half of Spain's working population were still employed in agriculture. Although the gap has narrowed greatly over the last 30 years, this delay in industrialization has had a major influence on the various aspects of Spain's industrial relations system. The most obvious signs of this influence are: the lack of any tradition of structured industrial relations and the relatively recent emergence of such a system; the minor role played until latterly by collective bargaining as a means of regulating terms and conditions of employment; and the considerable importance of the "agrarian question", both as a social problem and as an element of the labour market, in the development of industrial relations.

1.3 In contrast to the slow pace of the earlier period, since the 1960s Spain's economy has undergone rapid and profound change. Three very different phases can be distinguished in this period of accelerated modernization: the phase of expansion (1960-1973), during which annual GDP growth rates of around 7 per cent. were reached; the phase of serious economic recession (1974-1982), largely coinciding with the years of political transition, which was marked chiefly by a fall in employment and in the participation rate; and the phase of economic recovery, starting in 1983, the effects of which began to be felt in employment and economic activity from 1985 onwards. Underlying the differing features of

1

these separate phases, a common trend is discernible throughout the period, namely the integration of Spain's economy into the international context. From the policy of isolationism and "inward" growth which was pursued from the start of industrialization and taken to its extreme in the "autarky" of the early years of the Franco regime, the movement of events led, via various stages of progressive opening-up to the outside world, to Spain's accession to the European Community in 1986.

1.4 A brief description of those aspects of Spain's economic structure that are most relevant from the industrial relations point of view must mention, firstly, the wide diversity of the industrial sector, with production geared chiefly to covering the various elements of domestic demand. Secondly, as in the whole of Europe, many areas of industry (iron and steel, shipbuilding, textiles, automobiles, household electrical appliances, etc.) have been profoundly affected by the economic crisis, which resulted in the disappearance of many companies and in certain industries necessitated the adoption of conversion plans in the face of excess capacity and organizational deficiencies. Another facet of the industrial structure that should be included in this description is the highly capital-intensive nature of its production processes, which accounts for the sector's limitations as a source of job creation. As will be seen later, this feature of Spain's industry is discernible even in periods of strong economic growth.

1.5 As a result of the process of urbanization and the development of tourism, the construction sector saw a spectacular upsurge in the 1960s and early 1970s, becoming the main sector to absorb the surplus manpower no longer needed in agriculture. After suffering seriously from the impact of the economic crisis, the construction sector has again enjoyed a strong upturn in recent years, chiefly thanks to public infrastructure projects. From the standpoint of industrial relations, this sector is marked by a sharp division into small and large enterprises, often linked together by a widespread network of sub-contracting.

1.6 The contribution of the service sector to GDP has been around 50 per cent. since the 1960s, having risen dramatically to almost 60 per cent. in the 1980s. As in other countries, this is a particularly mixed sector of Spain's economy combining both long-established and new service activities, with a marked move away from the former towards the latter in the last few decades. Other relevant features of the service sector in Spain are the importance of activities connected with tourism and the strong growth, since the period of political transition, in public services. Despite this growth, the proportion represented by public employment in the service sector as a whole (approximately 27 per cent.) is still lower than in most other European countries. In absolute figures, the numbers employed by Central Government are close on one million; when the employees of public enterprises and of the Autonomous

2

Communities and municipal authorities are added, this gives a total of 1.9 million employees in the public sector.

1.7 During the period of modernization that began in 1960, agriculture has acted as the source of supply of the manpower and capital needed for urban economic development. At present, its share of GDP is under 6 per cent. But this decrease, and the shift in resources, must not be interpreted solely as evidence of the agricultural sector's decline: rather, it demonstrates the strong growth of the other sectors. And agriculture too has modernized during this period, in terms both of mechanization and of products and cultivation methods. What is more, its growth potential is considerable, and it has the advantage of recent integration into the Community context. In any case, for reasons that will be seen later the importance of Spain's primary sector in the industrial relations system is greater than its contribution to the economy as a whole would suggest.

1.8 These changes in Spain's economic structure have been correspondingly reflected (although with certain distortions) in the labour market and in the make-up of the working population. First of all, there has been a drastic fall in the agricultural labour force as a proportion of the total working population, which by 1989 was under 14 per cent. (with 24 per cent. employed in industry, 9 per cent. in construction and 53 per cent. in the service sector). But the overall decline in the agricultural labour force has not meant a process of rural exodus in all cases. It must also be borne in mind that one third of those working in agriculture are self-employed, mostly concentrated in the southern regions of Spain. In these regions the primary sector still plays an important part in the course of labour relations.

1.9 For the whole of the working population in the various sectors of the economy, the distribution between employees and the self-employed fluctuates around figures of 70 per cent. employees and 30 per cent. self-employed. The trend in recent years was for a proportionally larger increase in the number of self-employed, owing to the difficulty of finding a job during the years when the economic crisis was worsening. This trend appears to have halted in the late 1980s, with a slowing-down in the number of self-employed workers establishing new enterprises or setting up forms of association (co-operatives, workers' limited companies, etc.).

1.10 Apart from the impact on the sectoral make-up of the working population, the changes in Spain's structure of production have markedly altered the occupational structure, generating at the same time substantial occupational mobility of the labour force (re-training occasioned by a change of job or by the introduction of new production or work-organization techniques). A useful indicator of this change is the increase over the course of the 1980s in the number of workers with intermediate qualifications (100 per cent. increase) and higher qualifications (50 per cent. increase).

Despite this, the rest of the labour market suffers from serious deficiencies in the skill levels of the labour force, calling for major reform of the institutions that provide basic training and further training.

1.11 One of the principal factors that must be singled out when analysing the economic context of industrial relations in Spain is the incapacity of the production system to provide employment for the entire available labour force. This phenomenon, which is a constant factor underlying the whole course of modern-day developments, has manifested itself in various ways. The first of these is emigration, which has gone on incessantly since the late 1800s and reached a particularly high level, in the form of emigration to other Community countries, at the very stage of economic expansion that started in the 1960s. In round figures, this enormous emigrant flow, paradoxically coinciding with the years of strong growth in industry and the service sector, amounted to one million workers. The other manifestation of the chronic incapacity of Spain's economy to utilize the whole of its manpower resources is the level of unemployment resulting from the economic crisis. The stagnation of production activity and the return of emigrants together raised this figure in 1985 to 21 per cent. of the economically active population (some three million workers), revealing the full magnitude of this imbalance in employment.

1.12 In considering the unemployment figures in Spain, various other figures should also be taken into account; some serving to worsen the diagnosis of the situation, and others to improve it. The factors that worsen it include, in particular, the low participation rate of the section of Spain's population who are of working age (49 per cent. in 1988-1989); although this participation rate has risen substantially since 1985, the figure is still below the European average. The explanation for this lies in the limited representation of women in the working population, which did not reach the 30 per cent. mark until 1986; it must, however, be stressed that the participation rate of women has seen a spectacular rise during the past four years, exceeding 32 per cent. by the end of the 1980s. Other figures which adversely affect the diagnosis of unemployment in Spain but which at the same time are showing clear underlying signs of improvement are those for youth unemployment (under 40 per cent. by the end of 1988, as compared with 44 per cent. in 1985) and long-term unemployment (61 per cent. by the end of 1988, as compared with 64 per cent. at the end of 1987).

1.13 Data indicating an improvement in the real scale of unemployment in Spain include, firstly, a sustained trend of recovery that has been in evidence since 1985. This trend is expressed to some extent in the rate of unemployment, which fell by more than four per cent. between 1985 and 1989; but it is expressed above all in the rise in the participation rate and the drop in youth unemployment. Another fact pointing in the same direction is that the

4

unemployment figures are over-estimated, inasmuch as they are figures "recorded" or stated in public surveys which take no account whatever (in the unemployment detected by employment offices) or presumably very little account (in the unemployment reported by the quarterly Surveys of the Working Population) of undeclared employment in the hidden or "black" economy.

1.14 A final comment that should be made about the economic context of industrial relations in Spain concerns the geographical imbalance in the production structure. As regards employment, this imbalance is reflected in the high figures for migration within Spain. The overall level of unemployment thus conceals a very unequal distribution of surplus manpower among the various regions of the country; the surplus is very high in the agricultural regions of southern and western Spain but is (or was, until the recent economic crisis) lower in the north, where heavy industry is concentrated, and in the east, where there have been major centres of industries producing consumer goods since the early 1800s.

2. The legal framework of industrial relations

2.1 In 1976, Spain saw the start of a process of legal change which has profoundly altered the shape of industrial relations. The essential nature of this change, which was brought about by the transition from General Franco's dictatorship to the present parliamentary monarchy, is explicitly referred to in the 1978 Constitution, with recognition of "freedom of association and the right to form trade unions", the "right to collective bargaining", the "right to strike" and "free enterprise within the framework of a market economy".

2.2 This process of change launched by the political transition and the adoption of the Constitution has affected virtually every aspect of the legal framework of industrial relations: first and foremost, the status or legal position of the social partners or their representative bodies. The recognition of freedom of association immediately triggered the open, unrestricted activity of the trade unions and workers' "coalitions" which had previously existed in a precarious world where they were semi-clandestine organizations subject to intermittent repression. It also implied the extinction of the old regime's official Organización Sindical (Trade Union Organization) or "Vertical Union", characterized by the compulsory inclusion of both employers and workers in a complex network of corporatist bodies controlled by the state.

2.3 A second aspect of the legal framework which was affected by the reform launched in 1976 was intervention by the authorities in industrial relations. Overall, the state's role in this area of society has significantly diminished since 1976, as regards both regulatory and administrative intervention. The essential reason for this withdrawal by the authorities lies in the greater scope for freedom of action formally granted to the industrial relations organizations in the new legal and political context. As regards administrative intervention, account must also be taken of another reform concerning industrial relations: the transfer of many of the powers of intervention to the decentralized authorities of the regions or "Autonomous Communities".

2.4 Finally, the change in the legal framework of industrial relations has influenced two significant aspects of bilateral relations between the social partners. One of these is the scope of collective bargaining on terms and conditions of employment, which is much broader and more clearly defined than before. The other concerns the available means of defending labour interests, with workers and trade unions being given the "conventional" weapons of self-help (in particular, the right to strike) of which they had been deprived under the old political regime.

2.5 Twelve years on, this process of change is now virtually completed and there are signs that the forward thrust of industrial relations may soon be characterized not, as hitherto, by the creation and implementation of a "legal machinery" but by the activities of negotiation and participation which are the proper features of a working industrial relations system. The legal decisions taken in 1986 on the distribution of the "patrimonio sindical acumulado" (the assets accumulated by the official Organización Sindical during the Franco period) and the repayment of the "patrimonio sindical histórico" (assets seized from workers' unions in 1939) seem to symbolize the end of this period of change in the legal framework of labour relations.

2.6 Whether or not it is true, the mere assumption that industrial relations are entering a new phase in which the legislators are passing the torch to the employers' and employees' representative bodies suggests that the period which is coming to an end has been not only a period of legal change but also a period of change as regards the nature of the social partners and their attitudes and behaviour. The transformation of labour law can make it much easier to set up an industrial relations system and can also play a decisive role in determining the shape of that system. Yet not even such an important legal change as that of giving free rein to the social partners can, on its own, conjure out of the air the various elements of such a system.

3. Formation of the Spanish industrial relations system

3.1 As has just been stated, the years 1976-1986 saw not only a fundamental change in the laws governing labour relations but also the formation of an industrial relations system. Beginning with a situation in which the trade unions were fragmented and there were huge gaps not covered by employers' associations, this period saw the gradual consolidation of a definite structure of representation which now enables us to identify the social partners without any great difficulty. As regards the interaction of these representative bodies, both with each other and with the authorities, certain rules governing relations emerged during this period and have, with a few exceptions and reservations, made it possible to achieve some acceptable results as regards industrial peace and the reconciling of interests.

3.2 The particular shape of these elements of Spain's industrial relations system today has obviously not emerged purely by chance but is the result of the combined effect of various factors. One of these is the historical factor, which includes both the influence of the rules and traditions of the past and the ability of established interest groups to survive. A second factor was, and still is, the inclination of political institutions (parliaments, governments, public administrations, parties, etc.) to influence the structure of representation in industrial relations by selectively promoting certain trade unions or employers' associations. To these we can add a third factor which is an economic one: the coincidence of the formation of the industrial relations system with the crises and changes in production and trade following the 1973 rise in oil prices.

3.3 At first sight, it may seem that the representative bodies and institutional patterns of industrial relations in Spain have emerged and developed from nothing as a result of the recent recognition of freedom of association. The hypothesis is a credible one if we remember that Franco's was a long-lasting authoritarian regime which from the outset aimed to suppress all forms of employee and employer representation other than the official Vertical Union and seemed, at first, to have ample means of achieving that aim. However, the theory crumbles if taken to its ultimate conclusion. The Spanish case is certainly a good example of the fact that an industrial relations system can be created very rapidly out of a situation in which independent unions were formerly prohibited. But it is also an important illustration of the influence of history on this area of society. There is also the peculiar feature that this historical influence belongs to two very different eras: the period prior to the Civil War, whose representative organizations did not disappear, nor the memories of it, and the period of industrialization and growth between 1960 and 1975, which could be dubbed "the second phase of Franco's rule", characterized by a social climate and, in some aspects, official stance which differed markedly from those prevailing during the first two decades of the regime.

3.4 These historical influences did not mean that the ways open to political institutions for influencing elements of the industrial relations system were limitless, but they were nonetheless very great. In point of fact, the trade union and employers' organizations which existed when the transition began were of sufficient

7

importance to ensure that account was taken of them, but they were not strong enough to resist the power of political forces to shape and promote a particular system. Similarly, the traditions and practices of the social partners could not be openly suppressed or opposed, yet they were not well-rooted enough to withstand a planned operation to reform and modernize many aspects of them.

3.5 Political institutions have taken full advantage of this relative malleability of the various elements of the industrial relations system during its recent formation to point them in a certain direction. Opportunities to exercise this influence have not been lacking and have included, in particular, the transformation of labour law mentioned in the preceding section. Certainly, legislative regulation of the independent trade unions and labour rights serves the primary function of "democratizing" labour relations. But it could also serve an implicit secondary function of shaping the industrial relations system in a certain way. This, as we shall have a chance of demonstrating later, is what has actually happened.

3.6 As for the influence of the economic factor, it is anticipated here that the crises and changes in the production structure and trade since 1973 have been reflected first and foremost in the attitudes and behaviour of the parties involved in industrial relations and also, though less strikingly or directly, in the actual structure of representation. Of all the economic processes and events which have taken place over the past few years, the one which has had the greatest impact on this area of society has most certainly been the increase in the number of unemployed to some 20 per cent. of the economically active population. The social partners' reaction to this very high rate of unemployment, which has even reached over 40 per cent. for workers under the age of 25, has been on the one hand for workers' representatives to moderate the claims made in collective bargaining and, on the other, for the authorities and industrial relations organizations to re-arrange social priorities.

4. The actors of industrial relations: trade unions and employers' associations

4.1 Industrialization and economic growth during the period 1960-1975 were accompanied, in the sphere of industrial relations, by the appearance and spread of sources of independent trade union activity, concentrated first in enterprises and workplaces and then spreading to cover wider areas. These sources of activity acquired their first official coverage in the "bodies to promote labour harmony" in workplaces that were set up by legislation under Franco and called "jurados de empresa" (works councils), bodies which included representatives elected by the workers. Soon afterwards, "enlaces sindicales" (official workplace representatives), who were also elected by the enterprise workforce and

8

whose function was, on paper, to serve as a go-between or intermediary for the official Organización Sindical with the rank and file of workers, were utilized towards the same end of developing trade union activity in the real sense.

4.2 From the decentralized level of enterprises and workplaces, the representatives elected by the workers could move on to perform functions within the Vertical Union itself, in bodies officially responsible for reconciling the interests of employers and workers at sectoral and regional level. From the second half of the 1960s, full advantage was taken of this opportunity by the sources of trade union activity just mentioned, so that, during the final years of Franco's rule, it was often they who controlled the peripheral sections of the official Organización Sindical.

4.3 This trade union movement which emerged in the 1960s was, despite its inclusion in official representative bodies, clearly a form of political dissidence with the established regime. Its main protagonists were the "comisiones obreras" (workers' commissions), which were strongly influenced by the Communist Party but also included other opposition factions. Supporters of this policy of making use of available representative channels likewise included a trade-union organization also founded in the 1960s and called Unión Sindical Obrera (USO: Workers' Trade Unionist Confederation). At the time, however, this strategy of infiltration was opposed, for one reason or another, by the trade union bodies which had been broken up at the end of the Civil War, *i.e.* the Unión General de Trabajadores (UGT: General Workers' Confederation), which was affiliated to the Socialist Party, the anarchistic Confederación Nacional del Trabajo (CNT: National Confederation of Labour) and Solidaridad de Trabajadores Vascos (ELA-STV: Basque Workers' Solidarity), a trade-union exponent of Basque nationalism. Following a long period of inactivity, these trade union organizations too began to show signs of life in enterprises and workplaces during the final years of Franco's rule.

4.4 Although the Franco dictatorship did not substantially change its initial stance, the trade union front of opposition to the regime did, in those final years, enjoy a degree of tolerance because of its capacity to resist and also, to some extent, as a result of the attempts made at assimilation by the official Organización Sindical. Such tolerance was, at all events, a precarious state of affairs, alternating with or interrupted by relatively frequent periods of repression. This ambiguous situation of semi-clandestine activity, now tolerated and now repressed by the political powers, lasted until 1976, the year which marked the beginning of the period of political transition and saw the first steps being taken towards abolishing the official Organización Sindical and the announcement of the legalization of independent trade unions. These first steps were followed in 1977 by actual legal recognition of freedom of association and the right to strike, and continued dismantling of the Vertical Union. As already stated, this process of legal change culminated in and was consolidated by the adoption of the 1978 Constitution.

4.5 The development of the system of employer and employee representation during the years of political transition was marked not only by these legislative events but also by the expansion of the trade union movement's membership figures and organizations and the appearance of employers' associations. These two movements, representing different interests, were to follow different paths. The employers' associations subsequently opted for joining forces in a single organization: the Confederación Española de Organizaciones Empresariales (CEOE: Spanish Confederation of Employers' Organizations), which was founded in 1977 by the merging of various employers' confederations set up shortly before. The expansion of the trade union movement, on the other hand, followed the opposite path, with its various elements representing different ideological stances and occupational sectors dispersing to form separate organizations. The trade union structure resulting from this proliferation of organizations had a somewhat disjointed appearance in which it was possible to distinguish three distinct "strata" of trade unions: the "historical" unions, which dated back to before the Civil War and had re-emerged during the last years of Franco's rule; the trade unions founded in the 1960s on the basis of union activity in workplaces; and the newly formed trade unions, some affiliated to equally new political parties, others created with the more limited aim of protecting workers in their particular sectors.

4.6 When the period of political transition came to an end with the adoption of the Constitution and the launching of constitutional bodies, the process of formation of the system of industrial relations representation was not even nearing completion. For several years, this area of society remained fluid and saw a rapid succession of events. On the employers' side, the most important development was undoubtedly the consolidation of the CEOE as the employers' mouthpiece at national level. A milestone in this process of consolidation was when, in 1980, the most widely established employers' association among small and medium-sized enterprises, the Confederación Española de la Pequeña y Mediana Empresa (CEPYME: Spanish Confederation of Small and Medium-Sized Enterprises), joined the CEOE.

4.7 On the trade union side, the most remarkable event over the past few years has been the clarification of the landscape of representation, with the take-off of two national confederations (UGT: General Workers' Confederation; and CC.OO.: Trade-Union Confederation of Workers' Commissions), which won clear majorities in the 1980 elections of workers' representatives in enterprises and saw their positions confirmed in the 1982 and 1986 elections. This national dominance of two confederations, which tends to be projected onto each and every regional district by the mechanism of the "extension of representativeness" to the bodies included in each district, has led to the coining of the term "bi-unionism" to describe the structure of the trade union movement in Spain. If we are to use this term, it would in fact be more accurate to speak of "imperfect bi-unionism", since there are other trade union organizations which, although clearly minority groups in the system of industrial relations representation as a whole, are dominant in certain regions (e.g. ELA-STV in the Basque Country) or specific occupational sectors (e.g. USO, the Workers' Trade Unionist Confederation).

4.8 Another notable trend in the more recent history of the system is the stagnation in the growth of the unions following the brief period of expansion during the political transition in Spain. The most important manifestations of this phenomenon are: the low degree of unionization, which, according to the calculations that appear to be the most accurate, is less than 15 per cent. of the working population; the restriction of trade union representation to the traditional working-class core and its failure, with rare exceptions, to cross the barrier into new labour sectors (technical specialists, middle-management staff, skilled services, office staff, etc.); and, lastly, the financial inability of the trade unions to cover their own everyday running costs.

4.9 As regards internal organization, the most outstanding feature of the trade unions in Spain is their high degree of centralization, which is only partially offset by the activities of representative bodies within enterprises. With rare exceptions, it is the trade union confederations which set collective bargaining policy, take part in discussions with the authorities, are represented on the governing bodies of public social services, manage the bulk of the financial resources and are responsible for internal discipline. It is, therefore, not surprising that the major identifying feature of the "primary" trade unions is membership of one of the national confederations. Centralization is less marked on the employers' side, though the CEOE has played a more directive role in industrial relations than it has in its other areas of activity.

4.10 The framework of industrial relations representation as described in broad outline here has been shaped by various factors, some intrinsic and some extraneous to the organization and strategy of the trade unions and employers' associations. These factors will be analysed later. It does, however, seem appropriate to draw attention here to one internal factor to complete the description of the formative process of industrial relations representation in Spain. The fact is that a large number of regional and sectoral trade union bodies were set up under the impetus of the respective confederations, with a view to the rapid reconstruction of the trade union movement. A similar phenomenon, though limited to regional bodies, also occurred within the CEOE. This contribution of the confederations to the founding of the representative organizations which constitute their membership has been reflected, as might have been expected, in the centralization of representation and in the initial vigour of the trade union movement, a period of expansion which coincided, and not by chance, with the recruitment by the national confederations of the militant members and officials they needed to establish themselves at regional level.

5. The actors of industrial relations: workers' delegates and workers' committees

5.1 The tradition of employee self-help in enterprises and workplaces, which was orchestrated in the second phase of Franco's rule by making use of the channels offered by works councils and official workplace representatives, was not only maintained but became much stronger in the years of political transition, when the foundations of a new legal framework for industrial relations were being laid. With respect to the institutions representing employees at enterprise level, this reorganization signified the disappearance of official workplace representatives as a result of the abolition of the official Organización Sindical for which, on paper, they were supposed to serve as a go-between, and the conversion of works councils into "workers' committees" or "workers' delegates". The change of title was not, in this case, merely cosmetic: it was accompanied by a significant change in content. Workers' committees and workers' delegates were designed to represent and defend the interests of employees and thus consisted only of members belonging to the various groups of workers. By contrast, the former works councils, in accordance with their institutional duty to seek the common interest of the enterprise, had been of mixed composition, including representatives of the employer as well of the workers.

5.2 As happened in many other areas of labour law, the regulations issued on workers' committees and workers' delegates during the period of political transition formed the basis of the corresponding legislation passed after the Constitution had been adopted. Thus, the Estatuto de los Trabajadores (Workers' Statute) of 1980 maintained and still maintains the broad lines of the aforementioned regulations on employee representative bodies: appointment of workers' delegates in small enterprises and workers' committees in large and medium-sized enterprises; workers' delegates to be elected by the workers and workers' committees to consist of members elected by the various occupational groups; and responsibility of these representatives to defend the interests of the entire enterprise workforce. This legislation did not serve actually to set up these representative bodies, but rather to integrate and supplement certain aspects which had been omitted or covered insufficiently or ambiguously by the provisions introduced during the period of political transition. These included, in particular, the very important issue of the functions and powers of workers' committees and workers' delegates, which it is worth discussing at more length.

5.3 Among the many functions and powers of the unitary bodies representing an enterprise's entire workforce, the Workers' Statute establishes the right to disclosure of information on the enterprise's financial situation, expenditure and financial results; the right to consultation should the enterprise reduce or terminate its activities or introduce or modify systems of work organization, etc.; the power to monitor the employer's compliance with labour regulations; and, and this is truly extraordinary, collective bargaining at enterprise or workplace level. This authority to conduct collective bargaining extends not only to taking practical decisions jointly with the enterprise's management, but also to the concluding of actual collective agreements at enterprise level, that is, agreements of a broader and more systematic nature, formalized in writing, to regulate employment and working conditions. On paper, the authority of workers' committees and workers' delegates to negotiate such company agreements clashes with an equivalent bargaining power granted contractually to those trade unions which are firmly established in the enterprise. In practice, however, this collective bargaining power has in most cases been assumed by the unitary representative bodies and not by trade union representatives in the strict sense.

5.4 The tradition of collective representation at enterprise level, together with the important functions assigned to these representative bodies within enterprises by the Workers' Statute, could have given rise to a structure of representation in which industry-wide and national multi-industry levels were reserved for trade unions, while unitary representative bodies were responsible at enterprise level. However, this hypothetical situation in which one might witness the emergence of two separate systems to represent workers (on the one hand the trade unions and, on the other, unitary representative bodies within enterprises) has not materialized. On the contrary, the two forms of representation have become so closely linked that they might rightly be considered facets of a single system of representation. The factors connecting the two are various. One is the strong presence of the trade unions on workers' committees and among workers' delegates. Another is the major role attributed to the trade unions in the procedure for electing these representatives. A third is acknowledgement of the right of trade unions to set up their own representative bodies in workplaces, bodies which are connected organizationally with workers' committees when the trade unions concerned are well established in the enterprise.

13

5.5 For although the workers' committees and workers' delegates did not, in principle, have any connection with the organizational structure of the trade unions and even though this connection is still somewhat tenuous, Spanish law has, since the first draft of the Workers' Statute, recognized the trade unions' right to put forward candidates in the elections held periodically to appoint the members of these unitary representative bodies, in competition with any other independent candidates. Furthermore, success in these elections is vital for the competing trade unions, since "most representative union" status, with the advantages and power that brings, depends precisely on the electoral support gained in these elections. These two motives for putting forward candidates (being able to exert influence in the unitary representative bodies and acquiring the status of most representative union) explain why trade union organizations have fielded candidates in all the elections held in every enterprise and workplace in which they could expect a positive result. This, together with the workers' confidence in the trade union as an institution, explains the good electoral results achieved by trade union candidates. All trade union candidates who have stood in elections up to now have received very considerable support from the rank and file (securing some 90 per cent. of elected posts) and there is a growing trend for trade union candidates to oust "independent" candidates. So much so that these elections of workers' committees and workers' delegates have come to be called, incorrectly but symptomatically, "union elections".

5.6 The results achieved by trade union candidates in the elections of workers' delegates and workers' committees have been the trade unions' primary means of penetrating enterprises and establishing a functional connection with the respective unitary bodies representing an enterprise's entire workforce. In addition to this, however, labour legislation passed by the PSOE (Socialist) Government has established other means of penetration by, for example, granting established or most representative unions powers to initiate and manage "union elections" (1984 reform of the Workers' Statute) or making it possible to set up trade union branches within enterprises, with broad powers to carry on internal trade union activity to represent workers' interests (1985 Trade Union Freedom Act). To enable this latter function to be performed, provision has been made for "trade union delegates" to attend the meetings of workers' committees, with a view to co-ordinating and bringing together the two instruments by which the enterprise's workforce is represented.

5.7 To sum up, the hypothetical scenario of a dual system of representation, in which the various fields or levels of action are shared between different collective bodies, has not emerged in Spain; nor is it likely to emerge in the near future. The thrust of industrial relations and the trend in labour legislation are

14

inclining more in the opposite direction, with the trade unions having increasing influence over the unitary bodies representing workers. In line with this trend towards unionization, workers' delegates and workers' committees are becoming a subsystem connected with the unions by a multitude of organizational and functional links, and sometimes, in complete reversal of the path followed in the 1960s and 1970s, they are becoming a mere extension of the trade unions in the workplace.

6. The structure and process of collective bargaining

6.1 As mentioned earlier, the second phase of the Franco regime saw a certain trend towards the kind of industrial relations practices prevailing in industrialized democracies. The signs of this about-turn are perceptible, though with very marked differences, both in representative bodies and in collective bargaining practices. In the case of representative bodies, this trend was a result of the emergence of workers' "coalitions" which ended by forming a trade union movement of considerable strength. Yet these germs of trade unionism, which were based on workers' representative bodies at enterprise level and even infiltrated the official Organización Sindical, were never officially recognized as the independent trade union associations they actually were. The Franco regime's orthodoxy of state corporatism remained to the last, as evidenced by the regulations contained in a law as late as the Trade Union Act of 1971.

6.2 This same trend of effective liberalization was to emerge, though with fewer discrepancies between the law and practice of industrial relations, in regard to collective action taken by workers to control their employment and working conditions and improve their living standards. The classification of "workers' strikes" as a crime of sedition (1944 Penal Code) and the notion that the labour authorities had exclusive power to regulate employment and working conditions (1942 Labour Regulations Act) were superseded, in a remarkable change of approach, by recognition of the collective agreement as a means of improving the workers' situation (1958 Collective Agreements Act) and, as a result of this legal recognition, by acceptance of the initiation of collective labour disputes (Decree of 1962) and decriminalization of strikes (1965 reform of the Penal Code). The step which Franco's legislators refused to take as regards this aspect of collective labour relations was to legalize strikes. Although it ceased to be a crime as from 1965, the collective cessation of work continued to be considered an illegal act in breach of the contract of employment and, possibly, an offence against "public order". As a breach of or failure to comply with the contract of employment it was punishable by the employer, and penalties could include dismissal in the case of "active participation" in strike action. As a public order offence it was punishable by fines imposed by the authorities.

6.3 The structure and process of collective bargaining which emerged during the second phase of Franco's rule had some very peculiar features because of the singular nature of the legal and political framework within which they developed. The main peculiarity of the collective bargaining process was, as we have already indicated, the existence of legislation which discouraged strikes and other direct forms of collective industrial action. This did not mean that situations of open industrial conflict did not arise, but rather that they were accompanied by additional problems and tensions and quite frequently became political and social conflicts too.

6.4 As regards the structure of collective bargaining during this period, the essential factor to be borne in mind is the existence at the time of two completely separate and unconnected forms of collective agreement: the company agreement (negotiated by the works councils) and the industry-wide agreement (negotiated within the official Organización Sindical by "social" and "economic" representative bodies). Gradually, the forward thrust of collective bargaining was tending to reserve the company agreement for work/production units of a certain size, and to adapt the distribution of industry-wide bargaining units to the organizational structure of the peripheral administration of the Organización Sindical. These two paths of development led, in the early days of political transition, to a bargaining structure consisting of two separate elements: company agreements and industry-wide agreements, the latter being very highly fragmented and scattered.

6.5 The structure of collective bargaining today owes much to this historical inheritance. One resultant aspect is the division of negotiation between company agreements and industry-wide agreements, which together cover three quarters of all employees. Another is the separation or lack of co-ordination of these two types of agreement, each covering different segments or parts of work/production units. A third aspect is the fragmentation of industry-wide bargaining units, though negotiation practice over the past few years has taken a few steps towards redefining the scope of agreements and incorporating provincial agreements in national agreements.

6.6 Without losing sight of these persisting features, it should be noted that the current structure of collective bargaining in Spain is marked by some significant innovations. Probably the major innovation is the appearance and consolidation of national multi-industry agreements negotiated by the most representative trade unions and employers' associations at national level. The fundamental aim of these "summit" agreements, largely integrated on more than one occasion in agreements resulting from social concertation, has been to regulate certain aspects covered by collective bargaining at industry-wide or enterprise level as a concerted means of dealing with the consequences of the economic crisis. This framework-agreement function, which makes it possible to restrain (or at least hope to be able to restrain) labour costs, has been heeded in industry-wide and company agreements negotiated since.

6.7 Another notable feature of the structure of collective bargaining in Spain is the existence of two classes of agreement, depending on their range of applicability: the agreement with *erga omnes* force, which has general applicability to all members of the occupational group and not just members of the contracting organizations, and the agreement with limited applicability, which, in principle, covers only the employers and workers directly represented in the negotiating unit as a result of their membership of the contracting associations. Obviously, for a collective agreement to have *erga omnes* force, certain requirements regarding official recognition and procedure must be met, as laid down in the 1980 Workers' Statute; if these requirements are not met, the agreement is classed as an agreement of limited applicability, governed not by the Workers' Statute but by the general legislation covering representation and contracting, and is called an "extra-statutory" agreement.

6.8 If we were to seek antecedents to this peculiar feature of the structure of collective bargaining in Spain, *i.e.* the two channels of negotiation (the "statutory" channel, which results in a generally applicable agreement, and the "extra-statutory" channel, which results in an agreement of limited applicability) we might cite the "illicit" collective agreements which were sometimes negotiated during the Franco regime outside the framework of the works councils or official Organización Sindical. But today's dual negotiating channels owe more to the collective bargaining of the Second Republic than they do to that of the Franco regime; in addition to the negotiation of generally applicable collective agreements conducted by joint bodies chaired by the labour authorities, it was also possible, under the Second Republic, to conclude "negotiated agreements" whose scope was restricted to members of the contracting organizations.

6.9 Today, the industrial relations scene appears to be dominated by generally applicable collective agreements, usually signed by committees and delegates at enterprise level and jointly by the major trade unions at industry-wide level. We cannot, however, ignore the fact that a change in the composition or strategy of trade union or employers' representative bodies would lead to a substantial increase, more or less overnight, in the number and significance of extra-statutory agreements. A breakdown in the policy of joint action normally observed in this area by the two major trade union bodies would be enough to give rise to such a situation, at least as regards industry-wide agreements. In point of fact, at the level of national multi-industry agreements there has been an alternation of generally applicable agreements and agreements of limited applicability because of differences in the trade union policy followed with respect to these agreements by the major confederations, the UGT and CC.OO.

6.10 The combination of elements of change and continuity that can be observed in the current structure of collective bargaining in Spain can also be detected in the other component of the negotiation sytem, *i.e.* the process of drawing up and renewing agreements. The most outstanding difference from the previous situation here is undoubtedly recognition of the right to strike, which has eliminated the complication of labour disputes and episodes of repression, a complication that frequently arose during the final years of Franco's rule.

6.11 However, in addition to the change in the collective bargaining process brought about by recognition of the right to strike, a significant persisting feature should also be pointed out: the considerable effort that has to be devoted to negotiation, an effort which is certainly out of proportion to the absolute and relative numbers covered by agreements. There are two main reasons for this unwieldy negotiating machinery. The first is the custom of renewing agreements annually; this practice is beginning to die out but is still followed in many cases. The other reason is the lack of any connection or co-ordination between industry-wide and company agreements, which means that many aspects which could be negotiated just once at industry-wide level have to be discussed in every enterprise. To put this disadvantage into perspective, however, it should be pointed out that legislation and bargaining practice have established a number of mechanisms to alleviate the problem. These include the role that certain company agreements play as a model for others, the rule of temporarily retaining the substantive content of the previous agreement when it is impossible to conclude a new agreement, and the continuing validity of the statutory industry-wide regulations from the previous regime, which are maintained to supplement any regulatory areas not covered by collectively negotiated provisions.

7. Industrial conflict

7.1 The history of industrial relations in Spain, particularly in the period prior to 1936, contains few instances of negotiation or compromise between unions and employers; rather, it features numerous examples of strategies of outright imposition or resistance from the two sides. In a situation of this nature, the stances adopted by the social partners each reflect a mirror image of the other. On the employers' side, the stance is one of totally dominating labour relations, turning the contract of employment into a contract of acceptance and, in the event of a dispute, refusing to make any concessions and continuing to resist until the outcome is either victory or defeat. On the unions' side, likewise, the stance is one of rejecting all idea of compromise between offers and counter-offers, preferring to use "direct action" as a means of dictating employment and working conditions unilaterally. In Spain, these intransigent attitudes have been inspired or reinforced by an ideological view of industrial conflict, widespread in the traditional labour movement, whereby strikes are regarded as a kind of "revolutionary training ground", or even as the means of bringing about social revolution or the overthrow of a hostile political regime.

7.2 These attitudes and strategies promoted a spasmodic pattern of industrial conflict, usually occurring in a climate of strong tensions and public unrest, with prolonged and bitter disputes alternating with equally lengthy lulls and periods of inaction. The difficulty of institutionalizing and regulating strikes and labour disputes in the industrial relations system has been due in no small measure to the lack of an adequate legal channel for them during almost the whole of this period of history.

7.3 From 1975 onwards, partly as a result of the changed attitudes of the social partners and partly as a result of the changes in the legal framework, industrial conflict in Spain lost the insurrectional or all-out confrontational ingredients which had so often accompanied it up to 1936, and also the identity of being a struggle against the political regime which was a feature of labour disputes during the second phase of Franco's rule. Nevertheless, labour disputes have not entirely lost their political slant, even though its physiognomy and its significance may have changed.

7.4 The fact is that, with strikes legalized under the labour law system, industrial conflict.in recent years has taken the shape that might be expected of a trade union movement which has a small membership and scarce financial resources and is strongly inclined towards representation on public bodies: strikes are brief (often taking the form of intermittent strikes); they are usually accompanied by demonstrations or actions to attract the attention of public opinion (transport blockades are, perhaps, the preferred form of industrial action with this end in view); and they call more or less explicitly for support or mediation from the labour administration or the political authorities. With industrial conflict taking this shape, it is hardly surprising that it is labour disputes in the public sector that have become particularly important, especially in the public transport sector, where strikes have the greatest impact.

7.5 In so far as the strategic approach to industrial disputes adopted both by the unions and by the employers pays particular attention to their impact on public opinion and, thereby, on the political process, it may be said that industrial conflict in Spain has a political slant. On the part of the workers, strikes and other forms of industrial action are used both as a financial weapon against the employers and as a political weapon against the public authorities. For their part, the employers or relevant public authorities gear their reaction to concentrating on winning over public opinion because of the harm caused by industrial action affecting essential public services or the general body of consumers.

7.6 The political significance of industrial disputes in Spain is also underlined by the fact that collective bargaining usually seems to have taken place in a context of social concertation, with the more or less explicit participation of the Government. Up to 1986, these negotiations based on social concertation had varying results, but never led to mobilization of the workers; if they failed, the price in terms of conflict was paid in added difficulties for the collective bargaining process at industry-wide and company level. The crisis in social concertation that erupted in 1987 and 1988 had a very different outcome, and the unions' protest against the Government's economic policy culminated in a resounding episode of industrial conflict: the general strike of December 14, 1988.

7.7 It is perhaps still too early to venture a detailed assessment of the long-term repercussions of this strike on Spain's industrial relations system. In general terms it can be said that it emphatically marks the end of the system's formative period and of the climate of consensus that accompanied it, initiating a new phase in which the pattern and terms of exchange of relations between Government, parties and unions are beginning to change. More specifically, the traditionally close link between the PSOE (Socialist Workers' Party) and the UGT confederation has been broken, with the withdrawal of the latter's electoral support, and the Government's relations with the entire trade union movement are undergoing serious difficulties, with the announcement of a law regulating the right to strike. There have, however, been no major changes as regards collective bargaining and the level of conflict.

7.8 Two other features of industrial conflict in Spain should be mentioned in this general account. One is the limited role of the lock-out, which under current legislation may be used by employers only in specified circumstances in order to protect property and people on the work premises; the purpose of this was to put a stop to the spiral of confrontational action and resistance that was mentioned earlier. The other feature is the infrequent use of special independent means of settling labour disputes, such as conciliation, mediation and voluntary arbitration; there are, on the other hand, numerous collective disputes ''of rights'' (concerning the interpretation or application of existing regulations) which are dealt with by the courts. This lack of development of other formulas for conflict resolution that are unconnected with the public authorities clearly shows the influence of the interventionist tradition.

8. State intervention in industrial relations

8.1 From the first signs of the ''social question'' in Spain, the authorities promised to play a very active role in protecting workers and regulating industrial relations. For one reason or another, they postponed acting on these promises to intervene in the labour market for a number of years. Yet the ideologies and practices of the social partners (tending on the one side towards "direct action" and "social revolution" and on the other towards the "iron hand" and authoritarianism) did not create an atmosphere propitious to the regulation of labour relations by collective bargaining. After some delay, the promised intervention finally came and played its role in this area of social relations up to the end of the Restoration period, a role which became increasingly prominent under Primo de Rivera (1923-1929) and particularly during the Second Republic (1931-1936). This growing presence of the state made itself felt on two major counts: the passing of protective legislation, with ad hoc mechanisms to ensure its application, and the setting-up of a network of corporatist bodies (called "comités paritarios" (joint committees) under Primo de Rivera's dictatorship and "jurados mixtos" (joint councils) under the Second Republic) whose members were representatives of the employers' and employees' organizations, chaired by a public official.

8.2 The central role of the state in Spanish industrial relations, which, as we have seen, continued despite a succession of political regimes of differing tendencies, reached its peak during the first phase of Franco's rule when the Government, via the Ministry of Labour, took exclusive responsibility for the industry-wide regulation of terms and conditions of employment (the regulations issued were called "Labour Ordinances" or "Labour Regulations") and exercised strict control over certain decisions taken by enterprises in connection with staff management, such as the adoption of company rules, changes in employment relationships and dismissals. All this was in addition to the Ministry's power over the official union, the Organización Sindical, in that it controlled its structure and appointed its officials, and its general regulatory powers, which were virtually unrestricted.

8.3 The introduction of "collective agreements", which, in industrial relations, marks the beginning of the second phase of Franco's rule, signified the opening-up of certain areas to the collective autonomy of occupational groups. But the prevailing trend was still heavy state intervention. The Ministry of Labour retained its power to regulate employment conditions at industry-wide level, reducing the function of the collective agreement to one of merely improving on the statutory conditions. The formal acceptance of collective disputes, which did not, as we have already seen, go so far as the legalization of direct industrial action, was immediately followed by legal regulations governing the settlement of disputes, by virtue of which the authorities ended by imposing whatever final decision they deemed appropriate. In addition to all this, the courts were to hear any cases deriving from the interpretation of collective agreements; this meant that, given the increasing demands being made by workers, the judicial authorities had to intervene much more in labour relations. Finally to complete the picture, we have to consider the legislative and general regulatory powers of the higher organs of the state, which had to be used with great frequency in the early 1970s, and the additional opportunities for exerting influence which were provided by the "hierarchical" control of the official Organización Sindical, though these diminished as time passed.

8.4 As has already been pointed out, the period of political transition saw the beginning of a gradual reduction of administrative intervention in industrial relations and of legislative and official intervention in the regulation of minimum employment conditions. Thus, the power to regulate labour relations at industry-wide level was used only in exceptional cases, though past labour regulations or ordinances which had accumulated during the preceding regime were maintained and served to supplement collective agreements. Similarly, opportunities for the state to regulate employment conditions from the substantive point of view were virtually reserved for the legislators, who used them with restraint. Intervention by the labour authorities as regards collective labour relations was confined to defining the minimum level of service to be maintained in the event of strikes in essential public services, seeking settlements of collective labour disputes and provisionally controlling the legality of collective agreements.

8.5 So, the recent withdrawal of the state from some aspects of industrial relations did not imply the disappearance of its central role in this area of society. The labour authorities still have significant powers over labour relations within enterprises, such as authorizing collective dismissals caused by economic difficulties, or general changes in working conditions. Also, because there are still no effective extra-judicial mechanisms for settling disputes, the courts have a continuing role to play. Thirdly and most importantly, the suppression of public intervention in some areas has been partly offset by the appearance of intervention of a different kind. This includes social concertation and the promotion of a selective and centralized framework of employee and employer representation.

8.6 Since the late 1970s and early 1980s, social concertation, or the joint definition by the Government and the major trade union and employers' confederations of the broad lines of collective bargaining and important aspects of economic and social policy, has enabled the Government to shape the content of collective bargaining to remain within limits which are compatible with its economic objectives. The forerunner to this series of agreements based on social concertation was the 1977 Moncloa Pact, although this was actually a political pact between political factions rather than a true social contract. This preliminary political pact, which included practical compromises as regards pay restraint, was followed by other social contracts or pacts based on social concertation in the true sense, sometimes taking the form of tripartite agreements between the Government, trade unions and employers' organizations (1981), sometimes national multi-industry agreements between representative trade union and employers' confederations (1980, 1983) and sometimes a combination of the two (1984). In addition to this legal role, the Government has always participated fully in initiating and drafting these agreements.

8.7 The concessions granted in return for the pay restraint and industrial peace sought by the Government via social contracts have been of various kinds. One has been the influence exerted by the trade unions and employers'associations over labour legislation, which is clearly perceptible in the Workers' Statute and the Trade Union Freedom Act. Another is their participation in determining economic and social policy, hard evidence of which can be seen in the consultations preceding the submission to Parliament of draft State Budgets and the passing of regulations governing employment policy. A third is the right granted to the most representative trade unions and employers' associations to be represented on the constituent bodies of the social administration and part of the economic administration.

8.8 As a result of the combined effect of these contracted concessions, the industrial relations organizations have gained considerable institutional power and have had to concentrate a very sizeable proportion of their outside activities in these institutional areas. In any event, it is now misleading or even incorrect in this context to speak generally of "industrial relations organizations". In practice, it is the confederal bodies of the most representative trade unions and employers' associations who have benefited most from this institutional power, since it is they who are responsible for negotiating social contracts and who have been the main recipients of the concessions offered in return by the Government. Here, the interventionist line of social concertation becomes intertwined with the authorities' new policy on industrial relations, which is to promote a selective and centralized framework of representation. Certainly, social concertation not only requires but also encourages this type of framework of trade union and employer representation by concentrating decision-making and power in the upper echelons of certain organizations.

8.9 The state's principal means of promoting such a framework of representation have been the granting by law of "special status" to the most representative unions, and the legislators' choice of certain criteria of representativeness with a view to producing precisely the effects of selection and centralization. By virtue of their special status, the most representative unions have succeeded in securing the main advantages and powers granted by law to the trade unions, ranging from the negotiation of statutory collective agreements to a preferential entitlement to funds from the "patrimonio sindical acumulado". As a result of all this, in certain sectors and occupations designation as "most representative" has become a condition of survival in the trade union market. By virtue of the criteria of representativeness chosen by the legislators, unions which are members of the major national confederations have automatic access to this special status, while those which are not confederated or are not members of other confederations must have won over ten per cent. of places on the unitary representative bodies in the sector or district in question.

9. Description of the Spanish industrial relations system

9.1 Now that we have analysed the development and elements of the industrial relations system in Spain, it may be appropriate in this final section of the Introduction to attempt to give a general description of the system, summarizing its salient features. These are, in the author's opinion: 1) the rapid, state-assisted creation, at the end of the Franco regime, of the various elements of the system: representative bodies, bargaining practices and intervention by the authorities; 2) the fact that being a "voters' trade unionism" rather than a "members' trade unionism" naturally governs the activities of the unions in relation to the workers; and 3) the interconnection of action by the state (labour legislation, management of public social services) and by the employers' and employees' organizations (collective negotiation of conditions of employment), the most conspicuous illustration of which is social concertation, though it is also reflected in other aspects. These three features may be supplemented by a fourth: the relative weakness of the representative function performed by the unions and employers' associations at industry-wide level, which are restricted from above by the significant powers of the national confederations and from below by the tradition of the enterprise as the centre of negotiating activity.

9.2 The rapid formation of the industrial relations system was made possible by the easy process of re-establishing institutions and organizations dating from previous political regimes on new legal bases of freedom of association and the autonomy of the social partners. Inevitably, the bodies representing employers and workers played a very important role in this process, having to undertake the task of both reconciling interests and constructing or reconstructing their own organizational structure. We must not, however, forget the strategic intervention by the state in the development of the industrial relations system, establishing ground rules which facilitated the rapid creation of the system and implementing a clearly selective policy on representation. By 1987, after numerous "union elections" and continuing collective bargaining, the system was certainly well established, though there

24

were some worrying signs of bureaucratization and destruction of the basic associative fabric.

9.3 One of the reasons for the rapid formation of the industrial relations system in Spain (and, within the system, of the framework of representation) was, as stated earlier, the repeatedly good results won by the major confederations in the elections of workers' delegates and workers' committees. But the function of "union elections" in the system as a whole extends beyond this contribution to clarifying the trade union scenario. As already mentioned, these elections have also made it possible to build a strong, stable bridge between the trade unions and the unitary bodies representing the entire workforce within enterprises and workplaces. Yet another function of these elections has perhaps been even more important: that of legitimizing the position of some unions whose broad institutional powers contrast with their small memberships.

9.4 In seeking a name for a trade union situation such as that described here, the one that seems to be the most appropriate is "voters' trade unionism", since this underlines the significance of electoral results in the union context and at the same time suggests the blurring or disappearance of the importance of union membership. This replacement of a "members' trade unionism" by a "voters' trade unionism" is also reflected in two other important elements of the labour relations system: the generalized applicability of collective agreements irrespective of union membership, and the restrictions on union security arrangements (the closed shop, collective bargaining levy, etc.). Irrespective of the primary purpose they fulfil, these regulations have had the secondary effect of inhibiting two of the main incentives for individual union membership: pressure from the union side through collective bargaining and the worker's interest in the financial returns of union membership. With a legal framework of this kind, the motives for union membership are reduced (in the absence of any real pressure from the peer group's opinion, which is effective only in highly unionized work environments) to ideological affinity or the actual holding of representative office. It is therefore not surprising that, in Spain, only officials, activists and workforce representatives within enterprises tend to be trade union members.

9.5 The assistance provided by the state to help the industrial relations organizations to rapidly re-establish themselves carried the more or less explicit price of their collaboration in consolidating the new democratic regime and seeking a way out of the economic crisis. With the coming to power of a Socialist Government, this trading of assistance and collaboration between the state and the main employers' and employees' organizations turned into a relatively peaceful exchange of influences in their respective areas of activity. The state has conceded financial advantages and participation in its decisions on social and economic matters; the representative

25

bodies have until now consented, with varying degrees of difficulty, to bring their approach into line with the Government's economic objectives. Nobody can guarantee that this relationship of "political" exchange between the state and the industrial relations organizations will last in the medium or long term. There are, however, strong objective reasons in favour of its continuation, including the historical tradition of representation on public bodies, the advantages of industrial peace and the financially weak position of the unions.

9.6 One last feature which can be pointed out in this description of Spain's industrial relations system is the relative insignificance of the industry-wide level of collective bargaining, whose field of action seems to be squeezed between national agreements based on social concertation and the mass of company-level agreements. The reasons for this relative lack of bargaining activity at industry-wide level include, in particular, the absence of any connection or co-ordination between industry-wide agreements and company-level agreements; this lack of co-ordination, in its turn, is offset temporarily by the continuing validity of the labour regulations and ordinances passed under the previous regime. The effect of all these factors on collective bargaining is the virtual reduction of the field of application of industry-wide agreements to small and medium-sized enterprises and the frequent limitation of their content to the regulation of basic conditions of employment (pay levels, working hours, etc.).

9.7 The relative insignificance of the industry-wide level of collective bargaining is also reflected in terms of representative bodies, in that the industrial unions and federations are very much in the background in comparison with the confederations and the enterprise-level representative bodies. A similar phenomenon might have been expected to affect employers' organizations, to parallel this overshadowing of the industry-wide level in trade-union organizations. Yet this has not happened, probably because of the importance of the industry-wide level in relations between the employers' associations and the public authorities.

A

1. **"ABANDONO DE SERVICIO":** Occasional stoppage of or abstention from the performance of work. The term is usually reserved for the stoppage of work by **public servants** and by workers employed by enterprises contracted to carry out public works and services. Except in the case of a legal strike, deserting one's post or withdrawing services is in law a disciplinary or administrative offence and, if it occurs in essential services, may constitute a criminal act. See also **quitting the job**.

2. **ABANDONO DE TRABAJO — QUITTING THE JOB:** Cessation of work with the intention of not resuming it; sudden ending of the contract of employment by the worker without notice, demonstrated by a conclusive act or behaviour. Under current Spanish law it is deemed an irregular or unofficial form of resignation, in that the required notice is not given to the employer, who may therefore demand the appropriate compensation for damages. Some collective agreements provide for the loss, in such cases, of **end-of-service** *pro rata* **entitlements** to **special bonuses** and pay for **annual holiday** not yet taken. See also **"abandono de servicio"**.

3. **ABANICO SALARIAL — WAGE SPREAD:** Overview or graphical representation of the various levels or scales of the **pay/wage structure** within a sector, enterprise or certain group of workers. It indicates the pay differential between the various categories or posts within this unit and particularly between maximum and minimum levels. See **wage/pay**.

4. **ABI:** See **National Multi-Industry Basic Agreement of 1979** (Acuerdo Básico Interconfederal de 1979).

5. **ABOGADO LABORALISTA — LABOUR LAWYER:** A lawyer who assists and advises workers or their representative bodies in matters of labour law and **social security**. In the **legal procedure for labour cases**, the assistance of a labour lawyer is compulsory only for bringing appeals before the higher labour courts. In these advisory functions, labour lawyers are sometimes in competition with other professionals such as labour and social welfare officers or social workers.

6. **ABSENTISMO — ABSENTEEISM:** Non-attendance at work. Spanish legislation allows dismissal when a worker's absences, even if justified, coincide with a high rate of absenteeism among the entire company workforce. See **dismissal for objective reasons**.

27

7. **ABSORCION DE SUBIDAS SALARIALES — "ABSORPTION" OF PAY INCREASES:** Method of adjustment intended to prevent pay increases from being applied across the board irrespective of the previous level of pay. It means that the pay level existing prior to a pay increase remains unchanged if it is already above the level of that increase or, if it is lower, is increased only by as much as is essential to bring it up to the new level. This method of neutralizing pay increases is the general rule under Spanish law and therefore applies, in overall annual calculations, to the raising of the **national minimum wage** and also, in principle, to pay increments established in collective agreements and to **discretionary pay supplements**.

8. **ACCESO A LOS CENTROS DE TRABAJO — ACCESS TO WORKPLACES:** This term is normally used to refer to the right to enter and remain in work premises which the law grants to certain persons other than the enterprise's employees. The **Labour Inspectorate** has traditionally been entitled to free access, without prior notice and at any time, to any workplace or work establishment in order to conduct checks or investigations. Spanish law also grants the elected **union officials** of the **most representative unions** the right to enter workplaces to take part in trade union or workers' activities, provided they do not interrupt the normal functioning of the production process. **Workers' representatives** (workforce representatives and trade union representatives) are also entitled to free access to all the enterprise's premises in order to perform their functions, particularly that of monitoring working conditions and health and safety conditions. See **facilities for workers' representatives**.

9. **ACCIDENTE DE TRABAJO — ACCIDENT AT WORK/INDUSTRIAL ACCIDENT:** Physical injury suffered during or as a result of work. The definition of this term, coined in Spain by the first labour regulations, has gradually been broadened as a result of case law to include accidents while travelling (accidents "en route"), illnesses accompanying the consequences of an accident (concurrent illnesses) or caused by work (some of which would then be categorized as **occupational illnesses/industrial diseases**) and, in the absence of evidence to the contrary, any injury suffered during working hours and at the place of work. As occupational risks, accidents at work and industrial diseases enjoy better insurance protection than common or ordinary risks. In 1988 the number of serious industrial accidents in Spain was around 16,000; over the past few years the figures have increased in industry, construction and the service sector, and decreased in agriculture. See **health and safety, social security**.

10. **ACCION ASISTENCIAL — SOCIAL WELFARE ACTION:**
See **positive action**.

11. **ACCION POSITIVA — POSITIVE ACTION:** Action taken
to offset or neutralize the comparatively lesser chances of
employment or social integration of certain population groups
who are disadvantaged because of sex, race or some other personal
or social condition. The term ''positive action'' derives from the
American term ''affirmative action'' and is interchangeable with
the expression ''discriminación favorable o positiva'' (positive
or reverse discrimination), which means the elimination or
alleviation of situations of inequality suffered by various groups
in society. One of its main areas of implementation is vocational
training and employment, where in Spain it takes the form of
special employment programmes, **employment quotas** and
preferential employment directed particularly at young workers,
female employment, disabled workers and **older workers**.
Sometimes, the term ''positive action'' is used in contrast to the
term ''acción asistencial'' (social welfare action) to differentiate
it from the mere provision of aid or grants.

12. **ACCIONARIADO OBRERO — EMPLOYEE SHARE
OWNERSHIP:** Method by which workers participate in
ownership of the enterprise by acquiring shares, usually under
conditions which are more favourable than those prevailing on
the market. In comparison with other countries (particularly the
United States, United Kingdom and North European countries),
the method has been little used in Spain. See **workers'
participation**.

13. **ACOSO SEXUAL EN EL TRABAJO — SEXUAL
HARASSMENT AT WORK:** Sexually offensive behaviour or
repeated, unwanted sexual advances (also known as ''asedio
sexual'') in the workplace. In many cases, the offenders make
use of their superior position in the company hierarchy and the
opportunities this provides for influencing the employment and
working conditions of the victims. Spanish law recognizes the
right to protection against sexually offensive language or
behaviour, which can constitute grounds for the imposition of
disciplinary or even penal sanctions.

14. **ACTIVIDAD SINDICAL — TRADE UNION ACTIVITY:**
In its broadest sense, any activity performed by trade unions.
More narrowly used to refer to activities to defend and promote
workers' occupational interests, through legal means such as

collective bargaining, strikes or industrial action and participation or representation of interests in the enterprise or before the authorities (**representation on public bodies**).

15. **ACTIVISTA SINDICAL — UNION ACTIVIST:** See **trade unionist**.

16. **ACUERDO BASICO INTERCONFEDERAL DE 1979 (ABI) — NATIONAL MULTI-INDUSTRY BASIC AGREEMENT OF 1979:** Agreement signed on July 10, 1979 by the **UGT** and **CEOE** confederations with the aim of laying down some joint criteria on the basic shape of the industrial relations system following the 1978 Constitution. It achieved its aim of securing a role for the employers' and employees' organizations in the political process and in the sphere of employment, thus significantly influencing the labour regulations being drafted at that time, particularly the **Workers' Statute**.

17. **ACUERDO ECONOMICO Y SOCIAL DE 1984 (AES) — ECONOMIC AND SOCIAL AGREEMENT OF 1984:** Agreement signed on October 9, 1984 by the Government, the **UGT** workers' confederation and the **CEOE** and **CEPYME** employers' organizations to establish the outlines of economic and social policy for 1985 and 1986. It also included agreed commitments on pay increases, productivity and absenteeism, the structure and duration of agreements, and procedures for settling industrial disputes. See **social concertation**.

18. **ACUERDO INTERPROFESIONAL — GENERAL MULTI-INDUSTRY AGREEMENT:** Collective agreement which covers various occupations, sectors or branches of activity. In Spain, this term is commonly used to refer to agreements reached by trade union and employers' confederations. The term "acuerdo marco" (framework agreement) is used to refer to agreements on structure, rules of precedence and co-ordination between agreements; in addition to these procedural elements, they usually include substantive elements such as guidelines and basic criteria for collective bargaining at lower levels.

19. **ACUERDO MARCO — FRAMEWORK AGREEMENT:** See **general multi-industry agreement**.

20. **ACUERDO MARCO INTERCONFEDERAL DE 1980 (AMI) — NATIONAL MULTI-INDUSTRY FRAMEWORK AGREEMENT OF 1980:** General multi-industry agreement signed by the **UGT** and **CEOE** confederations on January 5, 1980

and renewed in 1981 with the participation of other union organizations. It laid down criteria and guidelines regarding the content of collective agreements in order to restrain pay increases, gradually reduce working hours and increase productivity. It also sought to define the outlines of the new industrial relations system by framing rules on the co-ordination of, precedence between and duration of collective agreements and on the establishment and functioning of trade unions in enterprises and workplaces. Part of its content was included in later labour laws.

21. **ACUERDO NACIONAL DE EMPLEO DE 1981 (ANE) — NATIONAL EMPLOYMENT AGREEMENT OF 1981:** Tripartite agreement signed by the Government, the **CC.OO.** and **UGT** trade union organizations and the **CEOE** employers' organization on June 9, 1981. It defined the outlines of economic and social policy and collective bargaining for the period 1981-1982, and established the bases for easing the restrictions on temporary contracts of employment in Spanish legislation and for the financial backing of the unions. See **social concertation**.

22. **ACUERDO SOBRE PARTICIPACION EN LA EMPRESA PUBLICA DE 1986 — AGREEMENT ON WORKERS' PARTICIPATION IN PUBLIC ENTERPRISES OF 1986:** Agreement signed on January 16, 1986 by representatives of public enterprises and the **UGT** confederation as a result of the commitments agreed upon under the **AES**. It extended trade union rights in public enterprises and introduced trade union participation in these bodies (and in the corresponding group enterprises) in the form of representatives on their Boards of Directors or on Information and Monitoring Committees set up for this purpose.

23. **ACUERDOS/PACTOS EN LA FUNCION PUBLICA — PUBLIC SERVICE AGREEMENTS AND "PACTS":** Terms applied to the different types of agreement that may be reached by public servants in negotiating their working conditions. "Agreements" bear on issues governed by the political organs of the state and must, therefore, be expressly and officially approved by these bodies before they can be declared valid and come into force, while "pacts" cover all other issues and, once signed, are directly binding on the parties. Public service agreements and "pacts" are covered by the 1987 **Representation of Public Servants Act**; their negotiation began in 1988, after the creation of the Joint Negotiating Committees provided for in the Act.

24. **ADHESION A UN CONVENIO COLECTIVO — ADOPTION OF A COLLECTIVE AGREEMENT:** Agreement by which the parties authorized to negotiate in a given **bargaining unit** accept the content of a collective agreement in force in another unit. It usually occurs because of difficulty in reaching a separate agreement or the convenience of adopting an agreement that is regarded as typical within the sector concerned.

25. **ADMINISTRACION DE TRABAJO — LABOUR ADMINSTRATION:** Public administration services and activities concerning social, industrial relations and employment policy. Labour administration came into being in Spain in the 1900s with the setting-up of the **Institute of Social Reform** and other administrative bodies that gave way in 1920 to the **Ministry of Labour**, which, under this or a similar name, remains to this day. A large number of the functions of labour administration are still performed by centralized state authorities but after the 1978 Constitution many of them were transferred to the regions or Autonomous Communities, which now have considerable powers in the sphere of industrial relations, health and safety at work and the management of employment policy. Labour administration in Spain has always been highly interventionist but, in return, has also encouraged the participation of the trade unions and employers' associations in areas or functions theoretically reserved for the authorities. See **corporatism, representation on public bodies**.

26. **ADMINISTRATIVO — OFFICE STAFF:** Workers who perform administrative, management, documentation, inspection or accounting tasks in an enterprise. Office staff are included in the category of **non-manual workers** or "white collar" workers and feature in industry-wide provisions as a specific **occupational group**; they are often classed together with **technical personnel**, with whom they are grouped for the election of **workers' committees**.

27. **AES:** See **Economic and Social Agreement of 1984** (Acuerdo Económico y Social de 1984).

28. **AFILIACION SINDICAL — TRADE UNION MEMBERSHIP OR AFFILIATION:** Subscription to and membership of a given trade union. Spanish law explicitly recognizes the right to join or not to join a trade union and declares null and void any negotiated agreements or decisions which

impose or impede membership or make employment dependent on membership or non-membership. See **union membership clauses**.

29. **AGENCIA DE COLOCACION — PLACEMENT AGENCY:** See **employment services**.

30. **AGENTES SOCIALES — SOCIAL ACTORS:** See **social partners**.

31. **AJUSTE DE PLANTILLAS — STAFFING ADJUST-MENT:** Adaptation of the size or skills of the workforce to new features of the organization of production, because of the introduction of a new production process, the start-up of new activities or rearrangement of the work system. See **labour flexibility**.

32. **ALARGAMIENTO DEL TRABAJO — JOB ENLARGE-MENT:** Adding to the tasks assigned to a particular **post/employment position/job**, with a consequent increase in their "horizontal dimension" or "scope" but, unlike **job enrichment**, without incorporating planning and control tasks. Job enlargement may serve to counter the monotony of narrowly fragmented jobs, and is also used with a view to increasing workers' motivation by attempting to provide them with a broader understanding and knowledge of the production process. See **work organization**.

33. **AMBIENTE DE TRABAJO — WORK ENVIRONMENT:** Physical and climatic circumstances or conditions (lighting, temperature, ventilation, humidity, cleanness, noise or vibration, etc.) of work.

34. **AMI:** See **National Multi-Industry Framework Agreement of 1980** (Acuerdo Marco Interconfederal de 1980).

35. **ANARCOSINDICALISMO — ANARCHO-SYNDICALISM:** Current within the **labour movement** and trade union movement, directly inspired by libertarian or anarchistic thinking. It rejects any collaboration with the authorities or negotiation with employers and favours direct or unilateral action, confrontation or conflict as the means of pursuing its objectives. In Spain, in contrast to its minority presence in other countries, it was one of the major currents in trade unionism in the early part of the century. See **National Confederation of Labour**.

36. **ANE:** See **National Employment Agreement of 1981** (Acuerdo Nacional de Empleo de 1981).

37. **ANTICIPO DE SALARIOS — ADVANCE:** Payment of wages before work has been performed or before wages are due; it constitutes an exception to the prevailing principle of payment of wages in arrears. Spanish law permits the payment in advance of future wages (up to a maximum of three months) to encourage the worker to accept a job. It also recognizes, under certain conditions, the employee's right to the payment in advance of wages earned but not yet due, corresponding to work already performed.

38. **ANTIGUEDAD — SENIORITY/LENGTH OF SERVICE:** Period of service completed by an employee within the same enterprise. Under Spanish law, seniority confers entitlement to certain **pay supplements** and determines the amount of **compensation for dismissal/severance pay** and **compensation for termination of the employment contract**. It is also usually taken into account in collective agreements as one of the factors relevant to the **promotion** of employees, as indicating experience and special commitment to the work. The **Workers' Statute** established ceilings for seniority supplements, in order to maintain the correlation between pay and performance.

39. **APOYO SALARIAL — WAGE SUPPORT: Job creation** measure whose purpose is to reduce wage costs by granting employers subsidies for every employee hired or paying part of the wage. It is normally used by the authorities to encourage the recruitment of population groups who have the greatest difficulty in obtaining employment, particularly young people. It has been much used in Spain over the past few years, particularly in employment schemes launched by the regions or Autonomous Communities.

40. **APRENDIZAJE — APPRENTICESHIP:** In the labour sphere, on-the-job training in an occupation or skill, following the instructions of an expert or specialist (master craftsman). In Spain, this form of **vocational training**, which derives from the old trade guilds, used to be provided under apprenticeship contracts, which have been replaced in recent years by **work-experience contracts** and **job-training contracts**.

41. **ARBITRAJE — ARBRITRATION:** Means of settling disputes or disagreements whereby an impartial third party issues a decision which in Spain is binding on the parties. It may be either

compulsory or voluntary, depending on whether there is a legal obligation to go to arbitration to resolve a particular form of dispute; it may be conducted in accordance with either existing legislation or the principles of natural justice; and it may be conducted by one or more arbitrators. Under the Spanish industrial relations system arbitration is rarely used, in spite of a certain legal tradition (Law of 1908) and the fact that recent legislation (1979) made provision for the creation of Labour Arbitration Tribunals (though they have not yet been established). Some collective agreements make provision for the possibility of referring disputes regarding their application and interpretation to a third party, usually following the unsuccessful intervention of the **joint collective agreement committee**.

42. **ARBITRAJE OBLIGATORIO — COMPULSORY ARBITRATION:** Form of **arbitration** whereby the parties are legally obliged to submit to the binding decision of a third party for the termination of a dispute or disagreement. Spanish law makes provision for this form of arbitration to be used in the case of strikes which, because of their duration or consequences or because of the attitudes of the parties, may seriously damage the national economy (**Labour Relations Decree-Law** of 1977). However, it has been used infrequently and until now only in the public sector.

43. **ARRENDAMIENTO DE SERVICIOS — CONTRACT FOR SERVICES:** Standard Civil Code contract whereby a person undertakes to provide a particular service for a fixed price. In the early years of the Industrial Revolution it was used for contracting waged labour, a purpose for which it was replaced by the **contract of employment**. It is now used mainly for contracting people in the liberal professions (lawyers, doctors, consultants, etc.), services external to the enterprise (accountancy, consultancy, etc.) or work of an occasional or marginal nature.

44. **ASAMBLEA — MASS MEETING:** Meeting of workers to discuss labour and trade union issues, often to conduct consultations or ballots on decisions relating to the **collective bargaining process** or the calling of **industrial action**. In Spanish law it is regarded as one of the means of collective action by the workers in a particular enterprise or workplace, although it mainly constitutes a channel of communication and information between workers and their representatives and a means of workers maintaining control over these representatives. Because of this, and the numerous requirements that have to be met before a meeting can be held, worker/workforce organization based on mass meetings is subject to a good deal of restriction.

45. **ASAMBLEA GENERAL — GENERAL MEETING:** See **union structure**.

46. **ASCENSO — PROMOTION:** Advancement of an employee to a higher category or grade. It is usually based on criteria of seniority, training, merit and ability and is often preceded by **merit-based selection**, performance appraisal or selection tests. See **occupational category** and **occupational classification**.

47. **ASEDIO SEXUAL — SEXUAL HARASSMENT:** See **sexual harassment at work**.

48. **ASISTENCIA SOCIAL — SOCIAL ASSISTANCE:** Various social welfare measures which complement or supplement basic **social security** cover. The main beneficiaries include socially underprivileged groups or those with little chance of obtaining employment or any other form of income (the disabled, refugees, immigrants, the elderly, etc.). In Spain, social assistance is provided through various channels, largely from the State Budget or the budgets of different public authorities. The contribution of the Autonomous Communities has become particularly important in recent years, with the introduction of the **social wage**.

49. **ASOCIACION EMPRESARIAL — EMPLOYERS' ASSOCIATION:** Group formed by employers to defend and promote their interests. In keeping with prevailing trends, employers' associations have played a vital role in the Spanish industrial relations system over the last 10 years, particularly in launching and fostering social concertation, consolidating and defining the features of collective bargaining and making proposals on labour laws. Legally, they are governed by the 1977 Employers' and Employees' Associations Act. In contrast with practice in other countries, in Spain they are not normally referred to as "unions"; nor are they covered by the legislation implementing the right to trade union freedom. See also **most representative employers' association, Spanish Confederation of Small and Medium-Sized Enterprises, Spanish Confederation of Employers' Organizations, employers' organizations**.

50. **ASOCIACION EMPRESARIAL MAS REPRESENTATIVA — MOST REPRESENTATIVE EMPLOYERS' ASSOCIATION:** In general, the employers' association with the most influence or largest membership in a given area. Under Spanish law, this status is granted to those organizations which can demonstrate most **representativeness** in overall terms;

specifically, those which cover a minimum of 10 per cent. of enterprises at national level or 15 per cent. within an Autonomous Community, provided that these enterprises employ the same minimum percentage of workers in the areas concerned. This status confers the legal right to have **representation on public bodies** and to negotiate **generally applicable collective agreements**. In contrast to the situation as regards trade unions, difficulties in applying these criteria and the lack of any reliable census of enterprises and employees have, up to now, impeded any precise identification of the most representative associations, though it is generally agreed that the **Spanish Confederation of Employers' Organizations** (**CEOE**) is the front runner. In collective bargaining, the notion of representativeness on the employers' side tends to be replaced in practice by the preparedness of workers' representative bodies to recognize a particular association.

51. ASOCIACIONES PROFESIONALES — PROFESSIONAL ASSOCIATIONS: See **occupational trade unionism**.

52. AUDIENCIA SINDICAL — TRADE UNION INFLUENCE: A trade union's ability to influence, call out or mobilize workers. Although it can be measured by various criteria, under Spanish law it is assessed on the basis of the support won in electoral ballots or consultations (**union elections**). Evidence of a specified electoral strength (**representativeness**) is required for access to certain areas of **trade union activity** (negotiation of **generally applicable collective agreements, representation on public bodies**).

53. AUMENTO SALARIAL — PAY RISE/PAY INCREASE: Increase in workers' **wages/pay** or remuneration. See **pay adjustment, national minimum wage**.

54. AUTOEMPLEO — SELF-EMPLOYMENT: Independent employment or employment on one's own account, whether as an individual or via companies consisting solely or mainly of workers (workers' **co-operatives, workers' limited companies**). The term has appeared recently in the context of **employment policy**. To encourage self-employment, Spanish law has provided for the lump-sum payment of unemployment benefits (''capitalization'') and the granting of aid to enterprises set up by workers, usually after they have been affected by redundancy.

55. **AUTOGESTION — (WORKERS') SELF-MANAGEMENT:**
Form of **workers' participation** in which workers assume
responsibility for the management and control of the enterprise.
Spanish history has witnessed several experiments in self-
management, the most radical being the collectives formed in
the Republican zone during the Civil War.

56. **AUTONOMIA COLECTIVA — COLLECTIVE
AUTONOMY:** Powers possessed and exercised by workers' and
employers' representative bodies to protect and promote their
own interests. In particular, power to draft internal rules on
organization, to regulate labour relations and to establish
procedures for resolving collective disputes and disagreements.
In its strictest sense, collective autonomy may take the form of
the right to **collective bargaining** over working conditions and
terms and conditions of employment. It is founded in the principle
of personal autonomy and is the opposite of the concepts of
heteronomy and interventionism (on the part of the authorities)
in regulating or shaping labour relations and in resolving labour
disputes.

57. **AUTORIDAD LABORAL — LABOUR AUTHORITIES:**
Authorities with powers and functions regarding labour relations
in Spain. They form part of **labour administration**, either in
central government or in the authorities of the Autonomous
Communities with jurisdiction in labour matters.

58. **AUTORREGULACION DE LA HUELGA — SELF-
REGULATION OF STRIKE ACTION:** Control of strikes by
means of collective bargaining and/or internal trade union
decisions and rules. Although there is in Spain trade union and
doctrinal support for this form of control, in practice the
development of its typical instruments (codes of conduct) and
indeed of other mechanisms (no-strike clauses, independent
procedures for settling disputes) has so far been very limited.
The only experiments in self-regulation have been in defining
minimum services within **essential public services**.

B

59. BAJA INCENTIVADA — VOLUNTARY REDUNDANCY:
Resignation or early cessation of employment of an employee,
encouraged by financial inducements such as **compensation for
termination of the employment contract** in excess of the
statutory amount, or supplementation of **social security** benefits.
It is usually offered to **older workers**, leading to **pre-retirement**
or **early retirement**. In Spain it has been used mainly in
enterprises undergoing rationalization or restructuring, but also
in growing or expanding enterprises as a means of rejuvenating
the workforce and, in general, to eliminate a labour surplus.

60. BALANCE SOCIAL — SOCIAL BALANCE SHEET:
Representation of a given enterprise's social and socio-economic
development. Modern versions attempt to cover not only the point
of view of owners and shareholders but also that of the workers
and other interested groups (consumers, suppliers, creditors,
public authorities, etc.). The social balance sheet and the
provision of socio-economic information in general have come
into being as a result of the change in the traditional notion of
the enterprise, which is no longer identified solely with the interest
of its owners (maximizing profit) and is seen as a "coalition of
interests" of various groups. This means that greater attention
has to be paid to its social aspects.

61. BANCO ECONOMICO — EMPLOYERS' SIDE: See **parties
to collective bargaining**.

62. BANCO SOCIAL — EMPLOYEES' SIDE: See **parties to
collective bargaining**.

**63. BANDA DE CRECIMIENTO SALARIAL — "PAY-
GROWTH BAND":** Method of regulating and forecasting **pay
rises/pay increases** using indicators or upper and lower limits
which take into account the rate of inflation and the retail price
index and which make it possible to adjust pay rises to the
circumstances prevailing in each sector or enterprise. It is a
procedure typical of centralized systems of collective bargaining
and **social concertation**. In Spain it was used quite widely in
the 1980s as a means of **pay restraint**.

64. BASE SINDICAL — RANK AND FILE: The mass of trade
union members; in the strict sense, all those who belong to a trade
union without holding office, as opposed to **union officials**. The
term is sometimes used to refer to the population of workers who,
without being members, follow the instructions of a union, vote
for its candidates, support its calls for industrial action and, in
general, are influenced by its activity as a representative body.

65. **BASES DE TRABAJO — BASIC PROVISIONS:** Basic provisions governing employment conditions in a given sphere (usually at enterprise, industry-wide or occupational level). Because they cover a particular industry or occupation, they have to respect the general minimum regulations established by law; because they are basic, they allow improvements to be made on the initiative of the parties to the contract of employment. This term, which has a long history in the Spanish system of labour relations, was first used to refer to the rules adopted by ''comités paritarios'' (joint committees) and **joint councils**; later it applied to the employment conditions laid down by **Labour Ordinances** and Labour Regulations. It is now less common and alludes mainly to the terms and conditions agreed in a **collective agreement**.

66. **BECA DE FORMACION PROFESIONAL — VOCATIONAL TRAINING GRANT:** Temporary subsidy, allowance or aid to cover the costs of apprenticeship or attendance at vocational training courses by the recipients of such assistance. In addition to its original purpose of promoting training and employment, this form of aid may also be used to assist or protect the unemployed. It is with this combination of purposes that it is used in Spain, particularly as part of the **Employment Training and Integration Plan**. This type of aid, funded by various public authorities, has increased considerably over the past few years.

67. **BENEFICIOS MARGINALES — FRINGE BENEFITS:** Set of payments and services provided by enterprises in addition to **wage/pay**. It sometimes corresponds to **payment in kind**, though its scope is usually broader, in line with the more up-to-date concept of **personnel management**: company cars, insurance policies and pension schemes, assistance with housing costs and education fees, covering of legal costs, etc. The use of this form of alternative pay, which is commonly received in Spain by **senior management** and, in general, by **professional and managerial staff** and specialists, is encouraged by tax advantages.

68. **BLOQUEO DE MERCANCIAS — BLOCKADING OF GOODS:** Pressure tactic consisting of physically preventing either the delivery to an enterprise of certain goods or the movement of goods manufactured and/or marketed by the enterprise. Such action may be taken independently or in addition to a **strike**. In Spain, where it is usually illegal, its use is uncommon. See also **boycott/blacking, industrial action**.

69. **BOICOT — BOYCOTT/BLACKING:** Industrial action in which workers appeal to the public not to purchase or use the products or services of a particular enterprise. It is legal in Spain as being covered by the constitutional right to freedom of expression, although it may lead to liability if it causes unjustifiable damage to other assets.

70. **BUENA FE — GOOD FAITH:** General principle that should govern compliance with all contractual obligations and, by extension, any other obligations deriving from employment relationships, whether individual or collective. Spanish law establishes breach of good faith (disloyal competition, the pursuance of criminal activities causing financial damage to the enterprise, the improper exercise of freedom of expression to the prejudice of the enterprise, deception or abuse of trust, etc.) as grounds for **disciplinary dismissal**. At collective level, Article 89.1 of the Workers' Statute obliges the parties to a collective agreement to abide by this principle in their negotiations (see **duty to bargain**).

41

C

71. **CADENA DE MONTAJE — ASSEMBLY LINE:** Production process in which the various work stations are distributed along a conveyor belt moving the product during the course of manufacture, so that each worker on the line performs a specific task or operation which is part of the process, repeatedly and usually at a fixed working rhythm and in accordance with a highly fragmented division of labour. It is an initial stage in the automation of work and is now being phased out by the introduction of new technologies and the use of new methods of **work organization** which pay greater attention to job satisfaction and worker autonomy. See **production-line work**.

72. **CAJA DE RESISTENCIA — STRIKE FUND:** Financial resources which trade unions use to offset the loss of **wage/pay** in the event of a **strike** and to cover strike costs. In Spain, because of their financially weak position very few trade unions provide for strike pay, with the exception of **ELA-STV**, which has always had a strike fund; this is one of the reasons why strikes tend to be short.

73. **CALENDARIO LABORAL — WORK CALENDAR:** Table indicating annual working days and public holidays. It is drawn up by the Government as a general guideline, but the Autonomous Communities and local authorities can then alter or add certain public holidays for their particular areas. In a narrower meaning, the term may also be used to signify the table that the management of an enterprise is obliged to draw up each year and display for employees' information, indicating the distribution of weekly and annual **working time** and **rest days**.

74. **CALIDAD DE LA VIDA DE TRABAJO — QUALITY OF WORKING LIFE:** The quality of life offered by the **work environment**, as well as the manner and conditions in which work is performed.

75. **CAMBIO DE PUESTO DE TRABAJO — INTERNAL JOB TRANSFER:** Movement from one post to another within the same enterprise, sometimes including a change of activity (**functional mobility**), occupational category or group (work of a higher or lower category) or even of place of work or residence (**geographical mobility**). Spanish legislation lays down that changes of activity must be within the same occupational group; authorizes movements to a post of lower category only in urgent, unforeseeable circumstances; permits a change to a post in another town (**transfer** or **temporary relocation**) only on technical,

organizational or production grounds; and, under certain conditions, grants employees the right to be classed permanently in a higher category once they have been classed in it on a temporary basis beyond a minimum period.

76. **CANON DE NEGOCIACION COLECTIVA — COLLECTIVE BARGAINING LEVY:** Sum that workers covered by a collective agreement must pay to the negotiating trade unions to cover bargaining costs. Under Spanish legislation **collective agreements** may establish the existence, amount and method of payment of this levy, though these must be expressly accepted, in writing, by each worker, a legal requirement that has impeded its use.

77. **CARGA DE LA PRUEBA — BURDEN OF PROOF:** Obligation to prove, in a case before the courts, the assertions made in the complaint. Under Spanish law the obligation lies in principle on the plaintiff, although there are various exceptions to this rule: presumptions in favour of the party who performs the act, inversion of the burden of proof, or transfer of the obligation to prove to the party appearing as the defendant (which applies, on the basis of constitutional case law, in cases of **discrimination**, sanction or **dismissal** on the grounds of trade union activity, particularly **disciplinary dismissal**).

78. **CARGO SINDICAL — UNION OFFICIAL:** Person holding a position of command, responsibility or confidence in a **trade union**; in the broad, colloquial sense, a workers' representative (member of a **workers' committee** or **workers' delegate**) in an enterprise or workplace. The senior officials of Spanish trade unions are usually the president, general secretary and national officers, who are generally elected or appointed by trade union Congresses or Meetings. Spanish legislation grants the elected officials of the **most representative unions** the right to time off or **leave of absence**, as well as the right to have **access to workplaces** and be present there to perform their duties.

79. **CARRERA — CAREER PATH:** Sequence of **posts/employment positions/jobs** held by a person during their working life, in one or more employing organizations. In Spain, workers' career paths have tended to develop within a single enterprise and have been particularly dependent on **seniority/length of service**.

80. **CARTA DE DESPIDO — LETTER OF DISMISSAL:** Written notification (letter, telegram or other suitable medium) of **dismissal**. According to Spanish legislation and case law, it

must contain both the cause and the date of dismissal, to enable the employee's legal defence. Failure to comply with these requirements renders the employer's action **unfair dismissal**.

81. **CARTA SOCIAL EUROPEA (CSE) — EUROPEAN SOCIAL CHARTER:** Treaty concerning social and labour issues signed within the Council of Europe on October 18, 1961, and ratified by Spain on April 29, 1980 with reservations regarding the interpretation and implementation of certain collective rights in order to ensure compatibility with constitutional regulations governing **public servants**. The declaration of social and labour rights prepared within the European Community during 1989 bears the same name.

82. **CATEGORIA PROFESIONAL — OCCUPATIONAL CATEGORY:** Grouping of tasks or jobs with uniform characteristics. The number and names of the categories within each enterprise are usually laid down in industry-wide provisions. Assignment to an occupational category determines the specific content of the work performed and the level of **wage/pay**. It is common for individual or collective agreements to assign workers to a "polyvalent" (multi-skill) category, which enables wider and more flexible use of their services. This is also the purpose of **occupational groups**, which combine various categories and mark the limit of a worker's **functional mobility**.

83. **CC.OO.:** See **Trade Union Confederation of Workers' Commissions** (Comisiones Obreras).

84. **CENTRALIZACION SINDICAL — CENTRALIZATION OF TRADE UNIONS:** Situation or tendency whereby important decisions and directives are usually issued by the **trade union confederation** bodies, with little or no participation by the rank and file or trade union bodies lower down the hierarchy. It is often an obstacle to **trade union democracy**. In Spain, centralization has in recent years been encouraged by legal factors: centralization of **collective bargaining**, prevalence of **social concertation**, the notion of **representativeness**; and by trade union practices or rules: direct affiliation to the confederation, restriction of the autonomy of federated or confederated trade unions, criteria for the distribution of funds.

85. **CENTRO DE TRABAJO — WORKPLACE:** Usually defined in law as an independent technical or organizational unit with its own productive purpose. As a concept it is extremely important for the application of many labour regulations and provisions:

geographical mobility, election of workers' representatives, formation of workplace branches, etc.

86. **CEOE:** See **Spanish Confederation of Employers' Organizations** (Confederación Española de Organizaciones Empresariales).

87. **CEPYME:** See **Spanish Confederation of Small and Medium-Sized Enterprises** (Confederación Española de la Pequeña y Mediana Empresa).

88. **CERTIFICADO DE TRABAJO — REFERENCE/WRITTEN TESTIMONIAL:** See **professional competence and status**.

89. **CESANTIA — SEVERANCE PAY:** Refers specifically to severance pay for civil servants. See **termination of the contract of employment**.

90. **CESE — CESSATION (OF EMPLOYMENT):** See **termination of the contract of employment**.

91. **CESION DE TRABAJADORES — PROVISION OF LABOUR:** Supplying or loaning of workers to another employer, usually with a view to avoiding the need to comply with the provisions of industry-wide agreements or generally evading labour laws. It is akin to mediation or intermediation in the contract of employment, and is sometimes concealed by means of the **sub-contracting** of labour, goods and services (labour-only sub-contracting). It may be of a temporary or permanent nature. Spanish law prohibits the temporary provision of workers, states that the persons by and to whom workers are provided are jointly and severally liable, recognizes the right of the workers concerned to be deemed to be employed by the enterprise of their choice, and lays down administrative and penal sanctions. A more pejorative term for this practice is ''**prestamismo**''. See **placement, temporary employment agency**.

92. **CGT:** See **General Confederation of Labour** (Confederación General de Trabajo).

93. **CIERRE PATRONAL — LOCK-OUT: Industrial action** taken unilaterally by the employer and consisting of the total or partial cessation of production activity. The premises may be physically locked or some other action may be taken to prevent the performance of work, *e.g.* the shutdown of power supplies, withholding of the materials or tools necessary for production,

etc. To protect the **right to strike**, Spanish legislation (**Labour Relations Decree-Law**, 1977) allows lock-outs only when persons or property are in danger, as a policing measure. Lock-outs appear to be a rare occurrence in Spain, where they tend to be used only when an enterprise faces grave economic difficulties or when persons or property are at serious risk. See **labour dispute/industrial dispute/trade dispute, employer's managerial authority/managerial prerogative**.

94. **CIRCULOS DE CALIDAD — QUALITY CIRCLES (QC):** Groups of workers formed either on their own initiative or in response to an invitation from the enterprise to discuss, at regular intervals, **work organization** and the **quality of working life**. Quality circles are still rare in Spain and those that do exist are very unevenly distributed among the various economic sectors. See **semi-autonomous work group**.

95. **CLASIFICACION PROFESIONAL — OCCUPATIONAL CLASSIFICATION:** Assignment of the worker to a particular **occupational group** or **category**. This decides the scope and content of many occupational rights and obligations: work content, the level of **wage/pay, career path** opportunities, etc. The traditional method of classification is based on the worker's **occupational skills** or experience. However, because of the effects of the technological revolution and new techniques of division of labour, and in order to escape the inflexibility of this method, classification using **job evaluation** is becoming increasingly common. Under Spanish law it must be agreed between employee and employer in accordance with the provisions of industry-wide agreements.

96. **CLAUSULA DE DESCUELGUE — GET-OUT CLAUSE/ESCAPE CLAUSE:** Clause often included in **general multi-industry agreements** or **product-sector or industry agreements**, affording enterprises that find themselves in economic difficulties total or partial release from the obligation to comply with the agreed terms, particularly as regards pay. Such clauses are normally used in situations of economic crisis and because of enterprise reorganization and restructuring processes. In Spain they have been only rarely applied, partly because of trade union opposition. The term "cláusula de desenganche" is also used.

97. **CLAUSULA DE DESENGANCHE — GET-OUT CLAUSE/ESCAPE CLAUSE:** Synonym of **cláusula de descuelgue**.

98. CLAUSULA DE PAZ — NO-STRIKE CLAUSE: See **collective agreement, obligational clauses**.

99. CLAUSULAS DE EMPLEO — EMPLOYMENT CLAUSES: Clauses aimed at guaranteeing or increasing the level of employment, whereby the employer undertakes not to reduce the number of employees (particularly by redundancy), to increase staffing levels by recruiting new personnel, to absorb the personnel of contracted enterprises, etc. They are usually **obligational clauses**, which means that failure to comply with them gives rise only to entitlement to compensation for damages. They are relatively common in **collective agreements** in the **public sector**.

100. CLAUSULAS DE SEGURIDAD SINDICAL — UNION MEMBERSHIP CLAUSES: Clauses of collective agreements whereby the employer undertakes to grant certain advantages or preferential treatment for unionized employees or members of a particular union, usually with a view to encouraging or guaranteeing trade union membership. English terminology tends to be used in Spain: "closed shop" (pre-entry closed shop, with union membership as a condition of recruitment by the enterprise), "union shop" (post-entry closed shop, where joining a union within a certain period after recruitment is a condition of employment) and "maintenance of membership" (maintenance of union membership as a condition of continuing employment). In a broad sense, this heading may include clauses on the **collective bargaining levy** and the deduction at source of **trade union dues** (a kind of check-off). Clauses which require or impose trade union membership are illegal in Spain because they are contrary to the right not to belong to a union.

101. CLAUSULAS NORMATIVAS — SUBSTANTIVE CLAUSES: That part of a **collective agreement** which has a direct normative effect on individual employment relationships. Unlike **obligational clauses**, clauses of this type continue on a provisional basis when the agreement has expired, they can be the subject of **extension** to other groups, and failure to comply with them is subject to administrative sanctions.

102. CLAUSULAS OBLIGACIONALES — OBLIGATIONAL CLAUSES: That part of a **collective agreement** which merely lays down obligations and undertakings for the parties to the agreement. One important clause of this type is the "cláusula de paz" (no-strike clause), whereby the parties undertake to refrain from engaging in industrial action for a certain period, normally the duration of the agreement.

103. **CNT:** See **National Confederation of Labour** (Confederación Nacional del Trabajo).

104. **COBERTURA DEL DESEMPLEO — UNEMPLOYMENT COVER:** Financial assistance for the unemployed. In Spain, official figures (produced by **INEM**) make a distinction between gross and net rates of cover, depending on whether unemployed agricultural workers are included. Both the gross and net rates fell between 1976 and 1988 but have been tending to recover over the past few years as a result of improved unemployment benefits. The rate of unemployment cover is an indicator of need, but a very rudimentary one since it does not take account of the increasingly diverse nature of the unemployed population. See **long-term unemployment, participation rate/activity rate**.

105. **CODIGO DE TRABAJO — LABOUR CODE:** Systematically arranged collection of all labour legislation in a single regulatory text. The only Spanish legislation to be promulgated under this title was Primo de Rivera's Labour Code (1926), which in reality was nothing more than a compilation of earlier regulations on **apprenticeship, accidents at work** and industrial courts, with the addition of Spain's first specific provisions governing the **contract of employment** (and some of its variations, such as the **seafarer's company service contract**). The past few years have seen a reawakening of interest in the drafting of a new Labour Code (a compilation of basic labour laws into which any later provisions would be incorporated, in the same way as the French Code du Travail); this scheme has yet to come to fruition.

106. **COGESTION — CO-DETERMINATION:** Form of worker participation in the management of an enterprise, usually through including representatives of the workforce in the enterprise's governing bodies, mainly the Board of Directors, either as a minority or with equal voting power. In Spain, on the basis of a Law of 1962 (repealed in 1980), a system of co-determination with workers having a minority voice was set up on an experimental basis in public enterprises and in private enterprises with more than 500 employees. The **Agreement on Workers' Participation in Public Enterprises** of 1986 was intended to initiate new methods of co-determination.

107. **COLEGIO PROFESIONAL — PROFESSIONAL BODY:** Type of occupational body whose aim is to protect and promote the interests of a particular occupational group, usually people exercising a liberal profession. In contrast to a **trade union**, membership is compulsory and the tasks of monitoring and

regulating exercise of the profession are delegated to it by the authorities. These professional governing bodies also provide assistance and protection for their members and tend to promote and defend professional interests, particularly when their members provide services under a contract of employment (*e.g.* doctors).

108. **COLOCACION — PLACEMENT:** As a general term, occupation of a post or entry into employment; in employer's terms, assigning a worker to a particular job. Placement requires prior information and organizational effort to match labour supply and demand, and private employment agencies were quick to emerge, but were gradually replaced by public employment offices. This regulatory process began in Spain with the Employment Service Act of 1931 and its principles still apply today. Current law prohibits private agencies (with the exception of **personnel selection agencies**) and gives public employment services (directed and managed by **INEM**) a monopoly over placement activities. In Spain, placement is governed by the principle of freedom of contract, as regards freedom to enter into a contract and freedom to choose the other party to the contract. Employers (whether in the public or private sector) have certain obligations regarding public employment offices, but they may make offers of employment specifying by name particular individuals they wish to hire as opposed to merely stating the number and type of workers required; they may choose among the workers registered with public employment offices (except where preferential rights exist for certain groups of workers or where compulsory hiring rules apply); and in many cases they may recruit individuals directly. There has recently been some questioning of the effectiveness of public placement procedures and calls have been made, reflecting the current trend towards flexibility, for an end to the public monopoly in this area, with the consequent opening-up of the field to private agencies, and particularly **temporary employment agencies**.

109. **COMISION — COMMISSION:** Remuneration which depends on the outcome of work performed either on a self-employed basis or as an employee. It is common in certain activities involving sales, the securing of customers or contracts and the like (*e.g.* commercial representatives). In the case of employees it is generally paid in addition to a fixed wage or salary, thus becoming a type of pay supplement, similar to bonuses or incentive payments.

110. **COMISION DE REFORMAS SOCIALES — COMMISSION FOR SOCIAL REFORM:** Commission set up in 1883 to study and promote the advancement and well-being of the working class, to channel relations between capital and labour and generally address social questions. It conducted numerous studies and surveys on the situation of the working class and drafted several labour regulations, which to a certain extent laid the foundations of Spanish labour law. The Commission was reorganized in 1890 and replaced in 1903 by the **Institute of Social Reform**; it was a first step in the development of Spain's **labour administration**.

111. **COMISION EJECUTIVA — EXECUTIVE COMMISSION:** See **union structure**.

112. **COMISION NEGOCIADORA — BARGAINING COMMITTEE:** Committee consisting of workers' and employers' representatives, formed to negotiate a **collective agreement**. For the negotiation of generally applicable collective agreements, Spanish law makes a distinction between the enterprise level or below (where the employer can negotiate with the workforce representatives or the **workplace branches** of the majority unions) and the multi-employer level (where only **trade unions** and **employers' associations** with a **representativeness** of at least 10 per cent. in the relevant bargaining unit or area are authorized to negotiate). The committee must not exceed a maximum number of members (12 or 15 for each party) and must represent the majority of workers and employers concerned. The rigidity of these rules has sometimes made bargaining difficult and in some cases has led to the signing of **extra-statutory agreements**.

113. **COMISION PARITARIA DEL CONVENIO — JOINT COLLECTIVE AGREEMENT COMMITTEE:** Committee that, under Spanish law, must be set up by the parties to a **collective agreement**, to deal with any disputes concerning the application and interpretation of the agreement and to perform any other functions assigned to it. It is often a requirement that appeals must be brought before these committees before they may be taken to court.

114. **COMISIONES OBRERAS (CC.OO.) — TRADE UNION CONFEDERATION OF WORKERS' COMMISSIONS (CC.OO.):** Major Spanish trade union body set up in the late 1950s through organizing on the basis of mass meetings and the coming-together of workers of various political and ideological

tendencies, mainly Christian, Socialist and Communist. It came to embrace the doctrines of the Spanish Communist Party (PCE), an organization with which it then shared its leaders but from which it has for some time now been tending to distance itself, because of the change in the Party itself (which is now part of the Izquierda Unida, a new political organization of united left-wing parties) and because of developments in the trade union movement in Spain. Its trade union structure and status as a leading workers' organization were mainly consolidated through the practice of individual members of the CC.OO. standing for election to representative posts in the **Vertical Union** (infiltration strategy or "entrismo"). In 1978, when **freedom of association/trade union freedom** was recognized in Spain, the organization held its first congress and constituted itself as a class-based union, with a highly centralized structure. The results of **union elections** indicate that it is losing its original status as the major trade union confederation to the **UGT**, though it still has sizeable electoral influence, including in the public service. In 1983, it claimed to have 716,000 members — 40.5 per cent. of all trade union members in Spain. It has never joined an international organization, though it has applied for membership of the ICFTU and ETUC.

115. **COMITE DE EMPRESA — WORKERS' COMMITTEE:** Organ of workforce representation in enterprises or workplaces with 50 or more employees; its purpose is to defend and promote employees' interests at work. In contrast to trade union representatives, its members (5-75, depending on the size of the enterprise or workplace) are elected by and from among all the employees (**union elections**) and hold their mandate for four years. Its powers and responsibilities include the right to negotiate company or workplace agreements; the right to information or consultation on financial, commercial and labour matters; responsibility for supervising and monitoring compliance with regulations on labour matters, social security, employment and health and safety; and the right to take administrative and legal action. Its members must observe **professional confidentiality**. In contrast to the situation in other countries, the role of the workers' committee in Spain is principally one of opposition, rather than of involvement in joint management. It occupies a central position in the Spanish industrial relations system both because of its powers and responsibilities and because of its ability to bring trade union activities and programmes into the enterprise and workplace, given that, although it is not union-based, it has from the start been influenced and even dominated by the **trade**

unions. See also **workers' delegates, facilities for workers' representatives, guarantees for workers' representatives, staff councils**.

116. **COMITE DE HUELGA — STRIKE COMMITTEE:** A body that must, according to Spanish law, be set up and appointed by workers and/or organizations taking part in a **strike**, its essential task being to direct the dispute and take all possible action to settle it.

117. **COMITE DE SEGURIDAD E HIGIENE — HEALTH AND SAFETY COMMITTEE:** Joint body responsible for promoting and monitoring the application of **health and safety** regulations, proposing measures to protect the life and physical well-being of workers and, where there is an imminent risk of accident, calling a halt to production. These committees consist of technical specialists, workers' representatives and persons appointed by the enterprise. They are compulsory in enterprises or workplaces with more than 100 employees and in those where particularly dangerous activities are carried on. Some of the committee's functions, particularly supervision and monitoring tasks, overlap with those of workforce and trade union representatives.

118. **COMITE EJECUTIVO — EXECUTIVE COMMITTEE:** See **union structure**.

119. **COMITE INTERCENTROS — MULTI-PLANT WORKERS' COMMITTEE:** Body representing all the employees of an enterprise which has several workplaces, with more than one **workers' committee** or with one such body plus **workers' delegates**. Its members are elected by and from among these workforce representatives, and its composition must be proportional to the strength of the different **trade unions** within its sphere of competence. Although it is not a body directly required by law (since both its setting-up and its powers and responsibilities are decided by a **collective agreement**), its role in the Spanish industrial relations system has been increasing over the past few years, particularly since its right to negotiate company agreements has been recognized in law. These committees are very commonly set up in large enterprises.

120. **COMITES PARITARIOS — JOINT COMMITTEES:** See **joint councils**.

121. **COMPLEMENTOS SALARIALES — PAY SUPPLE-
MENTS:** Pay components, distinct from **basic pay**, which are
added to basic pay under different headings: a worker's special
skill (personal supplements), the special circumstances of the work
or occupational activity performed (job or location supplements),
or improved output in terms of quality or quantity (quantity and
quality supplements). Sometimes they arise because of a special
way of calculating remuneration (sums payable at intervals of
more than a month: **special bonuses** and **profit-related pay**) or
a special form of remuneration (**payment in kind**). Both their
calculation and their amount are determined by collective
agreement or by the contract of employment. A concept borrowed
from the public service, pay supplements increase the complexity
of the pay/wage structure and the breadth of the **wage spread**.
They generally represent a large part of real earnings.

122. **CONCEPTOS SALARIALES — PAY COMPONENTS:**
Amounts that make up the **wage/pay**, essentially divided into
basic pay and **pay supplements** or **additional payments**. This
division makes it possible to adjust remuneration to suit each
worker or job, although it is sometimes nothing more than a way
of formalizing piecemeal rises, or is merely used to increase pay
by indirect or concealed means.

123. **CONCERTACION SOCIAL — SOCIAL CONCERTATION:**
Way of managing and tackling social and economic problems
within a given sector or in society as a whole; it is characterized
by negotiation or consultation between the authorities and the
most representative organizations protecting different interests,
particularly **trade unions** and **employers' associations**, the social
partners. Because social concertation follows some of the
principles of **corporatism**, it has also been called "neo-
corporatism" or "social corporatism". It is usually effected
through meetings, consultations or negotiations, and its fruits
include **social contracts** and tripartite agreements, which serve
as the framework of social and economic policy and sometimes
imply real legislative negotiation in that they prepare the text of
future laws or regulations. Social concertation featured very
frequently in the process of Spain's transition from dictatorship
to democracy (**Moncloa Pacts, National Employment
Agreement, Economic and Social Agreement**) and has had a
great impact on the Spanish industrial relations system, not only
because it directly addressed many labour issues, but also because
it encouraged harmonious relations between the trade unions and
employers' associations, established the basic framework of the
collective bargaining system, reduced industrial conflict and

consolidated the presence and role of the social partners. Even so, concertation has suffered marked vicissitudes and has alternated with periods of a breakdown of relations between Government and social partners. See **social dialogue**.

124. **CONCILIACION — CONCILIATION:** A dispute settlement procedure in which an impartial third party helps the parties to communicate and to dilute their differences. It differs from **mediation** and **arbitration** in that the conciliator is not required to make any specific proposals regarding settlement of the dispute, though it is in practice difficult to distinguish conciliation from mediation. Voluntary conciliation is rarely used in the Spanish industrial relations system. In the **legal procedure for labour cases**, it is the compulsory forerunner to a court judgement and has enabled the amicable settlement of many legal disputes, particularly in cases of dismissal and individual pay grievances and in certain sectors (construction, retail distribution, the hotel trade).

125. **CONCURSO DE MERITOS — MERIT-BASED SELECTION: Personnel selection** procedure in which the candidate's curriculum vitae and occupational background are assessed. It is used mainly in the public service, though it has also been applied to the employees of public administrative authorities and large enterprises, particularly those holding positions of responsibility or management posts.

126. **CONDICION MAS BENEFICIOSA — MOST FAVOURABLE CONDITION:** Principle with a long tradition in Spanish labour law, whereby it is compulsory to respect **terms and conditions of employment** acquired by unilateral concession on the part of the employer or by an individual agreement. This is associated with the *ad personam* guarantee clause often included in **collective agreements**, which protects individual conditions against any new collective regulations.

127. **CONDICIONES DE TRABAJO — WORKING CONDITIONS/TERMS AND CONDITIONS OF EMPLOYMENT:** Conditions or circumstances in which work is performed. Part of the **contract of employment** referring to the methods, hours and place of the performance of work and to the remuneration received in return. A distinction is usually made (particularly in the provisions of industry-wide agreements) between financial or pay conditions and conditions other than pay. Guaranteeing minimum, essential conditions for workers has been the traditional concern of labour legislation.

128. **CONDUCTA ANTISINDICAL — ANTI-UNION BEHAVIOUR/ANTI-UNION ACTIVITY:** Action or omission that is prejudicial to **freedom of association/trade union freedom**. It normally stems from acts or decisions by the employer, but may also originate from actions by employers' associations, public authorities and even trade unions or workforce representatives. A common example is **discrimination** in employment or in terms and conditions. Spanish law authorizes judges to order the immediate cessation of anti-union behaviour and provides for administrative or penal sanctions.

129. **CONFEDERACION ESPAÑOLA DE LA PEQUEÑA Y MEDIANA EMPRESA (CEPYME) — SPANISH CONFEDERATION OF SMALL AND MEDIUM-SIZED ENTERPRISES (CEPYME):** Main Spanish organization of small and medium-sized enterprises. It was set up in 1977 and has been a member of the **Spanish Confederation of Employers' Organizations** (**CEOE**) since 1980, which has enabled it to be a participant in the processes of **social concertation** and **collective bargaining** and to have **representation on public bodies**.

130. **CONFEDERACION ESPAÑOLA DE ORGANIZACIONES EMPRESARIALES (CEOE) — SPANISH CONFEDERATION OF EMPLOYERS' ORGANIZATIONS (CEOE):** Spanish employers' association set up in 1977 as an umbrella organization for more than 100 territorial associations/federations and about 50 industrial federations. According to its own figures, its members represent more than a million enterprises, which in their turn employ 75 per cent. of the working population. Its main governing bodies are the General Assembly, Management Council and Executive Committee. The President is elected every three years by the General Assembly. Its principal members, apart from **CEPYME**, include **FTN**, CONFEMETAL, CEIM and AEB. It is undoubtedly the most established and representative employers' organization in Spain and, as such, signs the majority of collective agreements and usually represents employers before the authorities and trade unions. Its work covers both labour and purely economic issues.

131. **CONFEDERACION GENERAL DE TRABAJO (CGT) — GENERAL CONFEDERATION OF LABOUR (CGT):** Breakaway organization from the **CNT**.

132. **CONFEDERACION NACIONAL DEL TRABAJO (CNT) — NATIONAL CONFEDERATION OF LABOUR (CNT):** Spanish trade union confederation set up in 1910 on the basis

of anarchistic or libertarian trade union groups and sectors. Although it was persistently banned and persecuted, it managed to consolidate its position as a major trade union force until the Second Republic (when it had some 1,200,000 members). After the long hiatus of the Franco regime, it re-emerged in the 1970s but has never regained its former influence and is now a minority organization. Its traditional strategy (rejection of negotiation and participation in favour of direct action) has aroused heated internal debate in recent years and promoted a number of breakaways; the most important of these led to the formation of the CGT (General Confederation of Labour). See **anarcho-syndicalism**.

133. **CONFEDERACION SINDICAL INDEPENDIENTE DE FUNCIONARIOS (CSIF) — INDEPENDENT TRADE UNION CONFEDERATION OF PUBLIC SERVANTS (CSIF)**: Trade union organization formed around 1980 from various independent public servants' trade unions. Its activities are currently confined to the public service, where it is the major representative body and has considerable electoral strength.

134. **CONFEDERACIONES SINDICALES — TRADE UNION CONFEDERATIONS**: Trade union organizations, also known as "central trade union bodies", which serve as umbrella organizations for smaller trade union associations, usually **industrial federations** and **territorial federations** but also occupational unions and unions covering specific groups of workers. They are generally national, although they are occasionally confined geographically to one Autonomous Community. Their activities tend to cover all economic sectors, though they are in some cases restricted to very specific sectors or categories (public service, **professional and managerial staff**, health-care workers). They are set up in response to workers' interest in joining forces, but their emergence may also be prompted by legal factors (**representativeness**), tradition, or the characteristics of the industrial relations system (**collective bargaining**). See **Trade Union Confederation of Workers' Commissions, National Confederation of Labour, Independent Trade Union Confederation of Public Servants, Galician Trade Union Confederation, General Workers' Confederation.**

135. **CONFLICTIVIDAD LABORAL — INDUSTRIAL CONFLICT (LEVEL OF)**: Refers particularly to industrial action and, more especially, **strikes**, measured not only in terms of their number or frequency but also in terms of the number of workers involved and the number of working days lost.

Industrial conflict in Spain eased during the 1980s, following the end of the political transition and the adaptation and conversion of the production system.

136. **CONFLICTO COLECTIVO DE TRABAJO — LABOUR DISPUTE/INDUSTRIAL DISPUTE/TRADE DISPUTE:** Disagreement or confrontation between employers and workers. Collective labour disputes may be disputes of rights (concerning application of an existing agreement or regulation) or disputes of interest (concerning regulation of a particular issue); a third party is usually called in to settle a dispute of rights, whereas direct use of **industrial action** is more common in the case of a dispute of interest. In Spain, **strikes** are the most common form of industrial action, with **pickets, boycotts, blockading of goods, transport blockades** and, on the employer's side, **lock-outs** trailing far behind; settlement through a third party essentially works through legal channels (see **special legal procedure for industrial disputes**), sometimes with the prior intervention of **joint collective agreement committees**; the use of **conciliation, mediation** or **arbitration** is very rare in Spain. It is intended that the **trade unions** and **employers' associations** should set up voluntary dispute-settlement procedures.

137. **CONGELACION DE SALARIOS — PAY FREEZE:** Prohibition or strict limitation of **pay rises**, as a result of an **incomes policy**. Legal limitation of pay rises was common in Spain during the 1960s and 1970s; nowadays it applies only to public sector employment, where ceilings are set for the pay levels fixed in **collective agreements**. During the 1980s, the policy has also been to freeze social incomes and **social security** benefits.

138. **"CONGLOBACION":** Criterion for establishing precedence between conflicting regulations or agreements on **terms and conditions of employment**: the one to be applied is that which is the most favourable overall. Nowadays it is mainly used to establish precedence between conflicting **collective agreements** that overlap with each other. It is the opposite of the criterion of accumulation (simultaneous application of conflicting regulations or agreements, selecting the most favourable individual provisions of each). Spanish law prescribes its use for both statutory regulations and negotiated agreements. The Italian term "conglobamento" is sometimes used.

139. **CONGRESO GENERAL — GENERAL CONGRESS:** See **union structure**.

140. **CONSEJO DE ADMINISTRACION — BOARD OF DIRECTORS:** The supreme governing body of joint-stock companies, appointed or approved by the general meeting of shareholders. In Spain, its members are not covered by labour law. It is the site of one of the forms of **workers' participation**.

141. **CONSEJO ECONOMICO Y SOCIAL — ECONOMIC AND SOCIAL COUNCIL:** Joint body consisting of representatives of the various interest groups, responsible for advising the authorities on economic and social affairs. Bodies of this type have traditionally existed in Spain. At present, the Constitution provides for the creation of such a council to assist the Government with economic planning.

142. **CONSEJO EJECUTIVO — EXECUTIVE COUNCIL:** See **union structure**.

143. **CONSEJO SUPERIOR DE LA FUNCION PUBLICA — SUPREME COUNCIL OF THE PUBLIC SERVICE:** Supreme representative body of the employees of public authorities, set up in 1984. It consists of representatives of the **most representative trade unions** and of the various public authorities. It is responsible for co-ordinating and advising on public-service matters, and serves as the general electoral council for elections of **public servants'** representatives. Police employees have a similar body of their own (Consejo Superior de Policía).

144. **CONSULTA — CONSULTATION:** Form of **workers' participation** whereby workers, through their representatives, voice their opinion on certain matters, usually before the enterprise makes a final decision. The fact that it does not lead to binding agreements usually distinguishes it from **collective bargaining**, though in practice consultation often implies negotiation. Spanish law grants workforce representatives the right to circulate information (usually in advance) on issues such as the restructuring of the workforce, the relocation of plants, reduced working hours, vocational training schemes, systems of organizing and monitoring work, time studies, the setting of bonuses and pay incentives, job evaluation, or a change in the legal status of the enterprise which would affect staffing levels. It also recognizes **trade union delegates'** right to be consulted before the employer takes any decisions affecting the employees in general and trade union members in particular, especially with respect to dismissals and disciplinary action.

145. **CONTRATO DE EMBARCO — SEAFARER'S COMPANY SERVICE CONTRACT:** The contract binding ship's officers and crew to a particular shipping company. In Spain, work on board ship or work at sea was initially covered by the Merchant Shipping Regulations; nowadays there is a **contract of employment** incorporating special rules on working hours, discipline, collective representation, etc.

146. **CONTRATO DE GRUPO — GROUP CONTRACT:** Contract entered into by the employer and a group of workers who work as a team and are usually represented by a leader or representative responsible for contracting work and distributing pay. As a form of **contract of employment**, its use is now restricted to a few sectors (construction, agriculture) or types of work (the performing arts). See **joint work**.

147. **CONTRATO DE RELEVO — HAND-OVER CONTRACT:** Type of **contract of employment** provided for under Spanish law where a newly recruited employee replaces on a part-time basis another employee taking **partial retirement**. It is a form of **work-sharing**, since it enables employees approaching **retirement** to reduce gradually their hours worked and to be replaced from among the unemployed. The rules are similar to those governing part-time contracts; it has a maximum duration of three years. See **part-time workers, job-sharing**.

148. **CONTRATO DE TRABAJO — CONTRACT OF EMPLOYMENT:** Agreement between employee and employer covering the performance of work on another's account, under conditions of dependence or subordination, in return for a **wage/pay**. The contract of employment has become standard practice in modern societies, in which there is growth in the demand for labour, an increase in the number of people whose only means of earning a living is through undertaking paid employment, and a wish by the authorities to tackle abuses in labour practices (the "social question"). Its predecessor was the **contract for services**, from which it takes its foundation in the freedom of labour (as opposed to servitude or slavery) and from which it differs in that it is accompanied by regulations protecting the worker (the weaker contracting party) by laying down minimum terms and conditions of employment that must be respected by the contracting parties. Since its full incorporation in Spanish legislation with the **Contracts of Employment Act** of 1931, the contract of employment has become increasingly widespread and has gradually replaced all other forms of contract (such as contracts for services, and other forms of commercial contract) used for contracting work on another's account. Most

of the working population now provide their services under a contract of employment: only **public servants**, personnel covered by special statutes or administrative provisions, persons practising the liberal professions and the self-employed use alternative formulas; even so, the last changes undergone by the production system have led to an increase in self-employment, partnerships and co-operatives which is particularly marked in certain sectors (*e.g.* the service industry). The contract of employment is the instrument that establishes and governs the **employment relationship** and it continues to be one of the key factors in **labour law** and the industrial relations system.

149. **CONTRATO DE TRABAJO EN PRACTICAS — WORK-EXPERIENCE CONTRACT**: Type of **contract of employment** that an employer enters into with a person who has recently acquired vocational qualifications, for the performance of paid work which at the same time enables them to apply and develop their vocational knowledge. It is governed by regulations similar to those applying to a contract of employment, though it is always a temporary contract and the **wage/pay** is usually lower. Work-experience contracts were introduced in Spain in 1976, as a means of absorbing young people into the labour market and for **personnel selection** and trial. These contracts have always received financial support, which has led to an increase in their use over the past few years.

150. **CONTRATO DE TRABAJO PARA LA FORMACION — JOB-TRAINING CONTRACT**: Type of temporary **contract of employment** that an employer enters into with a young person for the purpose of training them. It has, in Spanish law, replaced the contract of apprenticeship and is now one of the principal methods used for **personnel selection** and for absorbing young people into the labour market. The authorities have promoted this type of contract by providing financial support, which has led to an increase in its use over the past few years. Workers employed under job-training contracts have similar status to other employees, though their jobs are less secure and their terms and conditions of employment (particularly as regards **wage/pay**) are less favourable.

151. **CONTRATOS TEMPORALES — TEMPORARY CONTRACTS/FIXED-TERM CONTRACTS**: Types of **contract of employment** characterized by their fixed or limited duration. They are also called "contratos por tiempo determinado". As opposed to open-ended contracts for an indefinite period, they are suitable for non-permanent work or tasks within an enterprise,

or for the provision of certain business activities of a temporary nature. However, widespread use of temporary contracts is prejudicial to workers' interests in certain respects (such as career progression, **seniority/length of service, job security**) and, in general, to the effectiveness of protective labour regulations, and their use is therefore normally restricted. At present, Spanish law permits the use of this type of contract in three specific cases: when required by the nature of the work concerned (certain works or services, casual nature of the work, temporary replacement of workers entitled to have their jobs reserved for them, launching of new activities); on the grounds of **employment policy** (temporary job-creation contracts and **relief contracts**); and to promote entry into working life (**work-experience contracts** and **job-training contracts**). Over the past few years there has been a substantial increase in the relative number of temporary contracts, to around 20 per cent. of all contracts of employment currently in force.

152. **CONTROL OBRERO — WORKERS' CONTROL:** Expression used in the literature of the traditional **labour movement** for a strategy of influencing employers' decisions to bend them in a direction favourable to employees' interests. The aims of workers' control have been channelled through collective bargaining (the United Kingdom and the United States), intervention in employers' decisions through institutional bodies (Germany and Spain), or the adoption of industrial action (adversarial participation); they have also been reflected in the choice between purely trade union representation (**workplace branches** and **trade union delegates**) and bodies representing a company's workforce as a whole (**workers' committees**, works councils). However, since the Second World War, and particularly in West European countries, the two strands have gradually converged.

153. **CONTROLADORES LABORALES — EMPLOYMENT INSPECTORS:** Body of public servants responsible for monitoring compliance with labour laws in enterprises with fewer than 25 employees. They also collaborate with the **Labour Inspectorate**.

154. **CONVENIO COLECTIVO — COLLECTIVE AGREE-MENT:** Agreement reached through the **collective bargaining process**. In Spain this term applies particularly to **generally applicable collective agreements** (*i.e.* agreements with *erga omnes* force) drawn up in accordance with the requirements laid down by the Workers' Statute, while other agreements, which are

governed by ordinary contract law, are usually called "specially negotiated agreements", **extra-statuory agreements** or simply "pacts". The content of collective agreements may cover all types of issues within the field of industrial relations; they essentially concern **terms and conditions** of **employment** and other matters relating to the contract of employment (pay, working hours, working time, health and safety, occupational groups and categories, promotion, vocational training, selection tests, geographical and functional mobility, disciplinary procedures, etc.) or relating to the collective aspects of labour relations (trade union rights, the rights of workforce representatives, bargaining levels, the joint collective agreement committee, settlement of disputes concerning the interpretation and application of the agreement, no-strike clauses, etc.). The content of a collective agreement is usually divided into **substantive clauses** and **obligational clauses**, and into minimum or compulsory content and possible content. In the public service, agreements have marked peculiarities and are known as **public service agreements and "pacts"**. See **duty to bargain, collective bargaining structure, collective bargaining, parties to collective bargaining**.

155. **CONVENIO COLECTIVO DE EFICACIA GENERAL — GENERALLY APPLICABLE COLLECTIVE AGREEMENT:** An agreement which applies to all workers and employers in a given geographical area and sphere of activity, whether or not they are members of the contracting organizations or representative bodies. The generally applicable agreement, or agreement with *erga omnes* force, is the most common form of collective agreement in Spain, and has been so throughout the history of the Spanish industrial relations system. Its negotiation, content and effects are expressly provided for in Spanish law (Part III of the Workers' Statute), which is why the term "convenio estatutorio" (statutory agreement) is also used.

156. **CONVENIO COLECTIVO DE EMPRESA — COMPANY AGREEMENT:** An agreement which applies to all the employees of a particular enterprise or workplace. In Spain, its special nature lies in the fact that, on the employees' side, it can be negotiated by the workforce or trade union representatives within the enterprise, and there are more agreements of this type than of any other, covering a very large number of workers.

157. **CONVENIO COLECTIVO DE FRANJA — OCCUPATIONAL AGREEMENT:** Collective agreement whose application is confined to a group of workers defined on the basis of having the same or similar occupational skills. It can be at

enterprise or multi-employer level. It is usually negotiated by occupational unions, either directly or through their **workplace branches**. In Spain, after an initial period of reticence because of suspicions of **discrimination**, it has now gained acceptance. Such agreements exist, or are being negotiated, mainly in the public sector (*e.g.* airline pilots, train drivers).

158. **CONVENIO COLECTIVO DE SECTOR O RAMA — PRODUCT-SECTOR OR INDUSTRY AGREEMENT:** A collective agreement covering enterprises that carry on the same production activity or closely allied activities. In Spain, provincial-level industry agreements are the most important in terms of the number of workers affected, followed by industry agreements at national level. There is a recent trend towards the negotiation of general product-sector or industry agreements to replace **Labour Ordinances** as basic provisions.

159. **CONVENIO COLECTIVO EXTRAESTATUTARIO — EXTRA-STATUTORY AGREEMENT:** In Spain, this term is applied to collective agreements concluded outside the requirements of the Workers' Statute. In contrast to statutory agreements, extra-statutory agreements have only limited force, in that they apply only to members of the contracting organizations; what is more, according to case law their applicability is not automatic but depends on being incorporated as an implied term in the contract of employment. Up to now, extra-statutory agreements have essentially supplemented statutory agreements (particularly at enterprise and workplace level, in the form of **company "pacts"**). They become important in circumstances where there is a breakdown in union unity or where the employer or union strategy is to exclude a particular union from negotiations. See **bargaining structure, collective bargaining structure**.

160. **CONVENIOS DE LA ORGANIZACION INTER-NACIONAL DEL TRABAJO — ILO CONVENTIONS:** Instruments adopted by the International Labour Organization on a very wide variety of labour, social or trade union issues. In Spain, where their force is subject to official ratification and publication, they have since the 1930s played an important role in supplementing and interpreting national laws and regulations, particularly as regards the employment of women and minors, working hours and, more recently, trade union rights.

161. **CONVENIO ESTATUTORIO — STATUTORY AGREE-MENT:** See **generally applicable collective agreement, Workers' Statute, extra-statutory agreement**.

162. **COOPERATIVA — CO-OPERATIVE:** Association of people grouped together for purposes of production, provision of services or consumption. From the labour relations standpoint, workers' co-operatives are of especial interest; they receive protection and financial incentives from the authorities, being seen as an instrument of **employment policy** (as a form of **self-employment**) and in many cases a way of preventing the disappearance or liquidation of enterprises. The performance of work by their members is partly governed by the labour regulations governing work under a contract of employment.

163. **CORPORATIVISMO — CORPORATISM:** System of socio-political organization in which economic and social interests, including employees and employers, are represented directly within the political system by means of organized groupings or "corporations". The term may also be used in a pejorative sense to mean the behaviour of powerful interest groups which defend their members' interests without consideration of the general public good. As a political and social system, corporatism reached the height of its influence earlier in the century in certain European countries: in Spain, it shaped the structure of labour relations during Primo de Rivera's dictatorship and Franco's regime. Corporatist systems in this sense have now virtually disappeared, but in circumstances of economic crisis and social unrest there are clear signs both of the re-awakening of the corporatist spirit and of the growing involvement of representatives of producer groups (mainly the trade unions and employers' associations) in economic and social policy and in Government decisions regarding labour relations. These new trends are now called **social concertation**, neo-corporatism or neo-contractualism. See **social dialogue, national syndicalism, National Corporatist Organization**.

164. **CORTES DE TRAFICO — TRANSPORT BLOCKADE:** Pressure tactic consisting of interrupting the flow of traffic on roads or railways, with a view to publicizing a dispute. In the labour relations field it is normally used in **strike** situations and is common in large-scale disputes where, for instance, enterprises are undergoing reorganization or restructuring. It is in principle unlawful.

165. **COSTE LABORAL UNITARIO — UNIT LABOUR COST:** In macro-economic terms, the relation between pay and productivity. After the strong increase in real earnings in Spain during the 1970s, the rate of growth of labour costs has been falling over the past few years, as a result of pay-restraint policies

and the rise in **productivity**. Overall, labour costs fell from 73 per cent. of the value of the product in 1980 to 65 per cent. in 1986, which has allowed the recovery of gross profits in the Spanish economy. The terms ''coste unitario del trabajo'' and ''coste salarial unitario'' are also used.

166. **COSTE SALARIAL UNITARIO — UNIT LABOUR COST:** Synonym of **coste laboral unitario**.

167. **COSTE UNITARIO DEL TRABAJO — UNIT LABOUR COST:** Synonym of **coste laboral unitario**.

168. **CREDITO DE HORAS — TIME-OFF RIGHTS:** Amount of time granted to workers' representatives, during working hours and without any reduction in their pay or other entitlements, to perform their industrial relations duties. Spanish law allows each representative 15-40 hours per month, depending on the size of the workplace, though this number may be increased by collective agreement. It may also be agreed to credit the total number of hours to one representative or more, who may then be released from work. Time-off rights are one of the major **facilities for workers' representatives** (both workforce and trade union representatives).

169. **CSE:** See **European Social Charter** (Carta Social Europea).

170. **CSIF:** See **Independent Trade Union Confederation of Public Servants** (Confederación Sindical Independiente de Funcionarios).

171. **CUADROS — PROFESSIONAL AND MANAGERIAL STAFF:** Highly experienced or qualified workers who perform management or supervisory functions. They partly overlap with technical personnel. The specific nature of their occupational interests sometimes leads them to form their own unions (such as the Confederación General de Cuadros in Spain) or separate sections within the general trade unions. They are often among the **personnel excluded from a collective agreement**, or endeavour to negotiate **occupational agreements**.

172. **CUALIFICACION PROFESIONAL — OCCUPATIONAL SKILLS:** Combination of knowledge, experience and technical ability which equips a person for exercising a particular occupation or type of work. Such abilities are traditionally among the deciding factors as regards **occupational classification** and are also taken as the criterion for distinguishing between skilled workers and unskilled workers. See **job evaluation**.

173. CUOTA SINDICAL — TRADE UNION DUES: Member's financial contribution to the trade union; usually paid at regular intervals and calculated in proportion to pay, though the amount may also be fixed. Members' contributions are, in principle, the trade union's main source of funds, but in Spain they probably represent a small proportion of its income compared with state subsidies, funds distributed from **union assets** and the allowances and expenses received for **representation on public bodies**. It is relatively common for employers to undertake to deduct trade union dues directly from pay and pass them on to the union, a system known as "descuento de la cuota sindical" (check-off).

D

174. **DEBER DE NEGOCIAR — DUTY TO BARGAIN:** Duty of the parties to a collective agreement to accede to a request for negotiations when the request is legitimate, and to maintain positions that make it possible to reach agreement. Spanish law requires that workers' and employers' representatives bargain in **good faith**, and permits refusal of a request to bargain only when justified on legal or contractual grounds, when a current agreement exists, or in cases not involving the renewal of an existing agreement which has expired.

175. **DEBER DE NO COMPETENCIA — DUTY OF NON-COMPETITION:** Obligation binding employees not to undertake work on their own or another's account when it would constitute disloyal competition. Spanish law considers violation of this duty to be a breach of **good faith** and grounds for dismissal. It also allows for the parties to enter into a post-employment covenant in restraint of competition, whereby the worker undertakes not to compete with the employer once the contract of employment comes to an end. These restrictive covenants, which may not remain valid for more than two years, may be entered into only when the employer can prove a real industrial or commercial interest in so doing, and only in exchange for financial compensation.

176. **DECLARACION DE HUELGA — STRIKE DECLARATION:** Action by which the calling of a strike and the terms on which it is being called are communicated to the employer or to a third party. Under Spanish law, the employer and the **labour authorities** must be notified within a certain minimum period preceding the start of the strike: see **notice of strike**.

177. **DECRETO-LEY DE RELACIONES DE TRABAJO (DLRT) — LABOUR RELATIONS DECREE-LAW (DLRT):** Law of March 4, 1977, whose aim was to begin adapting Spanish labour legislation on industrial disputes, strikes, collective bargaining and dismissal to the social situation following Spain's political transition and to the economic changes of the 1970s. It was partially repealed by the **Workers' Statute**, but its provisions on strikes and industrial disputes are still valid, modified in its interpretation by the Constitutional Court's decision of April 8, 1981.

178. **DELEGADOS DE PERSONAL — WORKERS' DELEGATES:** Workforce representatives of employees in enterprises or workplaces with fewer than 50 and more than 10

employees, and of **public servants** in local authorities with fewer than 50 and more than 9 public servants. Their number varies between one and three, they are elected by majority vote of the entire workforce in so-called **union elections**, and they have the same powers and responsibilities, **facilities for workers' representatives** and **guarantees for workers' representatives** as members of **workers' committees** or **staff councils**. They play an important role in the Spanish industrial relations system, both because of the specific representational functions they perform and because although formally they are not a union channel of representation they are a means through which trade unions can influence an enterprise's activities. See **trade union delegates**.

179. **DELEGADOS SINDICALES — TRADE UNION DELEGATES: Trade union** representatives in the enterprise or workplace. This form of representation was introduced in Spain through collective bargaining and then passed into law in 1985 (**Trade Union Freedom Act**), where trade union delegates are defined as representatives of the strongest **workplace branches** in enterprises or workplaces with more than 250 employees; they are elected by and from among the trade union's members. They have the same **facilities for workers' representatives** and **guarantees for workers' representatives** as **workers' representatives**, and their functions are centred on **consultation** on matters relating to union members, defending members' interests before the employer, and acting as the communication channel between the employer and the union. Their role is becoming increasingly important, particularly in large enterprises with a marked trade union presence. See also **workers' delegates**.

180. **DELITOS LABORALES — CRIMINAL LABOUR OFFENCES:** Breaches of labour regulations classed as offences in the Penal Code. Many come under the heading of social offences, meaning forms of malicious behaviour that seriously prejudice the worker's occupational interests (particularly **job security**), such as **provision of labour, illegal traffic in labour** and involvement in illegal immigration. Other provisions on forms of behaviour classed as criminal offences protect **trade union freedom** and the **right to strike**, repress violent, coercive or intimidating action by **pickets**, and apply penal sanctions to certain breaches of **health and safety** regulations. See **labour offences**.

181. **DEMANDANTE DE PRIMER EMPLEO — FIRST-TIME JOB-SEEKER:** Person seeking their first employment or job. The term was coined in employment regulations and is used to

define the target group of certain **vocational training** and **job-creation** schemes, normally those aimed at **youth employment**. In Spain the number of first-time job-seekers has risen significantly over the past few years because of population growth and the increasing number of women joining the **labour market**. First-time job-seekers account for the greater part of the population who are unemployed (for the past few years, more than one third of those out of work have been young people under the age of 25).

182. **DEMOCRACIA INDUSTRIAL — INDUSTRIAL DEMOCRACY**: Term borrowed from English and used to mean both the aims and the means adopted by workers to have a voice in managing and controlling an enterprise. In Spain, the term **workers' participation** is more common.

183. **DEMOCRACIA SINDICAL — UNION DEMOCRACY**: Expression alluding to the application of democratic rules and guidelines in the government and functioning of a trade union. Under Spanish law, the internal structure and functioning of a trade union (described in detail in its **union rule-book**) must be democratic. Over the past few years the concept has come to be extended to external trade union activities to ensure that they are in accordance with the interests of all the workers represented. This means that it is becoming increasingly common for trade unions to submit their plans or decisions about collective bargaining, industrial action or participation in employers' decisions to the vote of all workers, not just their members.

184. **DEPENDIENTE MERCANTIL — SHOPWORKER**: Worker employed in retail and distribution establishments. This was one of the earliest sectors in Spain to be governed by labour regulations, particularly on **working hours** and **rest days**. Historically, this sector was characterized by the prevalence of **small and medium-sized enterprises** and hence relations of an almost family nature between employee and employer; over the past few years, however, the emergence of large establishments (chain stores and supermarkets) has brought a profound change in working patterns and practices (continuous working day, shiftwork, opening on public holidays) and has in many cases led to the setting-up of mini industrial relations systems with very particular forms of representation (**enterprise unions**) and **workers' participation**.

185. **DEPORTISTAS PROFESIONALES — PROFESSIONAL SPORTSMEN AND SPORTSWOMEN**: Persons who devote themselves on a regular basis to practising a sport on behalf of,

and under the organization and direction of, a sports body or club, in return for payment. In Spain, workers of this type were for a long time outside the scope of application of labour legislation, but their work is now fully covered by it (although as a **special employment relationship**). Numerous professional sports associations have emerged over the past few years; some of these (for example, the Spanish Footballers' Association (AFE)) are very well established and have attained a strong bargaining position. The signing of collective agreements has also started.

186. **DERECHO A LA INFORMACION EN LA EMPRESA — DISCLOSURE OF INFORMATION/RIGHTS TO INFORMATION:** The right of workers to receive regular information on company matters of concern to them as a group. Spanish legislation (mainly labour law but also company law) grants workforce representatives and **trade union delegates** the right to receive regular information on the enterprise's financial situation, trends in the sector to which it belongs, the forms of contract used, the number of temporary workers employed, sanctions imposed on employees and, among other matters, absenteeism and accident rates. See **workers' participation**.

187. **DERECHO A LA NEGOCIACION COLECTIVA — RIGHT TO COLLECTIVE BARGAINING:** Right granted by the Spanish Constitution to employees' and employers' representatives to regulate their own collective and individual labour relations. It implies support and protection of **collective bargaining**, as well as a degree of non-intervention by the Government in the conduct of industrial relations, thus giving **collective agreements** enough "space". This right is the very core of **collective autonomy**. Its implementation is essentially covered by the **Workers' Statute**.

188. **DERECHO DE HUELGA — RIGHT TO STRIKE:** Workers' right to suspend performance of their work as a form of action in an industrial dispute. Strikes were prohibited under Spanish law from the time of the Civil War until 1975, but were deemed to be a "fundamental right" in the 1978 Constitution. Current provisions governing the various aspects of strike action are contained in the **Labour Relations Decree-Law** of 1977. The right to strike is granted both to workers with a contract of employment and to public servants, with the exception of judges, magistrates, public prosecutors and police and military personnel. This right may be exercised (through a strike call, **notice of strike** and **strike declaration**) by trade unions, workforce and trade

union representatives and groups of workers. Strike action is co-ordinated by an appointed **strike committee**. Because of their aim, political strikes, strikes that are in breach of legally binding no-strike clauses and, very exceptionally, sympathy strikes are deemed to be illegal. There are also some forms of strike which, because of the methods used, are deemed to be improper use of the right to strike; these include working-to-rule, sit-ins, selective strikes and rotating strikes. In all strikes, there is an obligation to ensure the **safety and maintenance services** necessary for human safety and protection of the enterprise's property. There are additional restrictions on exercising the right to strike in **essential public services**, since in these cases a strike must be accompanied by government measures to ensure **minimum services**; exceptionally, in the event of possible harm to the national economy, the Government may bring about the ending of a strike by imposing **compulsory arbitration**. A legal strike suspends the contract of employment, maintains strikers' social security eligibility and prevents the imposition of employer sanctions. The employer may not replace the striking workers unless they fail to provide the necessary safety and maintenance services. In the event of an illegal strike or improper use of the right to strike, the employer may impose disciplinary sanctions on workers, provided there is proof that the worker actively participated in it. A strike is not defined as either legal or illegal by an administrative check prior to its occurrence, but only when the labour courts have to decide whether or not any sanctions imposed on the strikers by the employer are lawful.

189. **DERECHO DE REUNION — RIGHT OF ASSEMBLY:** In the labour field, this term is taken to mean the right granted under labour law to the workers of an enterprise or workplace to meet together or convene **mass meetings** to discuss and deal with subjects which concern them as a group; the right is also granted to the members of a **workplace branch**.

190. **DERECHO DEL TRABAJO — LABOUR LAW:** Branch of the law which covers all the principles and provisions governing industrial relations. It is divided into individual labour law and collective labour law. The subjects of individual labour law are the employer and the employee, and its basic institutions are the contract of employment and the individual employment relationship. Collective labour law includes the legal regulation of trade unions, employers' associations, workforce and trade union representatives, collective bargaining, representation on public bodies and workers' participation, and industrial disputes. Alongside these two fundamental components, labour law also

includes three blocks of provisions, governing the labour market and placement in employment, state intervention in industrial relations, and the legal procedure for labour cases. Social security can now be considered an independent branch, separate from labour law, though there are strong connections between the two, since social security law refers fundamentally to persons who work on another's account and maintains principles, concepts and institutions developed alongside labour law. In modern industrial relations systems, labour law performs three essential functions: the first is to protect the rights of workers as the weaker party to the contract of employment, which is manifested in the recognition of minimum, inalienable individual rights and collective rights whose purpose is to reduce the inequality between the parties to the contract, all of which makes labour law a compensating instrument and one of the major reflections of the ''social state''; the second is to confirm the economic and social legitimacy of the subjects of industrial relations, which finds its principal manifestation in the rationalization and regulation of the organizational authority and managerial prerogative of the employer and the powers of workers and their representatives to oppose them; and the third is to establish a balance between the interests of these subjects and those of the rest of the community, which is manifested first and foremost in the definition of the scope and bounds of industrial conflict. Spanish labour law emerged rather later than the systems of labour legislation in other EC Member States and went through its formative period in the first three decades of this century. Although historical development has been steady and continuous in some areas, such as the contract of employment, Spanish labour law has evolved in a very irregular and piecemeal fashion in comparison with legislation in other countries, essentially because of the Civil War. In fact, modern legal definitions of freedom of association, the right to collective bargaining and the right to strike do not appear in Spanish legislation until the Constitution of 1978.

191. **DERECHO NECESARIO — INVIOLABILITY:** Term used in referring to binding legal regulations which must be complied with and respected by parties to contracts or agreements between individuals. There are many regulations of this type in Spanish **labour law** and they are usually divided into regulations of absolute inviolability, which cannot be altered in any way by the parties, and regulations of relative inviolability, which establish a minimum and allow the parties to agree on more favourable conditions. This terminology is usually applied to statutory

regulations, but rules laid down by collective agreement are also inviolable for the parties to the contract of employment.

192. **DESCANSO SEMANAL — REST DAYS:** Period of rest during each working week. It has been one of the traditional demands made by workers, partly influenced by religious considerations (Sunday rest). Spanish labour law has recognized the right to a minimum period of weekly rest since the Law of 1904. At present all workers, with a few exceptions, are entitled to a minimum weekly rest of one and a half consecutive days, which may be extended by collective agreement or contract of employment and, in certain cases, saved up to form longer periods. The weekly rest period is very often the last two days of the week. In addition to Sunday or weekly rest, there are various paid **public holidays**; both are shown in the annual **work calendar**.

193. **DESCRIPCION DE PUESTOS DE TRABAJO — JOB DESCRIPTION:** Specification of the tasks and obligations of a particular post.

194. **DESCUENTO DE LA CUOTA SINDICAL — CHECK-OFF SYSTEM:** See **trade union dues**.

195. **DESEMPLEO — UNEMPLOYMENT:** Situation experienced by persons of working age who lack employment and who are actively seeking work. Depending on its cause, unemployment may be called "frictional" (caused by normal occupational mobility in an economic system based on freedom of labour and economic initiative); "technological" (caused by changes in production processes as a result of the emergence of new production methods or new plant and machinery); "structural" (caused by the cessation or reduction of production because of lack of demand for the product); or "cyclical" (caused by the stagnant and falling production of goods and services which is typical of periods of economic recession). From the point of view of its impact on workers, the most relevant classifications are those which distinguish between short-term unemployment and **long-term unemployment**; unemployment with and without financial assistance (whose relative proportions are indicated by the rate of **unemployment cover**); and total and partial unemployment (depending on whether it concerns the whole or only part of normal **working hours**). Most observers have judged mass unemployment to be the greatest problem faced by Spanish society in the 1980s and after: whereas in 1971 the rate of unemployment was below two per cent., during the 1980s it

climbed to around 20 per cent., with some three million people out of work. No matter how unemployment is analysed, Spain is, in relative terms, in a worse situation than any of its OECD partners, since even though the **participation rate/activity rate** in Spain is relatively low its rate of unemployment is the highest within OECD. This is explained by various factors, such as the high birth rate during the 1950s and 1960s, **return migration** and reductions in staffing levels as an employer reaction to increases in real labour costs. Unemployment in Spain predominantly affects young people and women, is mostly long-term, hits hardest at groups with the lowest skill levels and is unevenly distributed among regions and sectors. Since mid-1985, there has been a relative increase in the number of jobs, particularly in the service sector, and a slight fall in unemployment. The forms of financial assistance available (benefits, vocational training grants) are not, however, wholly adequate to meet the situations of need caused by this problem.

196. **DESEMPLEO REGISTRADO — RECORDED UN-EMPLOYMENT:** Unemployment which appears in the records and official statistics of the **INEM** as the recorded movement of labour. It is based on outstanding applications for work made through public employment offices. Certain categories may register as unemployed but are not recorded in unemployment figures: people who are already employed, are seeking a special form of employment (homeworking, work abroad, part-time work), are not immediately available for work (retired and disabled people and students) or are receiving agricultural unemployment benefit. Recorded unemployment in Spain rose sharply during the 1980s, mostly as a result of the economic crisis and the changes in the production system; however, there are other factors which have caused artificial inflation of the unemployment figures, such as the awarding of training grants and allowances to persons registered as unemployed and the implementation of job-creation schemes.

197. **DESEMPLEO DE LARGA DURACION — LONG-TERM UNEMPLOYMENT:** Unemployment which lasts for a prolonged period: one year (long-term unemployment) and two years (very long-term unemployment). It usually affects those groups with most difficulty in finding work (young people, older people, the disabled and women), particularly in certain sectors or geographical areas. The number of people in Spain affected by such unemployment gradually increased during the 1980s. As a result, vocational training programmes, job-creation schemes and financial assistance measures for the unemployed (particularly allowances) tend to be aimed at these groups.

198. **DESISTIMIENTO EMPRESARIAL — WITHDRAWAL BY EMPLOYER:** See **dismissal**.

199. **DESLIZAMIENTO SALARIAL — WAGE DRIFT:** Difference between pay rates incorporated in collective agreements and workers' actual earnings in a particular enterprise. It expresses the gap between the pay bill forecast for a given period and unit (i.e. enterprise, sector, entire economy) and the real level of wage costs. Wage drift is usually caused by supplements paid because of the specific characteristics of a job or a worker and to compensate for the impact of particular factors concerning the performance of work (such as overtime). It is one of the variables taken into account when pay increases are being negotiated or set.

200. **DESOCUPACION — UNEMPLOYMENT:** Synonym of **desempleo**.

201. **DESPIDO — DISMISSAL:** Ending or **termination of the contract of employment** by the unilateral decision of the employer. The term "desistimiento empresarial" (employer withdrawal) is also used. Progressive limitation of employers' power of dismissal in order to help guarantee workers **job security** has been a constant feature of statutory labour regulations, most of which moved from an earlier system of free dismissal to a system of dismissal for just cause or with justifiable reason. However, Spanish legislation, traditionally in favour of the latter system, has over the past few years been gradually extending the list of legal grounds or reasons for dismissal; the latest legislation even provides for a form of free dismissal. Three types of cause or reason can be used at present, and these have given rise in turn to three categories of dismissal: **disciplinary dismissal, dismissal for objective reasons** and dismissal for economic or technological reasons (**collective dismissal/redundancy**). Dismissal can be contested in the courts, where it may be declared to be justified dismissal, **unjustified dismissal** or **unfair dismissal**. Spain saw its greatest number of dismissals in the period 1978-1985, as a result of **industrial restructuring** and the reorganization of the production system. The current easing of this trend has been influenced by the reduction in the number of open-ended contracts of employment and the widespread use of temporary contracts.

202. **DESPIDO COLECTIVO — COLLECTIVE DISMISSAL/ REDUNDANCY:** Dismissal of a group of employees or all the employees of an enterprise which is motivated by a "collective" reason such as *force majeure*, technological restructuring, an economic crisis or closure of the enterprise. This form of dismissal

is typical of enterprises or production sectors undergoing **industrial restructuring** or reorganization. It requires observance of the **redundancy procedure** (also called the "expediente de crisis" or crisis procedure) and, except in the case of *force majeure*, where it is merely necessary to inform the labour authorities of the situation, in order to be valid collective dismissal must be agreed with the workforce representatives or, failing this, must be covered by prior authorization from the administrative authorities. This system, which is more protective than that laid down in EEC Directive No. 129/1975, has been criticized in recent years by the employers (**CEOE**), although the statistics indicate that there is little difficulty in obtaining such authorization and that procedures are usually negotiated by agreement between the parties. Workers subject to collective dismissal are entitled to compensation of 20 days' pay for each year of service, which is in some cases (*force majeure*, small enterprises, etc.) covered by the Wages Guarantee Fund (**FOGASA**). Collective dismissals are becoming much rarer in Spain now that the major processes of industrial restructuring have been completed.

203. **DESPIDO DISCIPLINARIO — DISCIPLINARY DISMISSAL:** Dismissal based on a serious, culpable breach of the contract of employment by the worker. It is the maximum sanction that can be imposed on the worker and is founded in the **employer's managerial authority**. Under Spanish law, grounds for disciplinary dismissal include unjustified absenteeism or lateness; insubordination or disobedience; verbal or physical aggression towards the employer, fellow employees or their families; persistent, wilful reduction of output; habitual drunkenness or drug addiction which have a detrimental effect on work; and active participation in an illegal strike. In addition to these specific grounds, there is the general one of breach of good faith, which by virtue of its breadth and vagueness has become the one most widely invoked. Dismissal must be notified in writing (by a **letter of dismissal**) and, where workers' representatives are involved, a disciplinary procedure must be started prior to such notification.

204. **DESPIDO IMPROCEDENTE — UNJUSTIFIED DISMISSAL:** Dismissal without any alleged grounds or without proof of the reason alleged by the employer. It entitles the worker to receive the back pay due (see **back pay awarded after dismissal appeal hearings**) and to be either reinstated or compensated by the employer. Where the employer's decision is based on legally acceptable grounds, it is classed as "despido procedente" (justified dismissal).

205. DESPIDO NULO — UNFAIR DISMISSAL: Failure to comply with the formal requirements laid down by law (or, where applicable, by collective agreement) renders dismissal "unfair" and obliges the employer to settle any back pay due and either reinstate or compensate the worker. Where the purpose is to deny the worker his or her constitutional rights, penalize him or her for exercising those rights or discriminate against him or her on trade union, ideological or other grounds, dismissal is classed by the courts as "radicalmente nulo" or "nulo radical" (void) and the employer is obliged in all such cases to grant **reinstatement** of the worker.

206. DESPIDO POR CAUSAS OBJETIVAS — DISMISSAL FOR OBJECTIVE REASONS: Dismissal arising either from certain changes in the organization of production (such as the elimination of particular jobs) or from factors which are not wholly within the worker's control but have an impact on **performance** (for example, incompetence, repeated although justified absence, inability to work with new technology). This form of dismissal was introduced into Spanish legislation in 1977 to broaden employers' scope for organizing work and deploying labour; its introduction was part of a series of measures to make labour law more flexible. In some situations (*e.g.* small enterprises) it is used instead of collective dismissal because it reduces the formalities involved and eliminates the need for prior authorization from the administrative authorities. A worker who is subject to this form of dismissal must be given **notice** of the decision within a stipulated minimum period, and is entitled to time off to look for another job and to compensation related to the length of service.

207. DESPIDO PROCEDENTE — JUSTIFIED DISMISSAL: See **unjustified dismissal**.

208. DESPLAZAMIENTO — TEMPORARY RELOCATION: Temporary transfer (also called "destacamento") of an employee to a workplace of the same enterprise which is located in a town other than that in which the employee normally works. Under Spanish law, the management of an enterprise may order temporary relocation only for technical, organizational or production reasons, for a maximum period of one year. These workers are entitled to **subsistence and travel allowances** and a minimum of four days' stay in their home town every three months. In some collective agreements the expression "comisión de servicio" is used to refer to occasional or special missions or relocations. See **geographical mobility, transfer**.

77

209. DESREGULACION — DEREGULATION: A term much in vogue in the economic debate of the 1980s to refer to pressures for the abolition of statutory regulations, including those which guarantee workers' rights, on the grounds that they are a constraint on enterprises' ability to compete. In its most extreme version, it propounds the elimination of **labour law** and the application of common or civil law regulations to industrial relations. See **labour flexibility**.

210. DESTACAMENTO — TEMPORARY TRANSFER: See **temporary relocation**.

211. DESTAJO — PIECEWORK: Payment system in which the **wage/pay** is determined on the basis of the units of output produced, irrespective of the time spent. It has in the past in Spain been a very common form of working but is now used only in certain sectors of production (construction, mining, agriculture) or certain types of activity (sorting, grading, etc.) in which the result can be checked by measuring product or work units and in which the worker can perform independently.

212. DIALOGO SOCIAL — SOCIAL DIALOGUE: Method of managing labour, social and economic issues by means of **consultation** and **social concertation** between the public authorities and bodies representing employees and employers. The expression derives from terminology used in the European Community. See **economic and social council, corporatism**.

213. DIETAS — SUBSISTENCE AND TRAVEL ALLOWANCES: Sums paid to employees to cover temporary relocation, maintenance and accommodation costs incurred as a result of their work activities. The amounts are usually laid down in a collective agreement or the contract of employment. They are not deemed to be pay. See **expenses**.

214. DIRECCION DE LA EMPRESA — MANAGEMENT: The function of directing, regulating and running an enterprise; it lies in principle with the owner. It may be exercised directly by the **employer** or delegated to other people (management personnel), which is customary when managerial authority is embodied in a collective group (*i.e.* in large companies and corporations). Spanish law grants the employer the authority to direct and control the enterprise's activities and lays down the worker's duty to obey the employer's orders; it also recognizes the right of **workers' representatives** to participation in certain decisions which directly concern the workers, without establishing a general right to representation on management bodies. Additional forms of participation are usually provided through **collective bargaining**. See **Agreement on Workers' Participation in Public Enterprises, board of directors, personnel manager**.

215. **DIRECTOR DE PERSONAL — PERSONNEL MANAGER:** Person in charge of a specialist department responsible for labour relations and the management of human resources in the enterprise. In Spain, the position and functions of personnel managers vary according to the size of the enterprise and the criteria and approaches governing personnel management. Small enterprises often do not have a personnel manager or else have a person who is responsible for other administrative or production tasks as well as personnel management. In large enterprises, the tendency is to appoint specialized personnel managers who are answerable to central management and are members of top-level management teams. Originally, the requirement for this job was an ability to manage and to maintain discipline; as time passed personnel management in Spanish enterprises was entrusted mainly to lawyers specializing in labour law, and nowadays personnel managers are tending to be people with increasingly diverse backgrounds and training.

216. **DISCIPLINA SINDICAL — UNION DISCIPLINE:** Conduct expected of members within a **trade union**; in a broader sense, **rank-and-file** compliance with the measures or instructions approved by union governing bodies. Discipline is important in highly unionized sectors and when representation within the enterprise is concentrated in union members, because the effectiveness of union decisions (particularly in the event of labour disputes) depends on it. It is less vital when representation involves all employees, irrespective of union membership, as is usually the case in Spain.

217. **DISCRIMINACION — DISCRIMINATION:** Distinction or difference in treatment; more especially, the treatment of a person or group of persons in a prejudicial or pejorative manner or as being inferior because of who they are and their ideas or beliefs. On the basis of the 1978 Constitution, Spanish labour law declares null and void any agreements or decisions implying any discrimination in employment or working conditions on the grounds of sex, ethnic origin, marital status, race, social status, religious or political ideas, membership or non-membership of

a trade union and language. In Spain the law also prohibits discrimination on the grounds that a person does not speak the language of the Autonomous Community in which they are working (in particular, Catalan in Catalonia). However, the law does not prohibit exceptions. Differences in treatment between unequal situations or aimed at correcting a real inequality are compatible with the principle of equality and non-discrimination; consequently, the law permits **preferential employment** and **employment quotas** favouring disadvantaged groups. See **positive action, indirect discrimination**.

218. **DISCRIMINACION FAVORABLE O POSITIVA — POSITIVE (REVERSE) DISCRIMINATION:** See **positive action**.

219. **DISCRIMINACION INDIRECTA — INDIRECT DISCRIMINATION:** Covert difference in treatment. It usually takes the form of arbitrary or unjustified imposition of requirements which in practice imply unfavourable treatment since they are applied only to groups who, because of their natural or social attributes, have greater difficulty in fulfilling such requirements. This form of discrimination is common in employment and in the application of terms and conditions (particularly pay), mainly through channelling certain groups (women) into lower-grade jobs and types of work (part-time) or demanding disproportionate occupational skills or qualifications from ethnic minorities. In Spain it has mainly affected women and nowadays is reflected principally in the greater difficulty women have in gaining access to management jobs and the lower pay they receive.

220. **DISMINUCION DEL RENDIMIENTO — GO-SLOW:** Form of industrial action or **labour dispute** consisting of an agreed and co-ordinated reduction in normal **productivity**; it generally serves as warning of a potential strike or can be classed as a concealed or incipient strike (sometimes in the form of a **work-to-rule**). A continued, wilful reduction in output is a ground for **disciplinary dismissal**. See **performance**.

221. **DIVISION INTERNACIONAL DEL TRABAJO — INTERNATIONAL DIVISION OF LABOUR:** Distribution and adjustment of labour between the production systems of the various countries competing on the international market; by means of this process each country specializes in the production of those goods and services which bring it comparative advantage, and imports the others.

222. **DLRT:** See **Labour Relations Decree-Law** (Decreto-Ley de Relaciones de Trabajo).

223. **DUMPING SOCIAL — SOCIAL DUMPING:** Practice adopted by certain countries of offering low wage costs in order to attract foreign investment. It is particularly worrying for countries (such as those of Western Europe) which, because of their long tradition of trade-unionism, have attained better living and working conditions and so have much higher labour costs.

E

224. **ECONOMIA INFORMAL — INFORMAL ECONOMY:** See **hidden economy**.

225. **ECONOMIA IRREGULAR — IRREGULAR ECONOMY:** See **hidden economy**.

226. **ECONOMIA OCULTA — CONCEALED ECONOMY:** See **hidden economy**.

227. **ECONOMIA SUMERGIDA — HIDDEN ECONOMY:** Sector of the economy which eludes administrative control and inclusion in official statistics; also known as the "economía irregular" (irregular economy), "economía oculta" (concealed economy) or "economía informal" (informal economy). Its essential motivation is to evade taxation and social security charges. It is calculated that as a proportion of the entire economy Spain's hidden (or "black") economy accounts for 20-25 per cent. of GDP; it is concentrated in the agriculture, service and consumer goods sectors; and it is particularly characteristic of work/production units with low levels of capitalization. It is encouraged by the relative inflexibility of the institutional framework and massive unemployment. Its parallel in the labour field is hidden, irregular or **undeclared employment**, which usually concerns the weakest group of workers, contributes to segmentation of the labour market, and is characterized by insecurity of employment, poor working conditions and little or no unionization.

228. **EDAD DE JUBILACION — PENSIONABLE AGE:** See **retirement**.

229. **ELA-STV:** See **Basque Workers' Solidarity** (Solidaridad de Trabajadores Vascos).

230. **ELECCIONES SINDICALES — UNION ELECTIONS:** Term used in Spain to refer to elections of workforce representatives in enterprises (**workers' committee** and **workers' delegates**) and in the public service (**staff council** and **workers' delegates**). They are held every four years. The use of the term "union" is technically incorrect, since the workers and their representatives need not necessarily be union members; it derives from historical factors: the elections of representatives in enterprises within the "Vertical Union" of the Franco regime were called "union elections"; from the prevalence of candidates put forward by **trade unions**: union slates; and from the use of

their results as a measure of **representativeness: trade union influence**. The trend shows a growing proportion of the vote in union elections going to the major confederations: **UGT** and **CC.OO.** in general, **ELA-STV** in the Basque Country, **CSIF** in the public service; and to the occupational unions within certain sectors (public administration) or in large enterprises, particularly public enterprises.

231. EMIGRACION — EMIGRATION AND INTERNAL MIGRATION: Geographical relocation of people, for employment and sometimes political purposes and either temporarily or permanently, within the same country (internal migration) or, more accurately speaking, to a foreign country. Emigration has been a constant feature in Spain since the early nineteenth century, with emigrants going originally overseas and later to other EC Member States. For many years, the outward flow of migrants offset labour surpluses, particularly in rural areas. Because of the economic crisis of the 1970s, however, recent years have seen a large drop in emigration figures, aggravating Spain's unemployment problems and causing a change of emphasis in migration laws, which are now concerned less with emigration than with protecting and assisting returning migrants. See **return migration**.

232. EMPLEADO — NON-MANUAL WORKER: Generically, the Spanish term means "employee". In its stricter and more widely used sense, it refers to an intellectual or white-collar worker as distinct from a manual or blue-collar worker. The term was used with this second meaning in early Spanish labour regulations; it has disappeared from current legislation, but is still used colloquially to refer to workers in certain sectors (services, retail and distribution) who perform certain types of work (administration, management, accounting) or have special qualifications (**technical personnel**). The number of non-manual workers as a proportion of the total working population is rising because of the growth of the service sector and the progressive mechanization of traditionally manual tasks.

233. EMPLEADOR — EMPLOYER: Person who provides employment or receives an employee's services. In Spanish law, an employer is defined as the person under whose organization and direction, and in accordance with a **contract of employment**, a worker provides services on another's account, of his own free will and in return for remuneration. An employer may be public or private, a natural or legal person, or a community of assets. Colloquially, the term "empresario" is more commonly used. See **enterprise**.

234. **EMPLEO — EMPLOYMENT:** Job, occupation, profession or **trade (craft).** The Spanish word has many meanings: it is usually synonymous with "trabajo" (work), though it sometimes coincides with **placement** and, to a lesser degree, with **occupational category** or rank. It has given its name to the area of public activity which is concerned with entry into working life, vocational training and intervention in the **labour market (employment policy).**

235. **EMPLEO COMUNITARIO — COMMUNITY EMPLOYMENT PROGRAMME:** Term commonly used to refer to programmes to counter **unemployment** which concentrate on works and services that are socially useful. The expression was first applied in Spain to a series of programmes to provide work for unemployed agricultural workers, which were run from the early 1970s until 1984 and then replaced by a combination of employment plans (Rural Employment Plan) and social welfare measures (**agricultural unemployment benefit**). At present the community programme formula forms part of **INEM** and Autonomous Community employment programmes, with the financial support of the European Social Fund.

236. **EMPLEO JUVENIL — YOUTH EMPLOYMENT:** Expression normally used to refer to young people's situation in the **labour market** and to **employment policy** measures which are directly concerned with their entry into working life. In the absence of a precise legal definition, for these purposes "young people" are deemed to be those members of the population under the age of 25. The problems of youth employment have been made particularly acute by the successive economic crises of the 1970s, strong population growth and reorganization of the structure of production, giving rise to youth unemployment levels in Spain of close on 50 per cent. The measures taken to tackle this situation and promote the recruitment of **first-time job-seekers** have included programmes providing financial incentives to encourage the use of temporary contracts; technical and financial assistance for enterprises; work experience; and **vocational training:** see also **Employment Training and Integration Plan.** Many of these measures have concentrated on promoting the use of **work-experience contracts** and **job-training contracts.** See **under-age workers/minors.**

237. **EMPLEO SELECTIVO — SELECTIVE EMPLOYMENT:** See **employment quota.**

238. **EMPRESA — ENTERPRISE:** Organization for the production of goods and services, normally with a view to making a profit. The term differs from **workplace** in that it refers neither to the place nor the technical unit in which production is carried on, but to the productive organization as a whole. Strictly, the Spanish term "empresario" (**entrepreneur/owner of an enterprise**) denotes the owner of an enterprise irrespective of whether they are the **employer**. See **employers' association, small and medium-sized enterprises, multinational corporation, public enterprise, group enterprise, free enterprise.**

239. **EMPRESA AUXILIAR — AUXILIARY ENTERPRISE:** Enterprise whose activity consists in performing works and services that form part of the activity of another enterprise ("principal" enterprise), serving as a complement or auxiliary through the negotiation of contracts and sub-contracts for labour, goods and services; common in sectors involving particularly complex or diversified production processes (*e.g.* iron and steel, construction, shipyards). Spanish law imposes the joint and several liability of the principal enterprise as regards outstanding pay due to the workers of auxiliary enterprises; some industry-wide provisions recognize their right under certain circumstances to become employees of the principal enterprise at the end of the contract. The concept differs from that of the "empresa de servicios" (service enterprise), whose activity consists in providing services (accounting, distribution, cleaning) for other enterprises. See **personnel selection agency, temporary employment agency, sub-contracting.**

240. **EMPRESA DE SELECCION DE PERSONAL — PERSONNEL SELECTION AGENCY:** Service enterprise which specializes in selecting workers on behalf of another enterprise. It usually participates in the placement process either as another enterprise's representative, selecting employees from available candidates, or as a point of contact between job-seekers and prospective employers (in the role of mediation or intermediation in employment). It is common for such agencies to be involved in selecting senior managers, professional and technical staff, middle-management personnel, white-collar workers and skilled personnel in general. Under Spanish law, these agencies are permitted to operate provided they fulfil certain conditions. See **placement, National Institute of Employment.**

241. **EMPRESA DE TRABAJO TEMPORAL — TEMPORARY EMPLOYMENT AGENCY:** Service enterprise whose purpose is to meet demands for temporary or casual labour from other

enterprises or organizations. It operates particularly in certain segments of the labour market (services in the home, seasonal or casual work, tasks requiring special skills, secretarial work, etc.) which are not satisfactorily covered by public employment offices. These agencies are implicitly prohibited in Spain by virtue of the legislation governing placement and penalizing **provision of labour**, though there are signs (advertisements in the press) that they have been operating for some time, often in the form of **personnel selection agencies** or **co-operatives**.

242. **EMPRESA IDEOLOGICA — IDEOLOGICALLY ORIENTED ENTERPRISE:** Enterprise characterized by the fact that it performs activities solely or mainly concentrated on the dissemination of religious, political, socio-economic or trade union ideas, beliefs or opinions (ideology). Its employees, or at least those occupying certain posts, are usually required to share this ideology.

243. **EMPRESA MEDIANA/PEQUEÑA — SMALL AND MEDIUM-SIZED ENTERPRISES:** Category of enterprises to which different legal provisions apply in some respects; labour regulations are also usually more flexible in their case. Spanish legislation does not make a precise distinction on the basis of the size of enterprises, but affords special rules on **termination of the contract of employment** (where the figures used are 25 and 50 employees); **workers' representatives** (where the figures used are 10 and 50 employees); and **trade union delegates** (where the threshold of 250 employees is used). Small and medium-sized enterprises usually form special **employers' associations**, and the intials PYME are often used in Spanish to refer to them.

244. **EMPRESA MULTINACIONAL — MULTINATIONAL CORPORATION:** Enterprise or **group enterprise** with headquarters and subsidiaries in several countries; its activity and its labour relations are therefore subject to the different labour laws of the various countries involved. Because of the difficulty of protecting labour interests at international level, some international bodies (OECD, ILO) have drawn up codes of practice on certain aspects of labour relations. The **trade unions** have also attempted to counteract these problems by forming **international trade union organizations**.

245. **EMPRESA PUBLICA — PUBLIC ENTERPRISE:** Enterprise which is wholly owned, or controlled by means of a majority share holding, by the state or one of its dependent bodies. In Spain as elsewhere, the size and economic importance of these

enterprises mean that their industrial relations have a marked influence on those in other enterprises. This in turn means that trade unions tend to use them as a testbed for possible innovations in their bargaining and participation strategies. Spanish public enterprises are usually members of the **CEOE** through the appropriate **employers' associations**. They are sometimes subject to stricter regulations regarding pay (pay ceilings). See **Agreement on Workers' Participation in Public Enterprises, public sector**.

246. **EMPRESARIO — ENTREPRENEUR/OWNER OF AN ENTERPRISE:** Strictly speaking, the owner of an enterprise. In the labour field, the term is used in Spanish as a synonym of "empleador" (**employer**).

247. **ENCUESTA DE POBLACION ACTIVA (EPA) — SURVEY OF THE WORKING POPULATION (EPA):** Survey of the employment situation in Spain conducted quarterly by the National Institute of Statistics (INE). It provides data on the economically active and inactive population; the number of people in employment and unemployed; and the participation rate, employment rate and unemployment rate by age group, sex, region or Autonomous Community, economic sector, occupational status (entrepreneurs or employers, the self-employed, employees and family workers) and length of time spent unemployed or seeking work. It usually differs in some respects from the survey of Recorded Movement of Labour (MLR) compiled each month by **INEM**. These two surveys are the main sources of statistics on the **labour market** in Spain.

248. **ENFERMEDAD PROFESIONAL — OCCUPATIONAL ILLNESS/INDUSTRIAL DISEASE:** Illness which is contracted at work or as a consequence of work; particularly prevalent in especially dangerous and unhealthy jobs or economic sectors (mining, steel industry, etc.). Together with **accidents at work/industrial accidents**, occupational illnesses constitute occupational risks, as opposed to common risks not related to work; they have been one of the main contingencies covered by **social insurance** and **social security** systems.

249. **ENLACES SINDICALES — OFFICIAL WORKPLACE REPRESENTATIVES:** See **works council**.

250. **ENRIQUECIMIENTO DEL TRABAJO — JOB ENRICHMENT:** Incorporation of planning or control functions in the tasks involved in a particular job to make it more varied and to increase the worker's self-motivation. It differs from **job**

enlargement in that it affects not the "breadth" or "horizontal dimension" of the job but rather its "depth" or "vertical dimension". See **work organization**.

251. **ENTREVISTA DE SELECCION — SELECTION INTERVIEW:** Method or technique of appraising the suitability of a candidate in a **personnel selection** process, based on conversation with them and observation of their reactions. Although sometimes questionable as a satisfactory guide to performance, it is the selection method most commonly used in Spain, particularly in the middle and higher strata of an enterprise's occupational hierarchy.

252. **ENTRISMO — INFILTRATION STRATEGY:** Practice adopted by individual members of the **CC.OO.** to gain influence within the **Vertical Union**, by standing for election to representative posts.

253. **ERGONOMIA — ERGONOMICS:** Combination of techniques directed at improving the relationship between people and the technological means of production and work. The aims of ergonomic studies are to reduce the physical and psychological pressures of the **work environment**, increase **productivity** and improve the **quality of working life.**

254. **ESCALA MOVIL DE SALARIOS — SLIDING PAY SCALE:** See **pay scale, wage spread**.

255. **ESCALA SALARIAL — PAY SCALE:** Chart showing the various pay ranges in an enterprise or in a particular industry, classified by groups, occupational categories or posts. It is usually included in industry-wide provisions, particularly collective agreements. The formula used for index-linking **pay adjustment** to guarantee workers' purchasing power is called "escala móvil de salarios" (sliding pay scale). See **wage spread**.

256. **ESCALAFON — EMPLOYEE RANKING:** List, chart or register of the personnel in an enterprise, group or occupational category, arranged according to seniority, merit or other criteria. It is a complete list, detailed and in hierarchical order, of the individuals in the **workforce** of a work/production unit. It is normally used for promotions and changes of category and is especially typical of the public service and large enterprises.

257. **ESQUIROL — SCAB/BLACKLEG:** Worker who continues to work when a strike has been called (in this case the term

"rompehuelgas", *i.e.* strikebreaker, also applies), or whose services are used for the **replacement of strikers**. The term is used pejoratively and is indicative of lack of solidarity or a breakdown in the workers' united action.

258. **ESTABILIDAD EN EL EMPLEO — JOB SECURITY:** Expression indicating degree of permanence or tenure of employment, as opposed to casual or precarious employment. In Spain, job security has been, and is still, one of the principles underlying labour regulations, and has led to regulations such as the preference for contracts of employment of indefinite duration, the prohibition on repeated renewal of temporary contracts, continuation of the contract of employment in the event of **transfer of undertaking**, and the requirement for justified reasons for **dismissal**. Effective job security depends not only on legal regulations but also on many other factors (economic, business, trade union, etc.). The past few years have seen the spread of the idea that some of the legal regulations protecting job security may impede economic growth and job creation; this has caused a noticeable trend in Spain towards making labour law more flexible, mainly by relaxing the restrictions on **temporary contracts/fixed-term contracts** and on justified reasons for dismissal. See **deregulation, labour flexibility**.

259. **ESTATUTO DE LOS TRABAJADORES (ET) — WORKERS' STATUTE:** Law passed on March 10, 1980, in accordance with the mandate laid down in Article 35.2 of the Spanish Constitution. It fundamentally altered Spanish labour legislation to suit the political and socio-economic situation which emerged in the 1970s. Except in strictly trade union matters, it is now the centrepiece of Spanish labour law. It differs from the Italian Workers' Statute of 1970, from which it took its name, in that it concerns the central aspects of the employment relationship, workers' participation and generally applicable collective bargaining. Compared with earlier Spanish labour legislation, it not only updated the industrial relations system but also made the regulations governing the contract of employment, mobility and termination of the contract of employment more flexible; permanently established workforce representatives as a means of workers' participation; and consolidated the status of collective agreements, as opposed to **Labour Ordinances**, as the principal source of industry-wide and occupational provisions. The Workers' Statute has been amended several times (1983, 1984, 1986 and 1989), usually to continue adapting labour regulations to changes in the production system and to strengthen the position of the most representative trade unions in the Spanish industrial relations system.

260. ESTATUTO SINDICAL — UNION RULE-BOOK: Set of rules drawn up by a **trade union** on its internal functioning and organization. Under Spanish law, they must state the union's name, purpose, objectives and scope; define its internal structure, financial organization, governing bodies and decision-making procedure; set out the conditions of membership and members' rights, obligations and guarantees; and describe amalgamation and disbandment procedures. Spanish law requires the rule-book to be deposited with the special public office set up for this purpose (the register of trade unions) as a prerequisite for the granting of legal status and permission to operate; this requirement also serves as a means of verifying a trade union's legality. See **union democracy**.

261. ESTRUCTURA DE LA NEGOCIACION COLECTIVA — COLLECTIVE BARGAINING STRUCTURE: Loosely, all the collective agreements in a collective bargaining system; in a stricter sense, the formal, practical relations between the various **bargaining units** and levels. The Spanish bargaining structure has, since 1958, been characterized by its relatively decentralized nature and by the large number of bargaining levels involved, notably the national product-sector level, the provincial product-sector level and the company/workplace level. Until the mid-1970s, the provincial product-sector level was the most important, in terms of both the number of agreements concluded and the number of workers affected. In terms of the number of workers affected this level is still the most important (with its 1000 or so agreements applying to two million workers), but recent years have seen growing importance attached to company and workplace agreements (some 2500, applicable to one million workers) and inter-provincial or national product-sector agreements (approximately 70, applicable to 1.7 million workers). In all, around six million workers are covered by collective agreements. The duration of agreements is usually 1-2 years. Spanish law leaves the parties free to decide on the bargaining unit, permits the most representative trade unions and employers' associations to establish rules on precedence and co-ordination between agreements by means of **general multi-industry agreements** and lays down that, in the absence of such agreed rules, an agreement may not, while it is in force, be affected by another agreement of differing scope (principle of non-concurrence). The parties are also free to decide on the duration of the agreement, although if no date of expiry is expressly stated the agreement is extended from year to year, unless otherwise laid down in the agreement itself.

262. ESTRUCTURA ORGANICA DEL SINDICATO — UNION STRUCTURE: The internal organization of a trade union, particularly its composition, operating rules and governing bodies. A union's internal structure essentially depends on the identity of its members and its field of action. The primary distinction is between trade union organizations which group workers directly (single organizations) and those which serve as umbrella organizations grouping unions operating at a lower level (aggregate organizations). The latter in their turn are divided into those which group unions on the basis of geographical or horizontal criteria (**territorial federations**), functional or vertical criteria (**industrial federations**), or both (**trade union confederations** or central trade union bodies). Operating rules mainly concern decision-making processes, disciplinary and monitoring procedures and, where applicable, relations between the various trade unions grouped together within a single organization. In Spain, union governing bodies are usually the "Congreso general" or "Asamblea general" (General Meeting or Congress), the highest management and governing body, which is convened every two to three years; the "Comité Ejecutivo", "Comisión Ejecutiva" or "Consejo Ejecutivo" (Executive Committee, Commission or Council), an elected governing body which is the highest decision-making body between General Meetings, and the "Secretaría General" (General Secretary), an executive post held by a single person. Spanish law requires a trade union to be structured and run according to democratic principles. See **union official, union democracy, union rule-book.**

263. ESTRUCTURA PRODUCTIVA — STRUCTURE OF PRODUCTION: Organization and distribution of the production system of a country or given geographical area. Its concrete features depend on variable factors such as who owns the means of production (public or private ownership), the relative importance of the different economic sectors (primary, secondary and tertiary), and the size of enterprises.

264. ESTRUCTURA SALARIAL — WAGE/PAY STRUCTURE: The way in which total pay is composed of its various elements; it may refer to a single employee or to a group of employees. In Spain, pay usually has a very complicated structure (**basic pay** plus **pay supplements** or **additional payments**); the purpose of this is to respond to the peculiarities or specific features of various types of work and to the bargaining power of the different groups or categories of employees. See **pay components.**

91

265. EXCEDENCIA — LEAVE OF ABSENCE: Situation in which an employee temporarily ceases to occupy a post or perform a job. It originated in the public service and then spread beyond this to become a special form of **suspension of the contract of employment** to allow employees to attend to family needs or public duties. Spanish law distinguishes between mandatory leave of absence, essentially provided to enable employees to perform public duties and union functions for the most representative trade unions, and discretionary leave of absence, which can be requested for child care or the performance of union functions and also when an employee has a minimum level of seniority. As a general rule, an employee who has taken discretionary leave of absence has a preferential right to any vacant post that may become available in the enterprise, while mandatory leave of absence entitles employees to have their post reserved for them. Collective agreements may extend or supplement the statutory regulations and often add additional grounds for leave of absence. Any clauses in collective agreements and regulations which impose this form of suspension of the contract of employment on women in the event of marriage are now deemed to be null and void, though they were frequently applied in the past.

266. EXPEDIENTE DE CRISIS — CRISIS PROCEDURE: See **redundancy procedure, collective dismissal/redundancy**.

267. EXPEDIENTE DE REGULACION DE EMPLEO — REDUNDANCY PROCEDURE: Procedure which must be followed when a contract of employment is to be terminated or suspended or when terms and conditions of employment affecting a group of workers are to be altered for economic or technological reasons or on grounds of *force majeure*. In Spain, such action requires the agreement of the workers' representatives or, failing this, prior official authorization. It is also called the "expediente de crisis" (crisis procedure) or simply "regulación de empleo" (adjustment of employment). This formula, which is particularly important in the case of **collective dismissal/redundancy**, has a long tradition in Spanish labour legislation and is accepted by the trade unions. It has over the past few years been contested by employers, who feel that prior authorization restricts their room for manoeuvre in personnel management, prevents them from taking decisions which fall within their own managerial and organizational authority, and is at variance with the system laid down in Community law (EEC Directive No. 129/1975 on collective dismissal).

268. **EXTENSION DE CONVENIOS COLECTIVOS — EXTENSION OF COLLECTIVE AGREEMENTS:** Administrative act or procedure whereby the applicability of a collective agreement is extended beyond the original bargaining unit. In Spain, this procedure is followed so that the provisions of an existing agreement can be applied to other sectors or areas in which, for certain reasons (lack of industrial relations bodies empowered to bargain, etc.), it is impossible to draw up a separate agreement. Because it implies adminstrative intervention, it is seen as being merely supplementary to collective bargaining and to **adoption of a collective agreement**, though it is used in preference to issuing **Labour Ordinances**. The extension of an agreement is a **labour administration** action and must be initiated at the request of an interested party; the National Collective Agreement Advisory Committee must be consulted before the extension procedure is carried out.

269. **EXTINCION DEL CONTRATO DE TRABAJO — TERMINATION OF THE CONTRACT OF EMPLOY-MENT:** Breaking-off or ending of the employment relationship. Under the Spanish industrial relations system it may occur for various reasons: relinquishment or annulment of the contract by the unilateral decision of one of the parties, with or without just cause (**dismissal** by the employer; **resignation, quitting the job** or justified annulment by the employee); agreement between the two parties (voluntary redundancy and early retirement); or as a result of an extraneous event which frustrates the contract or justifies its breaking-off (**invalidity/disability, retirement**, the simultaneous holding of jobs deemed incompatible in law, death, company closure, etc.). In some cases or sectors, termination is known as ''cese'' (cessation), and the financial rights deriving from termination or loss of employment are referred to as ''cesantia''. The statutory regulations governing termination of the contract of employment vary in each of these cases; sometimes, particularly when the annulment is unjustified or not motivated by their personal conduct, the injured party is entitled to **compensation for termination of the employment contract** (or **compensation for dismissal/severance pay**, where applicable).

F

270. FACILIDADES DE LOS REPRESENTANTES — FACILITIES FOR WORKERS' REPRESENTATIVES: Set of prerogatives and rights granted to **workers' representatives** to enable them to perform their functions. Under Spanish provisions, they include freedom of expression, freedom of movement and **access to workplaces; disclosure of information/rights to information** and the right to communicate information to the workers they represent; provision of a union room and a notice-board; and, in particular, **time-off rights** to enable them to perform their functions without prejudice to their rights in employment. See **guarantees for workers' representatives**.

271. FEDERACIONES SINDICALES DE INDUSTRIA — INDUSTRIAL FEDERATIONS: Trade union organizations which group unions operating at a lower level and belonging to the same industry or economic sector. In their turn, they normally belong to **trade union confederations**, in which they serve as a vertical or functional channel of organization. In Spain, the most powerful federations have traditionally been those covering metalworking, construction and wood, transport, textiles, food, chemicals, pensioners, mining and agriculture. Federations representing the tertiary or service sector have been gaining strength recently, particularly in some public services (e.g. education).

272. FICHA DEL TRABAJADOR — EMPLOYEE'S PERSONAL FILE: Document containing relevant occupational information about a worker: training received, employment experience, disciplinary action, pay increases, performance appraisals, etc. It is an aid to **personnel management**. See **professional competence and status**.

273. FICHAR — SIGNING IN AND OUT/CLOCKING IN AND OUT: Noting or recording the time at which workers arrive at and leave work. The aim is to monitor attendance and punctuality, and the method is frequently used in the public service and large enterprises. See **working hours**.

274. "FINIQUITO": Document certifying the **termination of the contract of employment** and the settling-up of the parties' respective rights and obligations, particularly as regards pay. Such documents are often drawn up in cases of termination of the contract of employment through voluntary redundancy or early retirement. The Spanish **labour courts** have repeatedly recognized their validity and their value as documentary evidence, except in the event of fraud or deception or of **waiver of rights** on the part of employees.

275. **FLEXIBILIDAD LABORAL — LABOUR FLEXIBILITY:** Ability to adapt the labour factor to general market conditions and the specific circumstances of the enterprise. Flexibility usually concentrates on the quantity of manpower used by the enterprise (numerical flexibility); the cost of the labour factor (pay flexibility); and the utilization of existing manpower, particularly as regards occupational or geographical mobility (functional flexibility). Over the past few years, because of the effects of the economic crisis and economic restructuring, employers and industries have made persistent demands for greater flexibility, which have been addressed both to the trade unions (to change their attitudes and behaviour) and to legislators (to reform or amend certain regulations which are seen as being excessively rigid). Since the late 1970s, this process has led in Spain to legal reforms such as the relaxation of restrictions on grounds for **dismissal** and on the use of **temporary contracts** and the adaptation of regulations governing working hours and **overtime** to the new requirements or characteristics of work/production units. At the same time, collective bargaining (guided here by national general multi-industry agreements or tripartite agreements) has attempted to restrain wage growth by adjusting pay increases to the particular situation of each enterprise or industry.

276. **FOGASA:** See **Wages Guarantee Fund** (Fondo de Garantía Salarial).

277. **FOMENTO DEL EMPLEO — JOB CREATION:** Element of **employment policy** aimed at increasing the number of available jobs and encouraging the conclusion of contracts of employment. In Spain, job-creation measures tend to include financial incentives for employers (lump-sum subsidies, reductions in social-security charges, tax exemptions or reliefs, etc.), but sometimes also modify or suppress certain labour regulations which may influence recruitment (temporary job-creation contracts). Such measures are often selective, being directed at particular groups, industries or geographical areas. Recent Spanish legislation contains many examples, mainly directed at the most disadvantaged groups on the labour market (young people, the disabled, older workers) and at geographical areas and economic sectors which are most in decline or have been worst affected by **industrial restructuring** or the economic crisis:

"Zonas de Urgente Reindustrialización" (Priority Redevelopment Areas) or "Zonas de Promoción Económica" (Economic Development Areas). The various administrative authorities and sometimes also the social partners collaborate in devising and implementing job-creation measures.

278. **FOMENTO DEL TRABAJO NACIONAL (FTN) — PROMOTION OF NATIONAL LABOUR (FTN):** Confederation of Catalonian employers' organizations, created in 1889 from the merging of two other bodies representing employers: Fomento de la Producción Española and Instituto Industrial de Cataluña. The Confederation currently groups together more than 300 employers' organizations representing some 80 per cent. of Catalonian enterprises. It is affiliated to the CEOE and has the second largest number of votes at the General Meeting (coming after CEPYME) though it is more strongly represented than CEPYME on the Management Board. Its governing bodies are the General Council, Management Board, Executive Committee and President.

279. **FONDO DE GARANTIA SALARIAL (FOGASA) — WAGES GUARANTEE FUND (FOGASA):** Fund modelled on similar European institutions, set up in Spain in 1976 to guarantee payment of **wage/pay** and **compensation for termination of the employment contract** when an enterprise becomes bankrupt or is in financial difficulties. Although its primary function is to insure accrued entitlements (it has sometimes been referred to as a form of pay insurance), it has also played an important role in the reorganization of enterprises and **staffing adjustment**, since it has often borne the cost of redundancies. The name refers both to the fund created for this purpose from employers' contributions and to the autonomous body dependent on the **Ministry of Labour** which is responsible for its administration. It essentially complies with EEC Directive No. 987/1980.

280. **FONDOS DE PENSIONES — PENSION FUNDS:** Accumulated wealth capitalized for the sole purpose of fulfilling and implementing **pension schemes**. A special administrative, financial and tax system has been established in Spain to encourage the setting-up of such funds and to ensure that they are properly run.

281. **FONDOS DE PROMOCION DE EMPLEO — EMPLOYMENT PROMOTION FUNDS:** See **industrial restructuring**.

282. **FORMACION CONTINUA — CONTINUING TRAINING:** Also called "formación permanente" in Spanish, this is training received throughout working life with a view to adapting, supplementing or updating original occupational skills or acquiring training or specialization to perform a different occupation, usually involving higher skills and social advancement. Spanish law makes provision for facilities, educational leave and financial assistance for this type of training, and recognizes the right to training and career progression. See **vocational training grants, time off, Employment Training and Integration Plan**.

283. **FORMACION OCUPACIONAL — OCCUPATIONAL TRAINING:** Training directed exclusively at learning a trade or occupation. It is usually given in enterprises or specialized centres or by the public employment services and tends to take the form of short, intensive courses whose content is strictly relevant to the occupation in question.

284. **FORMACION PERMANENTE — CONTINUING TRAINING:** Synonym of **formación continua**.

285. **FORMACION PROFESIONAL — VOCATIONAL TRAINING:** Teaching or instruction directly aimed at preparation for immediate entry to a trade or occupation. In contrast to former practice, in Spain vocational training is now given essentially by specialized centres, though a significant amount of training is still given in enterprises, through **job-training contracts, vocational training grants**, or work experience arrangements. Vocational training comes in many different forms: depending on its relationship with the general education system, it may be **vocational education** or **occupational training**; depending on its content, it may be basic or further training; depending on how it is run, it may be intensive or in the form of **sandwich courses**; and depending on when it is acquired, it may be initial or **continuing training**. Vocational training has recently assumed unexpected importance because the gradual and sustained transformation of the production system means that new occupations have to be learned and traditional skills adapted, particularly in certain economic sectors. There seems to be a general consensus that the resources devoted to vocational training in Spain are inadequate and that study programmes are out of date; as a result, agreements have recently been reached on the reorganization of vocational instruction (**Economic and Social Agreement**), various schemes for employment training and integration into working life have been launched (**Employment Training and Integration Plan**), and

general multi-industry agreements and collective agreements usually include numerous provisions on training courses and activities. For some time now enterprises have been required under Spanish law to pay a vocational training levy to fund training activities.

286. **FORMACION PROFESIONAL ALTERNADA — SANDWICH COURSES:** Form of **vocational training** which is alternated or combined with the performance of work, either during the same period (**job-training contract**) or by means of the temporary interruption of the employment relationship. It aims to combine and simultaneously apply theoretical knowledge and practical skills.

287. **FORMACION PROFESIONAL REGLADA — VOCATIONAL EDUCATION:** Form of **vocational training** given within the general education system by public centres or duly approved private centres. It is organized, run and managed by the public authorities responsible for general education. It combines instruction in strictly occupational skills with general or basic education. See **occupational training**.

288. **FORO DE EMPLEO — "JOB CLUB":** Meeting, conference or discussion group where information can be obtained on job opportunities or vacancies. These events tend to be occasional or informal and are normally organized on a private basis, often by employers interested in attracting skilled workers.

289. **FRENADO DEL RENDIMIENTO — WORKING FOR A LOOSE PIECE RATE:** Deliberate reduction of **performance** by a worker or group of workers, to conceal from the employer the real speed at which the tasks or operations of the job can be performed. It is habitual practice in **payment by results** systems and reflects the workers' belief that, otherwise, the **pace of work** will be increased as a result of **time-cutting**, without any alteration in pay.

290. **FTN:** See **Promotion of National Labour** (Fomento del Trabajo Nacional).

291. **FUERO DEL TRABAJO — LABOUR CHARTER:** Law of March 9, 1938 which, like other laws issued at that time (particularly its Italian equivalent, the Carta del Lavoro), gave solid form to the broad lines and principles of the Franco regime's social policy and labour legislation. It traced the main features of the future Organización Sindical Española (Franco's **Vertical Union**).

292. FUNCIONARIOS PUBLICOS — PUBLIC SERVANTS:
People who work for the public authorities, in accordance with administrative law (public service statute). They are not covered by labour law, though basic trade union legislation (**Trade Union Freedom Act**) applies to them. See **freedom of association/trade union freedom, personnel covered by special statutes, public service union**.

G

293. GARANTIAS DE LOS REPRESENTANTES — GUARANTEES FOR WORKERS' REPRESENTATIVES: Set of rules, measures and provisions intended to protect **workers' representatives** in carrying out their functions. The main guarantees are the prohibition of sanctions or **discrimination** because of the legitimate performance of their duties as representatives, and the requirement that the employer must follow a disciplinary procedure when imposing disciplinary sanctions for serious or very serious offences. See **facilities for workers' representatives**.

294. GESTION DE PERSONAL — PERSONNEL MANAGE-MENT: Aspect of **management** which is concerned with the acquisition and efficient use of human resources. See **personnel manager**.

295. GRATIFICACION — BONUS/ONE-OFF PAYMENT: Financial recompense or compensation for tasks or work. The term usually refers to the sums that an employee receives on an occasional basis or for a particular reason (better performance, exceptional tasks, etc.) although in some cases it has lost this original meaning and simply become the particular name in Spanish of certain **pay supplements,** such as **special bonuses**. See **discretionary pay supplements**.

296. GRATIFICACIONES EXTRAORDINARIAS — SPECIAL BONUSES: Pay supplements relating to a period of more than a month; also called "pagas extraordinarias" or, for short, "pagas extras" (special payments). Although they were originally exceptional or special supplements, they now form part of **wage/pay** and must be paid regularly as a right, which makes their name equivocal. Spanish law recognizes the right to two special payments, though this number is usually increased by the contract of employment or collective agreement. Their amount is normally negotiated individually or collectively. They may be paid in a lump sum, or monthly on a *pro rata* basis (**end-of-service pro rata** entitlements). **Profit-sharing** is a particular form of special bonus.

297. GREMIO — GUILD: Originally, word used in the pre-industrial era to refer to "corporations" or groups of the various members of a trade or profession, classed hierarchically into master craftsmen, skilled workmen and apprentices. Nowadays, the word is sometimes used in Spanish to denote the people who make up a particular sector of the economy, with a meaning similar to that of "ramo" (branch). It is used synonymously with "sindicato" (trade union) in some Latin American countries. See **free enterprise, profession**.

298. **GRUPO DE EMPRESAS — GROUP ENTERPRISE:** Group of enterprises which are legally independent but under single financial management. Also known in English as a "corporate group". The combination of formal independence with tactical unity creates various problems and anomalies as regards industrial relations, since it makes it impossible to define exactly who is the employer. In Spain, case law now deems responsibility to be shared by the various enterprises in the group; sometimes it is even treated as a single employer, for the purposes of the employee's **seniority/length of service** in the event of transfer from one enterprise to another and for the exercise of the **employer's managerial authority** and disciplinary powers. More problems are posed by the group enterprise in terms of collective representation, since Spanish law does not lay down any special rules. The 1986 **Agreement on Workers' Participation in Public Enterprises** provides for some forms of participation in group enterprises in the public sector. See **multinational corporation**.

299. **GRUPO PROFESIONAL — OCCUPATIONAL GROUP:** Set of similar occupations or occupational activities; it serves as a module for **occupational classification**, broader in scope than the **occupational category**. The concrete definition of an occupational group depends on the characteristics of each economic sector and is therefore included in its particular provisions, especially collective agreements. In Spain, the occupational group has been of little significance, since it has generally been used as a mere accumulation of occupational categories and a criterion for the generic classification of employees (manual **workers, ancillary employees, office staff** and **technical personnel**). It has now acquired greater importance, not only because the law sees it as setting the limits to **functional mobility** but also because it offers a means of making better and more flexible use of labour and increasing **job enrichment**. See **multi-skilling/polyvalence**.

300. **GRUPO SEMIAUTONOMO DE PRODUCCION — SEMI-AUTONOMOUS WORK GROUP:** Group of workers who are given a degree of freedom and autonomy in dealing with production and personnel matters within the group (allocation of jobs, quality control, sharing-out of incentive payments). The purpose is to improve production.

H

301. HOJA DE SALARIOS — PAY SLIP: See **pay statement**.

302. HORARIO — HOURS OF WORK: Specified daily timetable of **working time**, particularly the times of arriving at and leaving work. Various patterns can be used; a customary distinction is between **flexitime/flexible working hours** and fixed hours, according to the degree of discretion employees have over their own timetable. Hours of work usually relate to the entire workforce, though they may vary for different employees. Spanish law requires that they be included in the **work calendar** which must be drawn up and published each year by the enterprise. See **signing in and out/clocking in and out, overtime**.

303. HORARIO FLEXIBLE — FLEXITIME/FLEXIBLE WORKING HOURS: System whereby employees are given a degree of discretion over their own timetable of working time. This usually involves a core working time when presence is required, with flexibility over arrival and departure times. The system is sometimes also referred to as "horario variable" (variable working hours). Many Spanish **collective agreements** have introduced rules to make hours of work flexible.

304. HORAS EXTRAORDINARIAS — OVERTIME: Working time which exceeds the usual limits; colloquially, also called "horas extras" for short. In contrast to the situation in other countries, overtime in Spain is deemed to include all hours in excess of ordinary **working hours**, irrespective of whether these are established by law, collective agreement or the individual contract of employment. Spanish law restricts overtime to 80 hours per year (excluding any time spent preventing or repairing damage); makes overtime voluntary (which does not prevent it from being required by individual or collective negotiated agreement); and bans overtime at night (and at all times for **underage workers/minors**). Overtime attracts a minimum pay premium of 75 per cent., though it may be compensated by paid time off (as time off in lieu); collective agreements very often set a fixed amount for overtime pay, to make calculations easier. Habitual use of overtime can worsen unemployment rates, and many calls have been made for its reduction or abolition; in line with the idea of **work-sharing**, Spanish law authorizes the Government to reduce the maximum overtime limit or abolish overtime in certain economic sectors, and successive **general multi-industry agreements** have recommended the abolition of all overtime not necessitated by structural reasons or *force majeure*. As distinct from overtime, "horas recuperables" (make-up time) is intended to compensate for work that has not been done at the proper time, usually because of *force majeure*.

305. HORAS RECUPERABLES — MAKE-UP TIME: See **overtime**.

306. HUELGA — STRIKE: Collective action by workers consisting in the agreed withdrawal of their labour. It is normally directed against the employer, but Spain has a certain tradition of **political strikes** and socio-political strikes, often taking the form of a **general strike**. Nowadays, the main function of strikes is to back up the collective bargaining process and oblige the employer to comply with statutory or contractual regulations, though they also serve as a means of opposing government policies (politico-industrial strikes). In contrast to the situation in countries where other forms of industrial action (**pickets, boycotts, blockading of goods**, etc.) play a more important role, in Spain strikes occupy centre stage in **industrial action** and **industrial conflict**. Spain suffered numerous strikes during the 1970s and early 1980s, as a result of the political transition and the effects of the economic crisis on employment and working conditions: in terms of the number of working days lost, it was hit worse than any of the other major industrialized countries. Subsequently, the level of industrial conflict in Spain fell substantially, mainly owing to the effects of the general multi-industry agreements reached by collective bargaining. Approximately two million working days were lost in 1982, 1985 and 1986, while 1984 and 1987 (when there was a breakdown in social concertation) saw the figure rise to nearly four million. In recent years, the number of strikes occurring each year has fluctuated between 1000 and 1500, involving an average of one and a half million workers. In 1986 the worst-affected sector was the service sector, followed by industry. Strikes in Spain are usually short (in 1986 more than 70 per cent. of strikes lasted fewer than six working days), essentially because of the lack of **strike funds**. Strikes seem to be relatively effective: of some 900 strikes in 1986, more than 500 were called off by agreement between the parties, and of these more than 300 were won by the workers and approximately 200 ended in compromise between the two sides. Industrial conflict has recently become concentrated in the **public sector**, particularly in areas classed as **essential public services**, which has given rise to widespread debate on the best methods of preserving the rights involved. And closely related to this problem is the proposal to devise a new regulatory framework for strikes, which has been announced by the Government but rejected by the unions. See **arbitration, labour dispute/industrial**

dispute/trade dispute, right to strike, mediation, industrial peace, minimum services.

307. **HUELGA DE ADVERTENCIA — TOKEN STRIKE:** See **intermittent strike**.

308. **HUELGA DE BRAZOS CAIDOS — SIT-DOWN STRIKE:** Form of strike in which employees cease all work activities without abandoning their posts. The term reflects the employees' passive physical presence there.

309. **HUELGA DE CELO — WORK-TO-RULE:** Form of strike in which employees insist on strict and scrupulously detailed observance of regulations, instructions and working rules in carrying out their work; also called "trabajo a reglamento". It is actually a form of industrial action involving a disruption of the **pace of work** and, in particular, a **go-slow**, and is therefore sometimes likened to a **slow-down**. Although the law classes it as a strike, it is a practice often used in Spain, mainly in the public sector.

310. **HUELGA DE SOLIDARIDAD — SYMPATHY STRIKE:** Strike action taken by a group of employees to support the labour positions held in a **labour dispute/industrial dispute/trade dispute** which does not directly or immediately affect them. It usually occurs within an enterprise that has several workplaces or among a number of enterprises which specialize in the same activity and are located in the same geographical area. Sympathy strikes are legal under Spanish law as interpreted by the Constitutional Court, provided there is a minimum convergence of interest among the groups of employees involved.

311. **HUELGA EN PUNTOS CLAVE — SELECTIVE STRIKE:** Strike in which the members of the workforce who stop work are those who perform tasks without which the enterprise's entire production process must be brought to a halt. Also called "huelga neurálgica" in Spanish. Such action tends to be taken in enterprises and industries in which work activities are closely interrelated and interdependent (*e.g.* **production-line work**). Spanish legislation deems it to be improper practice because it causes unreasonable damage. It is to be distinguished from the **intermittent strike** and **rotating strike**.

312. **HUELGA GENERAL — GENERAL STRIKE:** Loosely, a strike characterized by the large geographical area and large number of occupational groups involved; more strictly, a strike

affecting all sectors of a country's economy, the major example being a national multi-industry strike. It is usually of a politico-industrial nature, constituting a form of protest against the Government. Spain has a certain tradition of general strikes, particularly during periods of dictatorship but also in democratic times, such as the one that occurred at the end of 1988. See **political strike**.

313. **HUELGA INTERMITENTE — INTERMITTENT STRIKE:** Form of strike in which employees alternate periods of work with periods during which they withhold their labour. Strike action is usually taken for several hours a day, several days a week or several days a month. For the strikers, it has various advantages over a continuous strike: it serves as a warning that conflict exists (''huelga de advertencia'', *i.e.* token strike), thus creating the possibility of its resolution; it allows pressure to be applied gradually; it has less impact on their **wage/pay**; and it makes it easier for them to communicate with each other and maintain unity, etc. This form of strike is legal in Spain, though it may be deemed to be improper practice if it causes unreasonable damage to the employer. It is to be distinguished from the **selective strike** and **rotating strike**.

314. **HUELGA NEURALGICA — SELECTIVE STRIKE:** Synonym of **huelga en puntos clave**.

315. **HUELGA POLITICA — POLITICAL STRIKE:** Strike which is aimed at the Government as a public authority, with a view to securing the satisfaction of purely political demands. Under Spanish law a political strike is deemed to be illegal and may constitute a crime of sedition if it seriously and intentionally undermines state security. It is to be distinguished from a politico-industrial strike, which is also aimed at the Government but only because the attainment of its labour objectives depends directly or indirectly on the authorities. This form of strike is not illegal, but may be deemed improper practice if it causes the employer unreasonable damage. Both political and politico-industrial strikes usually take the form of a **general strike**.

316. **HUELGA ROTATORIA — ROTATING STRIKE:** Form of strike which consists in the successive stoppage of work in different sections or by different groups of employees in the same workplace or enterprise. Its prime aim is to demonstrate the employees' backing of certain demands and to exert constant pressure, without bringing the production process to a total halt.

Rotating strikes are deemed to be improper practice under Spanish law. They are to be distinguished from the **selective strike** and **intermittent strike**.

317. **HUELGA SALVAJE — WILDCAT STRIKE:** In Spain, this term is used for strikes which involve obvious legal violations or irregularities in the way they are called or conducted: strike action taken unexpectedly or without advance notice; strikes accompanied by acts of violence; strikes which violate a no-strike agreement (**industrial peace**), etc. See **strike declaration, notice of strike**.

I

318. **ILE:** See **local employment schemes** (Iniciativas Locales de Empleo).

319. **ILT:** See **temporary incapacity for work/sickness absence** (Incapacidad Laboral Transitoria).

320. **IMPLANTACION SINDICAL — UNION STRENGTH:** In the broad sense, solidarity or significance of a **trade union**, in general terms or within a given sphere; in this sense, its meaning is similar to **representativeness**. Spanish case law, however, uses a narrower concept of union strength, based purely on the number of members or paid-up members. This concept has been used as the criterion for identifying those unions which may lawfully take certain forms of **industrial action**.

321. **INCAPACIDAD — INCAPACITY:** See **invalidity/disability**.

322. **INCAPACIDAD LABORAL TRANSITORIA (ILT) — TEMPORARY INCAPACITY FOR WORK/SICKNESS ABSENCE:** A temporary or transitory incapacity as opposed to permanent disability. Under Spanish law, temporary incapacity for work may last for a maximum of 12 months (which may be extended to 18 months), during which time the worker is entitled to **social security** health care and financial benefits, sometimes accompanied by supplements paid by the enterprise. When its maximum period expires, if the employee is still not cured and if the incapacity is still transitory the "temporary incapacity" situation formally changes into what is termed "provisional disability". See **invalidity/disability**.

323. **INCENTIVOS SALARIALES — PAY INCENTIVES:** Amounts or **pay supplements** added to **basic pay** to encourage employees to work harder or better. They can take various forms, depending on the type of activity or form of work organization: commission, **incentive bonus payments**, etc.

324. **INDEMNIZACION DE DESPIDO — COMPENSATION FOR DISMISSAL/SEVERANCE PAY:** Sum due to an employee because of **dismissal**, normally as compensation for damage. Under Spanish legislation, it must be paid in cases of **unjustified dismissal, unfair dismissal** or, in general, dismissal for reasons not attributable to the employee's conduct; the amount is laid down but varies according to the type of dismissal involved and the employee's length of service in the enterprise (45 days' pay for each year of service up to a maximum of 42 months' pay;

20 days' pay for each year of service up to a maximum of 12 months' pay, etc.). It may be increased under the terms of a collective agreement or contract of employment.

325. **INDEMNIZACION DE TERMINACION DE CONTRATO — COMPENSATION FOR TERMINATION OF THE EMPLOYMENT CONTRACT:** Compensation arising from the ending of the contract of employment. It is normally payable to the employee, who tends to be the party more detrimentally affected by termination of the contract, but employers may also demand such compensation if they can prove that they have been caused damage. The main provision under Spanish law is for **compensation for dismissal/severance pay**, but compensation may also be paid for termination of certain **temporary contracts, quitting the job,** failure to give the required **notice, retirement** of an individual employee, etc.

326. **INDIZACION — INDEX-LINKING/INDEXATION:** System for the automatic adjustment of financial quantities in accordance with a reference index: cost-of-living index, retail-price index, productivity, general economic situation, etc. It has frequently been used in Spain for regular **pay adjustment** (for example, by means of the ''sliding'' or index-linked pay scale), but has recently become less common because of its inflationary effects. Nowadays, index-linking is applied more to state **pensions**.

327. **INEM:** See **National Institute for Employment** (Instituto Nacional de Empleo).

328. **INFRACCIONES LABORALES — LABOUR OFFENCES:** Acts or omissions by employers which violate labour or social legislation. They may incur administrative or penal sanctions. In Spain, administrative offences, which are subject to sanctions imposed at the proposal of the **Labour Inspectorate**, are covered mainly by the **Labour Offences and Sanctions Act** of 1988, which describes various violations of labour legislation (particularly as regards work, health and safety, employment and social security) and categorizes them as minor, serious or very serious offences. The same Act states that administrative sanctions may include the imposition of fines of varying magnitude, and even temporary or permanent closure of the workplace. Offences which have greater social impact are categorized as **criminal labour offences** in the Penal Code and are subject to penal sanctions.

329. **INICIATIVAS LOCALES DE EMPLEO (ILE) — LOCAL EMPLOYMENT SCHEMES:** Measures aimed at creating jobs in the local area. Specifically, this is the name given to **job-creation** programmes run by municipal councils or local bodies within their area. They meet social needs at local level and utilize production resources that are unlikely to attract private enterprise. Such programmes are a common feature in Spain; they are normally subsidized by the European Social Fund and the various public authorities (sometimes in collaboration), and are mainly targeted at young people or the long-term unemployed.

330. **INSALUD:** See **National Institute of Health** (Instituto Nacional de la Seguridad Social).

331. **INSERSO:** See **National Institute of Social Services** (Instituto Nacional de Servicios Sociales).

332. **INSPECCION DE TRABAJO — LABOUR INSPECTOR-ATE:** Central government body responsible for monitoring and supervising compliance with labour and social legislation. Set up in 1906, it has since become part of **labour administration**. Labour Inspectors have rights of **access to workplaces** and to certain information kept by the enterprise and can issue official notifications (of infringement, settlement, etc.) and propose sanctions for violations of social legislation. They perform their functions essentially by visiting enterprises or workplaces; they are also officially empowered to institute legal proceedings and to act as mediators or conciliators in industrial and legal disputes. See **Employment Inspectors, labour offences**.

333. **INSS:** See **National Institute of Social Security** (Instituto Nacional de la Seguridad Social).

334. **INSTITUTO DE REFORMAS SOCIALES — INSTITUTE OF SOCIAL REFORM:** Institution similar to those in other countries, set up in 1903 to prepare labour legislation, to be responsible for its implementation and to promote the betterment and well-being of the working class, following in the footsteps of the **Commission for Social Reform**. It was to be one of the cornerstones of future **labour administration** in Spain: it conducted numerous studies on the labour situation, prepared draft labour laws, performed administrative functions and implemented labour regulations. In 1924 it was disbanded, with many of its functions being transferred to the Labour Council.

335. **INSTITUTO NACIONAL DE EMPLEO (INEM) — NATIONAL INSTITUTE OF EMPLOYMENT (INEM):** Administrative body coming under the **Ministry of Labour**, set up in 1978 to develop and follow up **employment policy**, to co-ordinate and run public employment offices and to administer the **unemployment** benefit system.

336. **INSTITUTO NACIONAL DE LA SALUD (INSALUD) — NATIONAL INSTITUTE OF HEALTH (INSALUD):** Body set up in 1978 to administer the provison of health care under the **social security** system. Its functions have been transferred to the Autonomous Communities with corresponding powers and responsibilities.

337. **INSTITUTO NACIONAL DE LA SEGURIDAD SOCIAL (INSS) — NATIONAL INSTITUTE OF SOCIAL SECURITY (INSS):** Body set up in 1978, replacing the former National Institute of Social Insurance (INP), to administer the **social security** system and, in particular, allocate financial benefits (except **unemployment** benefit). Its original responsibilities for the registration of enterprises and employee membership of schemes have since passed to the General Social Security Fund (TGSS).

338. **INSTITUTO NACIONAL DE SERVICIOS SOCIALES (INSERSO) — NATIONAL INSTITUTE OF SOCIAL SERVICES (INSERSO):** Body set up in 1978 to administer certain supplementary services of the **social security** system, particularly **social services**. Its functions have been transferred to the Autonomous Communities with appropriate powers and responsibilities.

339. **INTERLOCUTORES SOCIALES — SOCIAL ACTORS:** See **social partners**.

340. **INTERSINDICAL GALLEGA (INTG) — GALICIAN TRADE UNION CONFEDERATION (INTG):** Trade union organization set up in 1977 whose area of activity is confined to the Autonomous Community of Galicia. It describes itself as a revolutionary and class-based trade union and maintains relations with the World Federation of Trade Unions and various Portuguese central trade union bodies. In terms of electoral strength, it has become the third most important trade union in the region, though it appears to have lost some of its influence over the past few years as a result of internal disputes and splits.

341. INTG: See **Galician Trade Union Confederation** (Intersindical Gallega).

342. INVALIDEZ — INVALIDITY/DISABILITY: Physical or mental condition which makes a person totally or partially incapable of working, either as an employee or on a self-employed basis. Also known as "incapacidad" (incapacity), particularly if it is of short duration. Spanish law divides disability into several categories: temporary incapacity, from which the individual is likely to recover in the short or medium term (technically referred to as **temporary incapacity for work/sickness absence**); provisional disability (which more or less equates with long-term illness); and permanent disability (or disability in the true sense), where the reduction or loss of capacity is likely to be permanent. There are various degrees of permanent disability: partial disability, which makes it difficult but not impossible for the individuals concerned to pursue their usual occupation; total disability, which makes them unable to pursue their usual occupation; absolute disability, which prevents them from pursuing any occupation; and major disability, where they need a carer. Total and absolute permanent disability constitute grounds for **termination of the contract of employment**, though disabled workers retain an absolute right to preferential recruitment for their former post should they recover. **Social security** protection for the disabled consists of financial benefits and health care, which sometimes includes rehabilitation. Protection is more comprehensive when the disability has been caused by an **accident at work/industrial accident** or **occupational illness/industrial disease**. See **pensions**.

J

343. **JORNADA ANUAL — ANNUALIZED WORKING HOURS: Working time** measured in annual terms. In Spain, this unit of calculation has often been used in **general multi-industry agreements** (and from them in **collective bargaining**), which specified 1980 hours for 1981, 1880 hours for 1982 and 1826 hours 27 minutes for 1984. Current legislation recognizes this trend and provides for the possibility of setting working hours for the year, provided that the legally prescribed limits on daily **working hours** and the amount of **overtime** are observed: these are a maximum of nine hours' work per day, a minimum of 12 hours' rest between working days and a maximum of 80 hours' overtime per year. See **working hours**.

344. **JORNADA CONTINUADA — CONTINUOUS WORKING DAY:** Form of working in which daily **working hours** are not interrupted by a lengthy break for a midday meal. Spanish law deems a working day to be continuous if it includes less than an hour's break and, in this case, prescribes a minimum rest period of 15 minutes ("tea-break"), which is deemed to be working time if so stipulated by the parties to the collective agreement or contract of employment. This type of working day is common in certain types of work or activities (particularly in the service sector) and is the norm in the case of **shiftwork**. It is in contrast to the "jornada partida" (split working day), which is still typical of agricultural labour, shop work and small enterprises. The continuous working day that is shortened at certain times of year (summer) is called "jornada intensiva".

345. **JORNADA DE TRABAJO — WORKING HOURS:** Strictly speaking, **working time** measured by the day. In the broad sense, the time devoted to work, although working hours are not necessarily the same as actual working time, which is affected by other variables such as rest periods, **overtime, time off, annual holidays**, etc. Working hours may be measured on a daily, weekly, monthly or annual basis. The traditional notion of the working day (the literal meaning of this term in Spanish) is still used for certain types of work (temporary, casual or seasonal work) but is giving way to the measurement of working hours on a weekly or annual basis. Working hours are usually set by the contracting parties, though the state has long (since 1919 in Spain) set maximum limits, in order to protect workers' health and ensure that they have adequate rest periods, to improve the productivity and smooth running of enterprises and, more recently, to encourage **work-sharing**. These legal limits have been progressively lowered and have also been greatly improved on

by collective bargaining. In Spain, the legal maximum has gradually been shortened from an initial 48 hours per week (1919) to 44 hours (1976), 42-43 hours (1980) and 40 hours (1983), which is the current figure, though this is usually reduced by collective agreements which now tend towards a working week of 36-38 hours. The law also specifies **special working hours** for certain economic sectors (agriculture, mining, work at sea, transport, etc.) and certain types of work (starting up and shutting down plant, security work, caretaking, work in refrigerated chambers, etc.) and provides for longer or shorter working hours depending on the practical circumstances of each activity. Working hours are closely connected with other aspects of employment, essentially pay, whose amount (except in certain cases) is set on the basis of working time. See **annualized working hours, continuous working day, special working hours**.

346. **JORNADA INTENSIVA — COMPRESSED WORKING DAY**: See **continuous working day**.

347. **JORNADA PARTIDA — SPLIT WORKING DAY**: See **continuous working day**.

348. **JORNADA REDUCIDA — SHORT-TIME WORKING**: See **reduction of working hours**.

349. **JORNADAS ESPECIALES — SPECIAL WORKING HOURS**: Working hours whose length differs from those laid down as generally applicable to all economic sectors (normal or ordinary working hours). Spanish legislation makes provision for special working hours for certain types of work (security work, starting up and shutting down plant, etc.), certain economic sectors (transport, agriculture, etc.) and some **special employment relationships** (workers in the performing arts, commercial and sales representatives, domestic workers, etc.). Special working hours may also be set by collective bargaining or by the contract of employment. See **working hours**.

350. **JORNAL — DAY'S WAGE**: See **wage/pay**.

351. **JORNALERO — DAY-LABOURER**: Waged worker who provides his/her services by the day or for daily pay. It is a colloquial Spanish term, much used in the labour field and sociological literature to refer to casual workers in certain sectors, particularly agriculture.

352. **JUBILACION — RETIREMENT**: Cessation of employment and occupational activity on reaching a certain age, with

113

entitlement to financial compensation (retirement **pension**). Also called "retiro" (**pensioning-off/retirement**) and, less frequently, "vejez" (old age), though these expressions are more limited in meaning. Employees, public servants, self-employed persons and individual entrepreneurs may all take retirement; in the case of employees, it constitutes grounds for **termination of the contract of employment**. Under Spanish law, the general rule is that to qualify for formal retirement a worker must have reached a minimum age ("edad de jubilación", *i.e.* pensionable age) of 65 years and must have paid contributions for 15 years. While traditionally the worker could choose to carry on working after reaching the qualifying retirement age, it is becoming increasingly common, for reasons connected with **employment policy** or human resources management, for collective agreements to provide for compulsory retirement at a certain age, which was a long-established rule in the public service. For similar reasons, there are now often provisions which encourage workers (usually by means of financial incentives) to take **early retirement**, sometimes in the form of **partial retirement**. However, this trend towards early retirement has been restricted to certain sectors, industries or situations, without extending to the working population in general.

353. JUBILACION ANTICIPADA — EARLY RETIREMENT: Form of **retirement** that can be taken before the worker has reached the generally established pensionable age. The practice is very widespread in Spain, where it serves various purposes: it enables workers to cease employment earlier when their work is particularly dangerous or arduous; it facilitates industrial restructuring or reorganization and enables employers to cut surplus labour; and it promotes **work-sharing**. Collective agreements may (and often do) set other criteria for early retirement, usually with a view to lowering the average age of the workforce by offering older workers financial incentives to leave. See **retirement**.

354. JUBILACION PARCIAL — PARTIAL RETIREMENT: Gradual reduction of usual working hours as a precursor to full retirement. It eases the worker's transition from working life to retirement (gradual retirement) and at the same time enables new workers to enter working life. Spanish legislation has utilized this form of retirement, carrying entitlement to a (partial) pension, to encourage the occupational integration of unemployed young people by means of **hand-over contracts**.

355. **JUNTAS DE PERSONAL — STAFF COUNCILS:** This is the title given by Spanish legislation to the workforce representative bodies of **public servants**. Under the **Representation of Public Servants Act** of 1987, staff councils must be set up in all public administrative bodies, except in local bodies with fewer than 50 public servants, where the workforce is represented by **workers' delegates**. Their powers and responsibilities and the **facilities** and **guarantees for workers' representatives** granted to them are the same as those of **workers' committees**, on which their regulation is modelled.

356. **JURADOS DE EMPRESA — WORKS COUNCILS:** Bodies (headed by the employer or an employer's representative) for workers' participation and representation, set up during the Franco regime (in principle, as a workplace extension of the official **Vertical Union**). They were compulsory in enterprises or departments with more than 50 workers and served as an instrument of co-operation between capital and labour and as representatives of the official union in the workplace, together with the "enlaces sindicales" (official workplace representatives). With the passage of time they came to play a real part in representing and defending workers' interests, and the free **trade unions** utilized them effectively to extend their own presence. The councils disappeared with the return of **freedom of association/trade union freedom** (1977) and were replaced by the present **workers' committees** and **workers' delegates**.

357. **JURADOS MIXTOS — JOINT COUNCILS:** Joint bodies (with equal employee/employer representation) responsible for regulating employment and performing conciliation and arbitration functions within the corresponding occupational group. Although there were earlier indications they were actually set up in Spain in 1931, replacing the former "comités paritarios" (joint committees), for the purpose of regulating terms and conditions of employment (through **basic provisions**, or generally applicable corporatist collective agreements); preventing and settling labour disputes (including appeals against **dismissal**); examining and monitoring compliance with social legislation; and co-operating with public employment offices. See **corporatism**.

L

358. **LAUDO ARBITRAL — ARBITRATION AWARD:** Decision of the impartial third party or arbitrator to whom the parties have previously referred their disagreement. It is the outcome of **arbitration**. It may be made according to the principles of natural justice or on the basis of an existing regulation.

359. **LCT:** See **Contracts of Employment Act** (Ley de Contrato de Trabajo).

360. **LEY DE CONTRATO DE TRABAJO (LCT) — CONTRACTS OF EMPLOYMENT ACT (LCT):** Official title of the Spanish laws of 1931 and 1944 governing the **contract of employment** and the central aspects of individual employment relationships. The Law of 1931, which was based on the Preliminary Bill produced by the German labour lawyer Pothoff, represented the first systematic regulation of the contract of employment in Spain and was one of the most progressive laws of the period. In 1944, when Franco's dictatorship was already established, it was reviewed to bring it into line with the new regime and a large number of Labour Regulations were also introduced which eroded and reduced its original scope. In 1976 it was supplemented and partially adapted to the new situation in Spain by the Labour Relations Act, and in 1980 some of its provisions were repealed, with the others being reduced to regulatory status, by the **Workers' Statute**. Its replacement marked the end of a long and important phase of industrial relations in Spain.

361. **LEY DE INFRACCIONES Y SANCIONES (LISOC) — LABOUR OFFENCES AND SANCTIONS ACT (LISOC):** Law of April 7, 1988 which governs the powers of the Spanish public authorities to impose sanctions for breaches of labour and social legislation. It remedied the former fragmentation of regulations in the matter and incorporated the new (constitutional) principles of sanctioning powers into labour legislation. It was passed after a long legal and political debate on the extent of these powers and on state intervention in industrial relations in general. See **labour inspectorate, labour offences**.

362. **LEY DE ORGANOS DE REPRESENTACION DE LOS FUNCIONARIOS (LORF) — REPRESENTATION OF PUBLIC SERVANTS ACT (LORF):** Law of June 12, 1987 which governs **public servants'** rights to collective representation and participation in establishing their terms and conditions of employment, and their right of assembly, thus developing and

supplementing the **Trade Union Freedom Act**. The first public service **union elections** were held as a result of its entry into force. See **staff councils**.

363. **LEY DE PROCEDIMIENTO LABORAL (LPL) — LABOUR PROCEDURE ACT (LPL):** Title given to the successive laws which have governed the **legal procedure for labour cases** in Spain since 1958. See **conciliation, labour courts**.

364. **LEY GENERAL DE LA SEGURIDAD SOCIAL (LGSS) — GENERAL SOCIAL SECURITY ACT (LGSS):** Law of May 30, 1974 which is a recasting of earlier legal provisions on social security originating from the Basic Social Security Act of 1963. Part I contains general regulations governing the organization of the social security system (scope, funding, protective action, etc.); and Part II contains the basic rules governing the general scheme (applicable to workers in industry and services), which usually serve as a model or as supplementary regulations for special schemes (such as those for agricultural workers, the self-employed, etc.). Developed and supplemented by numerous regulatory provisions, the Act has undergone various amendments over the past few years in order to reorganize administration of the system, adjust the level of protection provided and introduce new regulations on **unemployment** benefits (Unemployment Protection Act of 1984, Pensions Act of 1985, etc.).

365. **LEY ORGANICA DE LIBERTAD SINDICAL (LOLS) — TRADE UNION FREEDOM ACT (LOLS):** Law of August 2, 1985 which develops the right to **freedom of association/trade union freedom** and regulates the formation of **trade unions** and their activities. In particular, it covers trade union representation at enterprise level (**workplace branches, trade union delegates**); the identification, responsibilities and powers of **most representative unions**; and negotiated agreements on the check-off system for collecting **trade union dues** and on **collective bargaining levies**. The Act was drawn up together with the 1984 amendment of the **Workers' Statute** in a legislative operation whose central feature lay in favouring the most representative trade union organizations. The Constitutional Court's decision of July 29, 1985 found the Act to be in accordance with the Constitution, with certain shades of interpretation.

366. **LGSS:** See **General Social Security Act** (Ley General de la Seguridad Social).

367. **LIBERTAD DE EMPRESA — FREE ENTERPRISE:** This is the term used for the right to economic freedom and access to markets and to the free exercise of entrepreneurial activities. In the field of industrial relations, it implies that the employer has certain rights to organize and manage labour. It is now expressly recognized by the Spanish Constitution, although this does not imply the total disappearance of state intervention in the market, nor does it prevent employees from having a voice in management decisions through **workers' participation** or **collective bargaining**. See **employer's managerial authority/managerial prerogative**.

368. **LIBERTAD SINDICAL — FREEDOM OF ASSOCIATION/TRADE UNION FREEDOM:** In Spain, after having been suppressed during Franco's regime trade union freedom was restored by the 1978 Constitution and developed in the **Trade Union Freedom Act**. The right to trade union freedom extends both to private sector employees and to **public servants**, though military personnel, members of the judiciary and employees of the fiscal authorities are excluded and there are some restrictions on members of the police force and security officers, who are prohibited from joining general trade unions. In addition to the right (collectively or individually) to form or join a union, trade union freedom includes the right not to be obliged to join a trade union ("negative" trade union freedom). It also embraces the right to engage in **trade union activity** and, in particular, the **right to collective bargaining**, the **right to strike**, the right to propose industrial action, the right to field candidates in **union elections** and the right to form union **workplace branches**. Special protection under Spanish law for exercising the right to trade union freedom includes the prohibition on suspending or dissolving trade unions except by a court decision; the declaration as null and void of any contractual clauses, regulatory provisions or company decisions which imply **discrimination** on trade union grounds; and the provision of preferential legal procedures. Majority legal opinion in Spain holds that employers are excluded from the scope of trade union freedom, their right to form and belong to associations resting in the more general right to freedom of association. See **union membership clauses, representativeness, trade union**.

369. **LIBRE CIRCULACION DE TRABAJADORES — FREEDOM OF MOVEMENT FOR WORKERS:** Right granted by EEC law to workers of the Member States to move freely about within Community territory for the purposes of employment, and not to suffer **discrimination** there as regards

employment or working conditions because of their nationality. See **foreign workers**.

370. **LICENCIA PAGADA DE ESTUDIOS — PAID STUDY LEAVE:** Exemption from work for a certain period for study or training purposes. Since the ratification of ILO Convention No. 140 (1974), Spanish legislation has recognized the right to career progression and vocational training in employment, which makes it possible for employees to take advantage of time-off rights, choose their work shift or, if necessary, adapt their working hours so that they can attend training courses or sit examinations. It is left to **collective agreements** to specify these rights and facilities.

371. **LISOC:** See **Labour Offences and Sanctions Act** (Ley de Infracciones y Sanciones).

372. **LISTA NEGRA — BLACKLIST:** General term alluding to any action taken by employers to identify workers known for their trade union membership or with a reputation for militancy, with a view to passing on the information to other employers to prevent these workers from being hired or encourage their dismissal. The word is based on historical practice, when employers kept and circulated an actual list of such workers. See **anti-union behaviour/anti-union activity**.

373. **LOLS:** See **Trade Union Freedom Act** (Ley Orgánica de Libertad Sindical).

374. **LORF:** See **Representation of Public Servants Act** (Ley de Orgános de Representación de los Funcionarios).

375. **LPL:** See **Labour Procedure Act** (Ley de Procedimiento Laboral).

M

376. MANDOS INTERMEDIOS — LOWER AND MIDDLE MANAGEMENT: General term used to refer to employees who perform management or supervisory functions on the orders or instructions of more senior management personnel. It usually covers "capataces"(overseers), "contramaestres" (foremen), "encargados" (supervisors), "jefes de taller" (workshop heads), "jefes de sección" (section heads) and "jefes de departamento" (heads of department). Their employment is governed by the general regulations but, compared with other employees, their attitude to their work is more coloured by the relationship of trust with the employer and individual agreements play a greater part in regulating their terms and conditions of employment.

377. MANO DE OBRA — MANPOWER: Term used to refer to the economically active population as a whole; from the management viewpoint, it constitutes the labour factor as one of the factors of production. The Spanish term originates from periods of history when the "obrero" (manual **worker**) was an important feature of the working population, and the expression is often still used to refer to this group. In legislation, it is sometimes used as a synonym of "trabajadores" (workers, *i.e.* employees as a group).

378. MASA SALARIAL — WAGE BILL: Total remuneration of all the employees of an enterprise or given unit; in its broader sense, the term refers to all labour costs (**wage/pay**; insurance costs and social security charges; certain non-pay components such as allowances or expenses, etc.). It is a significant variable in **collective bargaining** and **pay adjustment**, particularly in large enterprises or in product-sector agreements. It is also used in setting pay in the **public sector**.

379. MEDIACION — MEDIATION: Means of settling disputes whereby an impartial third party assumes the task of bridging the gulf between the positions held by the parties and making non-binding recommendations as to the settlement of their dispute. It differs from **conciliation** in that recommendations are made, and from **arbitration** in that these recommendations are non-binding. Under Spanish law, mediation is compulsory as a stage prior to the **special legal procedure for industrial disputes**. In a quite different context, the term also applies to the activity of establishing contact between those seeking and offering employment, with a view to the **placement** of job-seekers (mediation in the contract of employment). See **National Institute of Employment**.

380. **MEDICO DE EMPRESA — COMPANY DOCTOR:** Doctor contracted by the enterprise to provide medical and health care in the workplace. The doctor must hold an official certificate of competence to perform these tasks and is monitored and assisted in the work by **INSALUD**. Under Spanish law, industrial medicine services and company medical services must be set up in workplaces which have a large number of employees and where the work involves a high risk. The employer can ask the company doctor for **verification of illness** as regards an employee.

381. **MEDIDAS DE CONFLICTO COLECTIVO — INDUSTRIAL ACTION:** General term used to refer to collective pressure tactics by workers, particularly forms of action other than **strikes (pickets, boycotts/blacking, blockading of goods**, etc.), and also to pressure tactics or measures adopted by employers in situations of conflict, such as **lock-outs**. (In Spanish, the term also covers peaceful means of settling labour disputes, *i.e.* **conciliation, mediation, arbitration**, and in particular the **special legal procedure for labour disputes.**) Spanish law recognizes the right of workers and employers to take these forms of industrial action but, with the exception of strikes, they are used relatively infrequently in the Spanish industrial relations system.

382. **MEJORAS VOLUNTARIAS DE SALARIOS — DISCRETIONARY PAY SUPPLEMENTS:** Payments or supplements which the employer unilaterally chooses to add to the agreed or legally stipulated **wage/pay**, either individually or collectively. When they are a repeated and continuous practice they become established as a **most favourable condition** and cannot be unilaterally withdrawn or altered, though they may be "absorbed" by later pay increases. During certain periods when collective bargaining was prohibited in Spain (1939-1958), they served as the formal guise of collective agreements. See **"absorption" of pay increases**.

383. **MEJORAS VOLUNTARIAS DE SEGURIDAD SOCIAL — DISCRETIONARY SOCIAL BENEFITS:** Benefits which are voluntarily provided in addition to the basic protection afforded by the compulsory public system of social welfare or **social security**. They form part of "previsión o seguridad social complementaria" (supplementary welfare or social security arrangements). In Spain, they have usually been established by collective agreement and generally consist of additional financial benefits during temporary incapacity for work, retirement bonuses, supplementary pensions, etc. Their supplementary role,

121

particularly in the case of **pensions**, is also fulfilled by other forms of voluntarily agreed protection, such as that provided through social welfare bodies, **mutual insurance societies, pension schemes**, etc.

384. **MERCADO DE TRABAJO — LABOUR MARKET:** The set of relations whose objective is the supply of labour in exchange for payment. The salient feature of the Spanish labour market is the low **participation rate/activity rate** of the potential working population; this is partly attributable to the "discouragement" or withdrawal from the market of the most disadvantaged groups of the economically active population (married women, young people under the age of 19 and people over the age of 55) because of their poor employment prospects over the past few decades. It is also characterized by its strong segmentation or division into various population groups (parallel or segmented markets) to the detriment of certain groups. A third feature of the Spanish labour market is the relative importance of the **hidden economy**, where the supply of labour consists largely of the unemployed and groups who are not usually classified as being part of the economically active population (students, retired workers, housewives). In addition to all these factors, mention should be made of the trend towards standardizing pay levels and of the low rate of **labour turnover** in Spanish enterprises. See **provision of labour, temporary employment agency, National Institute of Employment, sub-contracting**.

385. **MERCADO INTERNO DE TRABAJO — INTERNAL LABOUR MARKET:** Labour market consisting of the human resources within a particular enterprise.

386. **MILITANTE SINDICAL — UNION ACTIVIST:** See **trade unionist**.

387. **MINISTERIO DE TRABAJO Y SEGURIDAD SOCIAL — MINISTRY OF LABOUR AND SOCIAL SECURITY:** Government department responsible for devising and implementing labour and social policy. The Ministry was preceded by various administrative bodies set up at the beginning of the century (in particular, the **Institute of Social Reform** and National Institute of Social Insurance) and was founded in the 1920s; since then it has, under various names, always been part of the state administration, constituting the nucleus of **labour administration**. It performs its functions through numerous services, independent agencies or management bodies (**Wages Guarantee Fund, INEM, INSS**, etc.) and through "peripheral

administrative bodies'' (provincial directorates). Many of its traditional powers and responsibilities have been transferred to the Autonomous Communities. The management of health services and health policy (**INSALUD**), as well as **social services** and social affairs (**INSERSO**), are now the responsibility of other Ministries (of Health and Social Affairs) or of the Autonomous Communities. All of this means that, basically, the Ministry is now responsible only for regulatory tasks, planning social and employment policy, managing the social security system and co-ordinating the various bodies responsible for labour administration. See **labour authorities**.

388. **MODERACION SALARIAL — PAY RESTRAINT:** The term used to refer to moderation in demanding and setting pay increases. This has over the past few years become one of the main instruments of the Government's anti-inflation policy. Pay restraint is usually implemented by setting maximum ''**pay-growth bands**'' or pay ceilings, either by collective agreement or by direct state intervention. In Spain, pay restraint has been attained essentially by means of tripartite or general multi-industry agreements and, for the **public sector**, through the State Budget Laws. Pay increases negotiated by collective agreement fell from 13 per cent. in 1981 to 6.5 per cent. in 1987; since 1987, in view of the strong growth of the economy and improved company profits, the trade unions have been demanding higher pay increases.

389. **MODIFICACION DE CONDICIONES DE TRABAJO — CHANGES IN CONDITIONS:** Changes in employees' obligations and tasks (in their **working conditions/terms and conditions of employment** generally), at the employer's instigation. Under Spanish legislation, which over the past few years has increased employers' powers in order to facilitate technological innovation and changes in **work organization**, temporary and/or minor changes may be decided unilaterally by the employer, while permanent and major changes must be agreed with the workforce representatives or, failing this, authorized by the labour authorities. See **functional mobility, geographical mobility, employer's managerial authority/ managerial prerogative**.

390. **MOVILIDAD — LABOUR MOBILITY:** General term used to refer to changes in the content of work (**functional mobility**) and the place of work (**geographical mobility**). It may relate to an individual enterprise (internal mobility) or to the entire **labour market** (external mobility).

391. MOVILIDAD FUNCIONAL — FUNCTIONAL MOBILITY: Mobility which concerns the object of work or the functions assigned to an employee. It may be vertical or horizontal, depending on whether or not it implies a change of **occupational category**. Under Spanish legislation, employers can change an employee's tasks provided that they observe the obligations arising from the contract of employment, the academic or occupational qualifications required for the job, and the tasks and duties proper to the employee's **occupational group**. When the change extends beyond this and is of a permanent nature, the employer must follow a special procedure for **changes in conditions**. If the change is temporary, the employer must comply with the conditions laid down for **internal job transfer**. See **labour mobility, geographical mobility**.

392. MOVILIDAD GEOGRAFICA — GEOGRAPHICAL MOBILITY: Mobility which concerns the place of work. Under Spanish law, employers can decide on changes in employees' place of work when they are to be made on technical, organizational or production grounds, although the employee's consent or prior official authorization is sometimes required.

393. MOVILIZACIONES — MOBILIZATION: Activities (meetings, demonstrations, distribution of posters and leaflets, etc.) to organize workers, particularly in preparation for an industrial dispute, and to bring the dispute to the attention of the general public and the authorities.

394. MOVIMIENTO OBRERO — LABOUR MOVEMENT: The organizations historically used by workers to defend their economic and social interests; the labour movement essentially comprises **trade unions** (and other workers' representative bodies) and the political parties which have traditionally represented the working class (Social Democratic, Socialist or Communist parties). The term has an old-fashioned flavour, not only because the word "obrero" (manual **worker**) is becoming increasingly rare in trade union language, but also because some of the parties which have traditionally championed the labour movement have become less class-oriented and are setting their sights on representing a broader range of interests. This has caused a separation between trade union organizations and purely political bodies and has resulted in the set of institutions which defend workers' interests being more commonly referred to as **trade unionism** or the trade union movement. In Spain, the labour movement in its traditional sense was at its height in the late nineteenth and early twentieth centuries, with the parallel creation of ideologically linked trade unions and political parties: socialist (**UGT** and PSOE), anarchist or libertarian (**CNT**, FAI, Syndicalist Party) and communist (PCE and associated trade unions). Now, as in other countries of Western Europe, the labour movement in its traditional sense is virtually restricted to **class trade unionism**, whose links with the parties of the Left are changing from vital bonds into relations focusing on political influence and exchange.

395. **MULTA DE HABER — DOCKING OF PAY/FINE:** Disciplinary sanction consisting in suspending or reducing pay without any corresponding interruption or reduction of work. It is expressly prohibited by Spanish law. See **suspension of employment and pay**.

396. **MUTUALIDADES DE PREVISION — MUTUAL INSURANCE SOCIETIES:** Bodies providing protection against collective or social risks, based on mutual benefit or co-operative principles. They are usually set up and funded within an occupational group or employers' organization. Mutual insurance was one of the first methods of providing cover for occupational and social risks (industrial mutual benefit) and although it is in the strict sense private and voluntary (independent mutual benefit societies), the authorities have made frequent use of the technique for the compulsory insurance of certain groups or for additional protection against certain risks or contingencies. Spain has a tradition of industrial mutual benefit (through friendly societies or mutual benefit societies, retirement funds and subsidies, company funds, etc.) as the basic form of protection in certain sectors (public service) and to replace or supplement the statutory public system of **social insurance** or **social security**. Nowadays, although these many different forms of protection still exist, mutual insurance tends to be an additional form of welfare or social security provision. See **discretionary social benefits, pension schemes**.

397. **MUTUAS PATRONALES — EMPLOYERS' MUTUAL INSURANCE SOCIETIES:** Associations set up by employers to pool their resources to provide protection against certain occupational risks. Spanish law makes them responsible for insuring against **accidents at work/industrial accidents** and **occupational illnesses/industrial diseases** and classes them as bodies co-operating with the public social security system, under the supervision and control of the **Ministry of Labour**.

N

398. **NACIONALSINDICALISMO — NATIONAL SYNDICAL-
ISM:** Political and social doctrine based on corporatist principles
and certain communitarian theories of enterprise (largely imported
from Germany and Italy), which was the main ingredient of the
socio-political system of the Franco regime. Its institutional
manifestation was the Organización Sindical Española (Spanish
Trade Union Organization), sometimes called the Comunidad
Nacional-Sindicalista del Estado (State National Syndicalist
Community) and also known as the Sindicato Vertical (**Vertical
Union**), the term which is most commonly used and most
accurately depicts the organization. The doctrine had little
theoretical foundation and its supremacy as an ideology waned
noticeably in the second part of Franco's rule; its institutions
remained, however, until **freedom of association/trade union
freedom** was restored in Spain in 1977. See **works councils**.

399. **NEGOCIACION COLECTIVA — COLLECTIVE BAR-
GAINING:** System of autonomous regulation of industrial
relations; more strictly, a process of negotiation between the
employer or employers' associations and the workers'
representative bodies (**parties to collective bargaining**), with a
view to reaching agreements to regulate individual and collective
relations (**collective bargaining process**). Collective bargaining
now occupies a central position in the Spanish industrial relations
system, despite its troubled early days during the first few decades
of the twentieth century and despite the fact that one of its
distinctive features has been the important part played by state
legislation in determining its structure, development and effects.
Until 1936 basic collective bargaining was dominated by **joint
committees** and **joint councils** whose members, in addition to
workers' and employers' representatives, included government
officials with major decision-making powers. After the hiatus of
the Civil War and following a period during which collective
bargaining was banned, an unusual system of collective bargaining
emerged (Law of 1958) in which the state maintained a high
degree of involvement: the parties who were legally authorized
to bargain had to operate within the confines of the **Vertical
Union** created by the Franco regime (a public body, membership
of which was compulsory); the process of negotiating and
administering collective agreements was tightly controlled by the
administrative and legal authorities; and each agreement applied
to all workers and employers in the sector concerned. This model
of generally applicable collective bargaining, which remained
virtually unaltered until 1977, constituted a powerful means of
regulating industrial relations, although co-existing with Labour

Ordinances. Since the 1978 Constitution (in which the right to collective bargaining is enshrined in Article 37.1), collective bargaining has undergone profound transformation and acquired greater genuine effectiveness in regulating labour relations, although the current system retains a number of features from the old system, such as the legal preference for generally applicable normative agreements and the major role played by the judicial institutions in administering and implementing agreements. One of its important innovations is the extension of collective bargaining (**Representation of Public Servants Act of 1987**) to **public servants**, though with markedly special features (**public service agreements and "pacts"**). See **collective agreement, extra-statutory agreement, collective bargaining structure.**

400. **NEGOCIACION COLECTIVA ARTICULADA — ARTICULATED BARGAINING:** Form of collective bargaining in which various **bargaining units** in a given sphere of operation are linked in some way. It involves defining the matters that may be negotiated by each unit and establishing the relationship (or "articulation") between the different units, according to rules set by collective agreements at a higher level, usually national and **general multi-industry agreements**. Spanish law grants the most representative trade unions and employers' associations certain powers to define such levels of articulation through general multi-industry agreements and procedural agreements, but these powers have only rarely been exercised.

401. **NEGOCIACION PERMANENTE — CONTINUOUS BARGAINING:** System whereby collective bargaining continues after a **collective agreement** has been signed and during its period of validity, mainly because the agreements reached are "open-ended" and require later additions. It differs from static bargaining, in which collective agreements are deemed to be "closed" agreements which can be renegotiated only on expiry. The British system is an example of continuous collective bargaining, whereas the Spanish system must obviously be classed as a static model.

402. **NOMINA DE SALARIOS — PAY LIST:** See **pay statement**.

O

403. OBRERO — WORKER: In general terms, the Spanish term "obrero" refers to a person who performs works or services under the direction of another person, with the same meaning as "trabajador" (worker in the sense of an employee). But its more precise meaning is a manual or blue-collar worker, as opposed to a **non-manual worker** or white-collar worker. The term was much used in early labour regulations but has virtually disappeared from modern legal texts; it is now used only colloquially or in industrial sociology. In industry-wide regulations, it is used to refer to certain categories of worker such as **unskilled workers/labourers** and **skilled workers/craft workers**.

404. OCUPACION DEL CENTRO DE TRABAJO — SIT-IN/OCCUPATION OF THE WORKPLACE: Form of industrial action where workers remain in the workplace, even outside working hours and against the employer's orders. It may be autonomous or independent **industrial action** but is often used to reinforce or accompany **strikes**. It is particularly common when there is a threat of the enterprise closing down or of the workforce being cut on economic or technological grounds.

405. OFERTA DE EMPLEO ADECUADA — SUITABLE OFFER OF EMPLOYMENT: Offer of employment which suits the worker's skills or occupational qualifications. Under Spanish law, the rejection of a suitable offer of employment by a person in receipt of **unemployment** benefit can give rise to the supension or even loss of entitlement to such benefit.

406. OFERTA PUBLICA DE EMPLEO — PUBLIC SECTOR VACANCIES LIST: List of vacant posts in the various parts of the public administration, for both people employed as public servants and those who have ordinary contracts of employment. It is a means of organizing and rationalizing the processes of **personnel selection** and **career progression** of public sector employees. It is drawn up and published at the end of each budget period.

407. OFICIAL — SKILLED WORKER/CRAFT WORKER: Worker with average qualifications who is assigned tasks or work involving a degree of initiative or responsibility. Skilled or craft workers are usually classified as a subgroup or category of "obreros" (manual **workers**), which is in turn divided into various grades (first, second, etc.) according to occupational skills, the degree of responsibility involved in the work or other similar factors. The Spanish term "oficial" dates back to the time of craft guilds and is most used in particular economic sectors (construction, wood, metalworking, etc.).

408. **OFICINA DE COLOCACION — PLACEMENT OFFICE:** See **employment services**.

409. **OFICINA DE EMPLEO — EMPLOYMENT OFFICE:** See **employment services**.

410. **OFICIO — TRADE (CRAFT):** Combination of occupational skills equipping a person to do a particular job; by extension, a person's usual occupation, work or profession. It has been one of the criteria used for defining occupational groups and categories (grouping of various crafts or trades) and for forming **trade unions** ("sindicato de oficio", *i.e.* craft union), particularly during the early stages of industrialization and of the trade union movement. Nowadays, the classification of workers by craft or trade is no longer significant and has in the trade union world (except in the case of **occupational trade unionism**) been superseded by organization on the basis of industry or economic sector.

411. **OGSH:** See **General Ordinance on Health and Safety at Work** (Ordenanza General de Seguridad e Higiene).

412. **OIT:** See **International Labour Organization** (Organización Internacional del Trabajo).

413. **ORDENANZA GENERAL DE SEGURIDAD E HIGIENE (OGSH) — GENERAL ORDINANCE ON HEALTH AND SAFETY AT WORK:** Regulation of 1971 which set the basic rules in Spain governing **health and safety** at work. It contains a very full list of regulations and prescriptions, though it is probably little suited to the new features of the production system. It has over the past few years been supplemented by numerous regulations directed specifically at certain industries, occupations or types of work, many of which implement EEC Directives and Regulations. There are signs that the Ordinance is being or will come to be replaced by more up-to-date legislation.

414. **ORDENANZAS LABORALES — LABOUR ORDINANCES:** Regulations which govern terms and conditions of employment and working conditions in enterprises, branches of industry and economic sectors. They originated during the Franco regime to replace the **basic provisions** adopted by **joint councils**, and are the most obvious reflection of the regime's interventionist and authoritarian attitude and its radical opposition (particularly in

the early years) to manifestations of **collective autonomy** and, in particular, to **collective bargaining**. They were initially called Labour Regulations but this was changed to "Labour Ordinances" in the 1960s. Their role as basic industry-wide or occupational regulations is tending to be taken over by **collective agreements**, given that current legislation allows them to be replaced entirely by agreements and authorizes the Ministry of Labour to repeal them. Only in extreme cases may the Government issue new Ordinances. See **extension of collective agreements**.

415. **ORGANIZACION CORPORATIVA NACIONAL — NATIONAL CORPORATIST ORGANIZATION:** System of industrial relations representation and participation in public institutions which was in force in Spain during Primo de Rivera's dictatorship (1923-1929). It consisted of a vast pyramid of public bodies, with the **joint committees** of employers and workers forming the base. Its inspiration lay partly in principles drawn from the system of craft guilds and "corporations", as well as in the communitarian and corporatist theories characteristic of its time.

416. **ORGANIZACION DEL TRABAJO — WORK ORGANIZATION:** Term referring to the way in which an enterprise functions. It is used in collective agreements to indicate various aspects or problems of human resource management (monitoring attendance and absences, assessing performance, job evaluation, adapting to technological change, functional and geographical mobility, elimination of jobs, etc.). In a stricter sense, however, the term refers to the way in which the operations necessary to the production process are divided among workers, *i.e.* the division of labour within the enterprise. In Spain, work organization was marked by the late introduction of the methods and techniques of Taylorism (based on scientific management); it was not until the 1960s that typically industrial forms of organization emerged, mainly in larger enterprises. During the years of the economic crisis, faced with unstable markets and fluctuating levels of economic activity, Spanish enterprises sought more flexible forms of organization. This has led to the growth of the **hidden economy**; far-reaching technological renewal; large-scale elimination of jobs; and progressive segmentation of the labour force, with a core of permanent workers (on whom an investment in training is made to obtain maximum functional flexibility) and a group of peripheral workers with greater insecurity of employment.

417. **ORGANIZACION INTERNACIONAL DEL TRABAJO (OIT) — INTERNATIONAL LABOUR ORGANIZATION (ILO):** Organization created in 1919 by the Treaty of Versailles and now linked with the United Nations Organization; its aim is to improve workers' material and intellectual conditions.

418. **ORGANIZACIONES EMPRESARIALES — EMPLOYERS' ORGANIZATIONS:** Generic term used to refer to any grouping of employers in the defence of their interests. Employers' organizations which operate in the Spanish industrial relations system are usually specifically called **employers' associations**. Alongside or in opposition to these associations, employers sometimes channel their interests through other collective organizations, such as official chambers (of trade, agriculture, etc.).

419. **ORGANIZACIONES SINDICALES INTERNACIONALES — INTERNATIONAL TRADE UNION ORGANIZA-TIONS:** Organizations which bring together **trade unions** of various countries. The most representative are: the International Confederation of Free Trade Unions (ICFTU); the World Confederation of Labour (WCL), which took over from the earlier International Federation of Christian Trade Unions (IFCTU); the World Federation of Trade Unions (WFTU); and, more recently in Europe, the European Trade Union Confederation (ETUC).

P

420. **PACTO COLECTIVO DE TRABAJO — NEGOTIATED AGREEMENT:** In the general sense, the Spanish term "pacto colectivo de trabajo" means a **collective agreement**. It is, however, used with a more specific meaning to refer to collective agreements with limited applicability (**extra-statutory agreements**) or to agreements negotiated within the enterprise to improve on the provisions of higher-level agreements. See **company "pact"**.

421. **PACTO DE EMPRESA — COMPANY "PACT":** Term used in Spain for **extra-statutory agreements** whose purpose is, at enterprise or workplace level, to improve on the provisions of a **collective agreement** concluded at a higher level. Company "pacts" deal mainly with pay.

422. **PACTO DE PERMANENCIA EN LA EMPRESA — MINIMUM-STAY CLAUSE:** Arrangement whereby employees undertake to maintain their employment relationship for a minimum period. It is one of the few cases in which the law allows the employee to undertake not to terminate the contract of employment. Spanish legislation permits such arrangements, provided that they do not last for more than two years and that the employee has received specialist training at the enterprise's expense. Failure to comply may give rise to compensation for damages. See **resignation**.

423. **PACTO SOCIAL — SOCIAL CONTRACT:** Agreements between the Government and the most representative trade unions and employers' associations to establish the basic framework of social and economic policy and involve the signatories in its implementation, particularly as regards pay. Social contracts have been very common in Spain in recent years, where they are usually referred to as **social concertation** or tripartite agreements.

424. **PACTOS DE LA MONCLOA DE 1977 — MONCLOA PACTS OF 1977:** Agreements reached in October 1977 between the Spanish Government and delegates of the most representative political parties to set the basic shape of economic and social policy during political transition. They established the framework of policy on pay, employment and social security during the early years of the democratic regime. They are seen as democratic Spain's first **social contract** or tripartite agreement.

425. **PAGA DE BENEFICIOS — PROFIT-RELATED PAY:** See **profit-sharing**.

426. **PAGAS EXTRAORDINARIAS — SPECIAL PAYMENTS:**
See **special bonuses**.

427. **PAGO CON EFECTO RETROACTIVO — BACKDATED PAY:** Clause usually included in collective agreements in Spain, whereby it is agreed that **pay rises/pay increases** will be awarded retrospectively as from the date of expiry of the previous agreement, should the replacement agreement enter into force at a date later than that.

428. **PAGO DEL SALARIO — PAYMENT OF WAGES:** Disbursement to employee of **wage/pay** due. The payment of earnings has traditionally been covered by legal guarantees to ensure that they are actually received and to avoid withholding of pay or fraudulent practices by the employer. Current Spanish law refers to agreed terms and conditions or to usual practice as regards the place and time of payment (although it sets a maximum period of one month for payment of regular wages) and permits payment in legal tender, by cheque or by a similar method through financial institutions, which is now common practice. The legal guarantees ensuring that pay is actually received lie in the fact that it is protected against seizure (up to the amount of the **national minimum wage**, it must be given preference over the employer's other debts), and that it will be paid by the **Wages Guarantee Fund** in the event of insolvency or financial difficulties for the enterprise. The law also recognizes the employee's right to receive **advances**. The payment of wages must be recorded on a **pay statement**.

429. **PARO — STOPPING WORK/UNEMPLOYMENT:** Situation resulting from the suspension, interruption or termination of the performance of work; in general, absence or lack of work. In its most common meaning, the Spanish term "paro" is synonymous with "desempleo" or "desocupación" (**unemployment**), but it sometimes also applies to the cessation of work caused by a **labour dispute**, and specifically by a **strike** by employees or by a **lock-out** by employers ("paro patronal").

430. **PARO PATRONAL— STOPPAGE IMPOSED BY LOCK-OUT:** See **lock-out, stopping work/unemployment**.

431. **PARTE EMPRESARIAL — EMPLOYERS' SIDE:** See **parties to collective bargaining**.

432. **PARTE LABORAL — EMPLOYEES' SIDE:** See **parties to collective bargaining**.

433. PARTES DE LA NEGOCIACION COLECTIVA — PARTIES TO COLLECTIVE BARGAINING: Each of the sides who take part in the **collective bargaining process**; a distinction is made between the employees' side (''parte laboral'', also called ''banco social'') and the employers' side (''parte empresarial'', also called ''banco económico''). They may each be composed of one or more elements, and together constitute the **bargaining committee** for a given agreement. Spanish legislation on **generally applicable collective agreements** stipulates that only workforce representative bodies (or trade union bodies, provided they are in the majority) are empowered to bargain at enterprise level, and that only trade union and employers' organizations possessing a minimum status of **representativeness** are empowered to bargain above enterprise level. Majority representation status within the scope of the agreement is a requirement for both the employees' and the employers' side in all cases. There are no legal restrictions on the negotiation of agreements with only limited applicability.

434. PARTES PROPORCIONALES — END-OF-SERVICE *PRO RATA* ENTITLEMENTS: Components of remuneration which are paid on termination of the contract of employment and whose amount is calculated in proportion to the time worked; they form part of the final settling-up of pay that is generally recorded formally in the ''**finiquito**'' document. They usually correspond to **annual holiday** pay, **special bonuses** and other pay components which cover periods of more than a month.

435. PARTES SOCIALES — SOCIAL PARTNERS: Organizations representing collective interests which in this capacity act as signatories to **social contracts** or take part in processes of **social concertation**. They are also called social actors (''agentes sociales'' or ''interlocutores sociales''). The term usually refers to trade unions and employers' associations.

436. PARTICIPACION EN BENEFICIOS — PROFIT-SHARING: Form of remuneration which is calculated on the basis of the profits made by the enterprise. It usually takes the form of a separate pay component which is additional to fixed or basic pay (**pay supplement**). Spanish law includes profit-sharing among pay supplements which, along with **special bonuses**, are paid at intervals greater than a month. Profit-sharing was originally a means of financial participation similar to **employee share ownership**; with the passage of time, however, its connection with the enterprise's trading results has in many instances been broken, so that it has become a fixed pay component, usually payable on an annual basis (profit-related pay).

437. PARTICIPACION EN LA EMPRESA — WORKERS' PARTICIPATION: General term used to refer to all the means or activities by which employees influence the employer's decisions that affect their labour interests and/or participate in the management of the enterprise. In its broadest sense it also covers ways in which workers participate in ownership of the enterprise or in its financial results (**employee share ownership, profit-sharing**), and what is known in Spain as "external participation", which does not include worker involvement in the enterprise's management bodies or procedures. The main channels of workers' participation under the Spanish industrial relations system are **collective bargaining** (the typical form of external participation); the rights to information and **consultation** granted to trade unions and workforce and trade union representatives; and the various forms of **co-determination** and monitoring of management which the most representative trade unions are entitled to operate under the **Agreement on Workers' Participation in Public Enterprises of 1986**.

438. PARTICIPACION INSTITUCIONAL — REPRESENTA-TION ON PUBLIC BODIES: Participation of organizations or interest groups (including trade unions and employers' associations) in public bodies or institutions and, more broadly, in functions of public relevance or scope. It is typical of systems inclined towards **social concertation** or concerted economic planning. Spain has a long tradition of such participation: current legislation includes it among the rights and prerogatives of the most representative trade unions and employers' associations.

439. PATRIMONIO SINDICAL — UNION ASSETS: All the financial property, rights and obligations of a **trade union**. Members' **trade union dues** are normally the main source of income and under Spanish law are protected from sequestration. The expression is important when a distinction is being made between "patrimonio sindical histórico" and "patrimonio sindical acumulado". The former are the assets seized from the independent trade union organizations (**UGT, CNT, ELA-STV**) after the Civil War (Political Liabilities Act of 1939), which were returned (or the corresponding compensation paid) to their former owners under a Law of 1986. The latter are the assets accumulated in various ways (compulsory dues, state grants, etc.) by the now defunct official **Vertical Union** of the Franco regime, which have since 1976 been being distributed to the trade union organizations,

135

particularly those with most representative status. In recent years, trade unions have been granted funds from one or other of these sources.

440. **"PATRONAL"**: Word now almost disappeared from legal usage in Spanish but still used colloquially and in trade union circles, meaning "employers" collectively; by extension, it is used adjectivally in the sense of "pertaining to employers", for example in the expression "cierre patronal" (**lock-out**). See **employers' association**.

441. **"PATRONO"**: Alternative word in Spanish for "empleador" or "empresario" (**employer**), used in early labour regulations but now rarely found.

442. **PAUSA EN EL TRABAJO — BREAK:** Interruption of work which is authorized by law, custom or collective agreement. Provision is usually made under Spanish law for **continuous working days** to include a break of at least 15 minutes ("tea-break").

443. **PAZ LABORAL — INDUSTRIAL PEACE:** Absence of **industrial conflict**, particularly strikes. The term is normally used in connection with the period for which a collective agreement is in force, since Spanish law prohibits **strikes** and **industrial action** aimed at altering the negotiated provisions of an agreement. The term "paz social" (social peace) is often used synonymously, although this refers particularly to the impact of industrial conflict on society as a whole.

444. **PENSIONES — PENSIONS:** Financial benefits paid at regular intervals, usually for life; their purpose is to protect people against situations of need or lack of income deriving from permanent cessation of employment or the death of a family's main earner. Spain has since the early twentieth century had a public pension system which initially covered very specific risks but was later expanded and reorganized in accordance with the criteria laid down by the Basic Social Security Act of 1963. The current system provides pensions for permanent invalidity, retirement, widows, orphans and other family survivors, as well as **welfare benefits**. Pensions, and essentially those for permanent invalidity and retirement, now account for the greater part of expenditure on the public social security system. This has in recent years led to the introduction of more stringent eligibility conditions; the establishment of more comprehensive grounds for disqualification when other benefits are being received; the imposition of ceilings

and exceptions as regards adjustment or updating (introduced by successive State Budget Laws); and the promotion of private welfare schemes (**mutual insurance societies**, etc.) to supplement or replace public provision, and private pension plans (**pension funds** and **pension schemes**). See **agricultural unemployment benefit**.

445. **PENSIONES ASISTENCIALES — WELFARE BENEFITS:** Financial benefits whose purpose is to protect people against situations of need, and eligibility for which does not depend on previous contributions or qualifying periods. They are usually granted to the elderly, the handicapped and people suffering from long-term **unemployment** or **invalidity/disability**, provided that they have no other financial income, benefits or resources. In Spain, these benefits are paid by both the social security system and the various public authorities (particularly Autonomous Communities and local bodies). See **social wage**.

446. **PENSIONISTA — PENSIONER:** Persons who receive a **pension** (usually paid by public bodies and schemes) and who have in most cases (**retirement**, absolute **invalidity/disability**) permanently ceased being economically active. The number of pensioners has been increasing in both absolute and relative terms in recent years because of the gradual expansion of welfare systems and the fall in the birth rate. In Spain, the number of pensions paid by the social security system increased from some 4.5 million in 1981 to 6 million in 1989. Under Spanish law pensioners are not permitted to form their own trade unions, but they can join existing unions and form other types of association. This means that their union membership and mobilization strength are relatively high in Spain, leading them to form special federations within the major trade union organizations which, in the **UGT** and **CC.OO.**, represent six per cent. and eight per cent. respectively of total membership. Special associations have also been founded and have in more than one instance been recognized by the authorities as social partners.

447. **PEON — UNSKILLED WORKER/LABOURER:** Term referring to workers with few or no **occupational skills** who perform functions that require no special skill; their work is usually limited to helping other more specialized workers. Historically, it has been common practice to hire their services by the day, and this is the origin of the expression ''peonada'' (**unskilled labour**).

448. **PEON ESPECIALIZADO — SEMI-SKILLED WORKER:** A worker who acquires special ability or familiarization in performing certain simple actions or operations. This knowledge is usually acquired in the enterprise or workplace.

449. **PEONADA — UNSKILLED LABOUR:** Day's work done by an **unskilled worker/labourer** or **day-labourer**; gang of unskilled workers or labourers working on a particular job. The term is traditional in Spanish in certain economic sectors (particularly agriculture and the construction industry).

450. **PERFIL PROFESIONAL — PROFESSIONAL/OCCUPA-TIONAL JOB PROFILE:** Description of the characteristics a worker must possess for a particular job (experience, aptitude, attitude to work, leadership or social skills, etc.). It is indispensable for thorough **personnel selection** and to establish **vocational training** needs.

451. **PERIODO DE PRUEBA — PROBATIONARY PERIOD:** Initial phase of the employment relationship during which the parties are able to discover and test each other's suitability and characteristics and to decide whether the contract of employment is to continue. The probationary period is of particular significance under regulatory systems which favour the open-ended contract of employment and demand justification for dismissal, since it is in those circumstances that it is most important for employers to have an opportunity to break off a contract of employment *ante tempus* and at will. Spanish legislation allows the parties to the contract of employment to make a written agreement arranging a maximum probationary period of 15 days to six months, depending on the worker's occupational skills. The contract of employment is in full force during this period, but the parties can withdraw at will. Collective agreements may (and usually do) contain clauses governing probationary periods.

452. **PERMISO DE TRABAJO — WORK PERMIT:** Authorization that non-nationals have to obtain in order to carry on gainful employment in Spain, either in a self-employed capacity or as an employee. A work permit must be accompanied by a visitor's or residence permit and its period of validity and the occupational and geographical areas it covers may vary. The granting of a work permit is, in principle, dependent on the person concerned securing an administrative authorization if they intend to work in a self-employed capacity or a written undertaking from their prospective employer if they intend to work as an employee. Both the initial granting of a work permit and its renewal also depend

on many other factors, such as the condition of the labour market, any shortfall in national manpower, reciprocal agreements with other countries or (in the case of work in a self-employed capacity) potential for creating jobs. Spain's full accession to the EEC implies the withdrawal of this requirement for Community nationals. Certain types or groups of workers (workers in the performing arts, diplomats, etc.) are also exempt from this requirement and people from certain countries (Latin Americans, Filipinos, Andorrans, Equatorial Guineans and Sephardim) have a preferential right to work permits. The number of permits issued by the Spanish authorities has been relatively stable since 1977 (50,000-60,000 per year, mostly for work as an employee). See **foreign workers**.

453. **PERMISOS — TIME OFF:** Generic term applied to the various situations in which an employee is allowed by law or with the employer's consent to be temporarily or briefly absent from work; the term ''licencia'' has the same meaning. The right to time off under certain circumstances has gradually been extended so that work under an employment contract is compatible with the demands of the employee's family life and social life. Spanish law recognizes employees' right to paid time off for marriage, the birth of a child or death of a relative, moving house, the fulfilment of public duties, and carrying out trade union functions or the functions of a workforce representative. Time off may also be granted to enable an employee to sit examinations and provision is also made for employees to absent themselves from work for one hour per day or to reduce their working hours, with a corresponding cut in pay, to nurse an infant or care for a minor. These rights may be governed and extended by collective agreement or by the individual contract of employment.

454. **PERSONAL — PERSONNEL:** All the employees of a business unit. For the purposes of worker representation, Spanish legislation divides personnel into two major groups: technical and administrative employees, and skilled and unskilled workers.

455. **PERSONAL DE ALTA DIRECCION — SENIOR MANAGEMENT:** Group of persons who exercise managerial authority in the enterprise within the objectives laid down by top-level management bodies. This group does not include persons who are members of the board of directors, nor those who perform management or control functions of only limited scope within the enterprise. Senior management personnel differ markedly from other occupational groups, both in their terms and conditions of employment and in their professional interests.

For this reason, historically they were excluded from Spanish labour legislation; nowadays, their employment is classed as a **special employment relationship** and governed by special labour regulations, although terms and conditions continue to be settled primarily by individual negotiation. Senior management personnel are not included in employee representative bodies, they do not usually join trade unions and they are usually excluded from collective bargaining.

456. **PERSONAL ESTATUTARIO — PERSONNEL COVERED BY SPECIAL STATUTES:** Expression applying to those whose employment relationship is governed by special regulations or statutes which do not permit the individual negotiation of terms and conditions and restrict the potential for collective bargaining. It is mainly used to refer to health and ancillary personnel who work in institutions and centres within the state health system, under the protection of the relevant Personnel Statutes (doctors, health technicians, ancillary workers, etc.). Recent Spanish legislation is beginning to assimilate such personnel with **public servants**, though they are still in a somewhat anomalous situation, coming somewhere between public servants and workers governed by ordinary labour law.

457. **PERSONAL FUERA DE CONVENIO — PERSONNEL EXCLUDED FROM A COLLECTIVE AGREEMENT:** Workers who by virtue of the particular nature and location of their work are excluded from the scope of application of the relevant collective agreement. Their terms and conditions are usually regulated by individual negotiation. **Senior management** personnel have traditionally been excluded; more recently it has also been common practice to exclude employees on work-experience and job-training contracts and some employees on temporary contracts, although in this last case the courts have judged such exclusion to be discriminatory.

458. **PIQUETE — PICKET:** Group of workers physically present outside a place of work during a **strike** to hand out information about the strike, persuade other workers to join the strike, and call for financial support and solidarity. Picketing is usually aimed at workers affected either directly or indirectly by the dispute, but may also be aimed at the enterprise's customers and the general public. It is common in economic sectors in which workplaces are widely scattered (*e.g.* construction and retail distribution). Picketing is legal under Spanish law, provided it does not involve violence or coercion, which may make it a criminal offence.

459. **PLAN DE FORMACION E INSERCION PROFESIONAL (PLAN FIP) — EMPLOYMENT TRAINING AND INTEGRATION PLAN (PLAN FIP):** Annual planning of Government activities and programmes for **occupational training**. The Plan was first introduced as a result of legislation on **employment policy** and of the undertakings made by the Government in the **Economic and Social Agreement of 1984**. It usually includes programmes for vocational training and integration into the labour market; educational refresher courses and sandwich courses; occupational training in rural areas and sectors undergoing restructuring; and rehabilitation training for particular groups of workers who have difficulty in finding employment (*e.g.* socially marginalized groups, ethnic minorities, the disabled, returning emigrants) or re-training needs (the self-employed, members of co-operatives). The Plan is administered by **INEM**, in collaboration with other public authorities, private institutions and trade union and employers' organizations.

460. **PLAN DE FUTURO — ENTERPRISE PLAN:** Programme or scheme drawn up by an enterprise for the pursuance and development of its activities, normally with a view to overcoming economic difficulties. An enterprise plan is usually part of a reorganization process or **industrial restructuring** and is generally drawn up in collaboration with the enterprise's workforce, since it often requires the employees' agreement to pay restraint and staffing adjustments.

461. **PLAN FIP:** See **Employment Training and Integration Plan** (Plan de Formación e Inserción Profesional).

462. **PLANES DE PENSIONES — PENSION SCHEMES:** Schemes whose purpose is to arrange for the future provision of annuities or lump-sum payments for retirement, invalidity, survivors, widows and orphans. Pension schemes are set up voluntarily, are deemed by Spanish law to be of a private nature and may be on an individual or collective basis. They may be set up and administered by corporations, companies, enterprises, associations, trade unions and bodies or groups of any kind and may take various forms. If they are set up by enterprises for their employees, they form part of the ''sistema de empleo'' (employment system) and the workers covered by them participate fully in their management. Pension schemes have long existed in Spain, have recently been regulated by law and have been accorded significant tax relief. They are likely to be an important ingredient of collective bargaining over the next few years. See **pension funds, social welfare**.

141

463. PLANIFICACION DE RECURSOS HUMANOS — HUMAN RESOURCE PLANNING/HUMAN RESOURCE MANAGEMENT: All the activities directed at rationalizing and systematizing the acquisition, use, development and maintenance of an enterprise's workforce. It presupposes the existence of a broader corporate planning framework within the enterprise and consists of two successive and interdependent stages: manpower planning, whose aim is to ensure that the size and skill levels of the workforce are appropriate to the enterprise's needs at any given moment, and career development, which involves planning the assignment of employees to posts in accordance with their skills and potential for advancement and with likely changes in posts within the enterprise. It is estimated that in Spain most enterprises with more than 200 employees now carry out medium-term human resource planning.

464. PLANTE — PROTEST: Form of **industrial action** consisting in a refusal to work or a disruption of the correct performance of work. It arises suddenly and unexpectedly and its purpose is usually defence or resistance against the employer or the authorities, often as a precursor to more drastic forms of action (**strike**). Although not found in legal terminology, the word is widely used in Spanish trade union jargon.

465. PLANTILLA — STAFFING LEVEL/STAFF COMPLE-MENT/WORKFORCE: Body of permanent employees, both non-manual and manual, of an enterprise (also called "trabajadores de plantilla"); the **personnel** of the production unit. The term is normally used when reference is being made to changes in the number or compositionof an enterprise's personnel (**staffing adjustment**, workforce flexibility).

466. PLATAFORMA REIVINDICATIVA — LIST OF CLAIMS OR BARGAINING PROPOSALS/"PLATFORM": Expression used in Spain to refer to all the demands put forward by workers' representatives during **collective bargaining**. In company or workplace agreements, the list is usually drawn up and/or approved by a **mass meeting** of the workers. It is general practice to include demands that are likely to be relinquished or reduced at a later stage, the basic aim being to include as many as possible of the demands that have been formulated by the various groups of workers represented in the negotiations, to give the other party the impression that concessions are being made, and initially to obscure the issues which are genuinely the most important to the workers' side.

467. PLENO EMPLEO — FULL EMPLOYMENT: Situation in which the economic system provides employment for all those seeking it; the notion is compatible with a certain amount of frictional **unemployment**.

468. PLURALIDAD SINDICAL — TRADE UNION PLURALISM: Synonym of **pluralismo sindical**.

469. PLURALISMO SINDICAL — TRADE UNION PLURALISM: Simultaneous independent existence of several unions covering the same area; also referred to in Spanish as "pluralidad sindical". Trade union pluralism requires recognition of the right to **freedom of association/trade union freedom** as an essential condition and is usually caused by very diverse factors, generally of an ideological or political nature but sometimes religious, regional or linguistic. The situation in Spain is one of trade union pluralism, although with a tendency for most unions to be concentrated in two major central bodies (**UGT, CC.OO.**); a trade union movement structured in this way is sometimes referred to as "bisindicalismo" (a two-union system).

470. PLURIEMPLEO — MULTIPLE JOBHOLDING/MOON-LIGHTING: The practice of holding two or more jobs at the same time. It has always been relatively common in Spain, mainly because of the low level of wages. Owing to the serious unemployment problem, measures have been taken over the past few years to reduce or eliminate the practice, both through incompatibility rules (for **public sector** employees) and through more stringent methods of checking records in the **social security** system, since a second job is often not declared. It can also be ruled out by a sole-employment clause agreed between the parties to the contract of employment, though this tends to be done only in the case of highly skilled jobs.

471. PLUSES SALARIALES — ADDITIONAL PAYMENTS: Pay components added to **basic pay**. In the Spanish context, they are broadly speaking the same as **pay supplements**, but strictly speaking the term usually refers only to certain supplements which are paid for the quality or quantity of work performed or are paid occasionally or for reasons concerning a particular enterprise or area (additional payments negotiated under the existing collective agreement, special allowances for transport and housing, bonus payments for punctuality, shift premiums, etc.). The term is also used to refer to supplements or special payments which are paid in a given enterprise for no formally specified reason.

472. **PODER DE DIRECCION — EMPLOYER'S MANAGERIAL AUTHORITY/MANAGERIAL PREROGATIVE:** The powers attributed to the employer to specify and organize the work to be performed in an enterprise. This authority is rooted in the **contract of employment** and, to a lesser extent, in the recognition of **free enterprise** under the Spanish Constitution. In addition, it consists of a broad range of powers such as the authority to select, promote and discipline employees, and the authority, in exceptional circumstances, to introduce substantial changes in the employee's obligations on a temporary, individual basis, otherwise known as *ius variandi*. In addition to the limitations imposed by state regulations and the contract of employment, the employer's managerial authority is most significantly affected by the provisions of collective agreements. Recent Spanish legislation has extended this authority, giving employers greater flexibility and more scope to act at their own discretion, although also granting **workers' representatives** certain powers to influence its exercise. See **management, changes in conditions, labour mobility, senior management**.

473. **POLITICA DE EMPLEO — EMPLOYMENT POLICY:** Aspect of social and economic policy whose aim is to achieve a balance between labour supply and demand. Employment policy includes a broad range of measures and activities: **job creation, work-sharing**, administration of **placement** and public **employment services**, and **occupational training**.

474. **POLITICA DE RENTAS — INCOMES POLICY:** Aspect of economic and social policy whose aim is to control the level of incomes in line with the country's economic and social objectives. Incomes policy in Spain has over the past few decades centred on restraining growth in **wage/pay** to control inflation. The past few years have also seen the increasing participation of representatives of interested groups (essentially the trade unions and employers' associations) in determining incomes policy (**social concertation**).

475. **POLIVALENCIA — MULTI-SKILLING/POLYVALENCE:** Ability to perform a range of different tasks, thus permitting greater **labour flexibility**. In Spain, collective agreements usually include provisions encouraging multi-skilling.

476. **PRACTICAS DE FORMACION — WORK EXPERIENCE:** Arrangement whereby trainees or students are given short-term placements in enterprises or workplaces. It is part of a training formula in which studies and work are co-ordinated and

alternated. The **Employment Training and Integration Plan** promotes work experience for **vocational education** students.

477. **PREACUERDO — DRAFT AGREEMENT:** Preliminary agreement drafted with a view to future negotiations. It is a common feature in Spain in the processes of **social concertation** or **collective bargaining**, and its content is usually confined to procedural matters and the basic issues for the coming negotiations. The term is also used to refer to an agreement that still requires ratification before it can become applicable. It lacks the binding force of a collective agreement.

478. **PREAVISO — NOTICE:** In the field of industrial relations, prior notification usually in the context of **termination of the contract of employment** or intention to take industrial action (**notice of strike**). Spanish legislation includes numerous provisions requiring notice of termination of the employment contract, the most common requirement being that at least 15 days' notice must be given in the event of withdrawal from contracts which are valid for more than a year; individual or collective agreements may extend this requirement to cover other eventualities. Failure to give notice may result in the offending party having to pay compensation for damages.

479. **PREAVISO DE HUELGA — NOTICE OF STRIKE:** Period of time which must elapse between the communication to the employer and **labour authorities** of a **strike declaration** and the actual start of the strike. Its twofold purpose is to enable the employer and third parties to take measures to prevent the strike, and to allow for further negotiations to take place to settle the dispute. Spanish law requires a minimum of five days' notice, unless the strike concerns enterprises responsible for providing public services, in which case ten days' notice must be given. Strike action taken without giving notice is deemed to be improper practice.

480. **PREFERENCIA DE EMPLEO — PREFERENTIAL EMPLOYMENT:** Preferential treatment as regards placement in or occupation of a job. Spanish legislation prohibits **discrimination** in employment in principle, but permits the adoption of special measures to assist the occupational integration of groups of workers with special employment difficulties (young first-time job-seekers, the disabled, older workers, women with family commitments, etc.). It also grants priority for re-employment to workers who have been on **leave of absence** or who are fit to return to work after a period of **invalidity/disability**. See **employment quota**

481. PREJUBILACION — PRE-RETIREMENT: Situation prior to retirement in which workers who have ceased employment receive benefits equivalent to a retirement pension until they reach the statutory pensionable age. These benefits are usually granted to workers nearing retirement age who cease working as a result of industrial restructuring or who are in a situation of long-term unemployment. It is similar to **early retirement**, but differs in that it does not imply the final cessation of occupational activity.

482. PRESCRIPCION — LIMITATION (OF ACTION): Under Spanish law, loss or lapse of rights and of the possibility of bringing legal actions, as a result of the passing of time. The aim is to ensure the smooth flow of legal proceedings and to eliminate situations of potential disagreement or instability. In the labour field, exercise of rights and of the possibility of bringing legal actions is subject to shorter limitation periods than in the case of ordinary actions and rights. Labour law sometimes uses the term "caducidad" (expiry), which is similar to limitation but governed by more stringent conditions.

483. "PRESTAMISMO": See **provision of labour**.

484. PREVISION SOCIAL — SOCIAL WELFARE: This term has traditionally been used to refer to the public systems which were set up in continental Europe in the late nineteenth and early twentieth centuries to provide cover against social risks; these systems took over from earlier welfare schemes and charitable organizations and used insurance techniques. In this sense, social welfare is a generic name for the various types of **social insurance** and the forerunner of present **social security** systems. Nowadays, in Spain it includes all the independent and voluntary mechanisms, bodies and systems which supplement the protection provided by the public **social security** system: **mutual insurance societies**, social welfare bodies, industrial foundations, friendly societies, **pension schemes** and **pension funds**, and **discretionary social benefits**. It also goes under the general name of "seguridad social complementaria" (supplementary social security). See **social assistance, social services**.

485. PRIMAS — INCENTIVE BONUS PAYMENTS: Element of pay intended to encourage employees to increase output or **productivity**. Also known as **pay incentives**. They constitute one of the elements of the variable component of pay.

486. **PROCESO DE LA NEGOCIACION COLECTIVA — COLLECTIVE BARGAINING PROCESS:** The exchange of offers and counter-offers (usually conducted by a **bargaining committee**) between the workers' side and the employers' side, to reach a collective agreement. Under Spanish law, the collective bargaining process must observe the **duty to bargain** in **good faith**.

487. **PROCESO ESPECIAL DE CONFLICTOS COLECTIVOS — SPECIAL LEGAL PROCEDURE FOR INDUSTRIAL DISPUTES:** Special summary court proceedings to resolve **labour disputes/industrial disputes/trade disputes** concerning the interpretation or application of a provision. They must be preceded by an attempt at **conciliation** and/or mediation by the labour authorities. These special legal proceedings may be initiated by trade unions and workforce representatives and by employers or employers' representatives. They are particularly important for settling disputes over the application or interpretation of collective agreements and have given rise to a considerable body of precedents on collective labour law in Spain. See **legal procedure for labour cases**.

488. **PROCESO LABORAL — LEGAL PROCEDURE FOR LABOUR CASES:** Judicial channel for resolving labour grievances or disputes. The distinguishing features of the legal procedure for labour cases, which first emerged as a special form of civil procedure, are that it grants greater powers to the judge and places more emphasis on the principles that it should be free of charge and that the judge can deliver a decision orally, either immediately after the hearing or within a very short period; the purpose is to facilitate workers' access to the judicial system and to provide a rapid solution to labour problems. In Spain, the first regulations on the legal procedure for labour cases were introduced in the early twentieth century with the legislation on industrial tribunals; the current regulations are contained in the **Labour Procedure Act**. Some disputes over labour issues are settled through proceedings under administrative law, for appeals against acts of the labour administration authorities, appeals against regulations on minimum services in the event of a strike, appeals against administrative sanctions, etc. See **limitation (of action)**.

489. **PRODUCTIVIDAD — PRODUCTIVITY:** Productivity at national level is usually measured as the ratio between GDP and the employed population, and at company or firm level as the ratio between output and the number of employees or number

of man-hours used. The level of productivity has been a very topical issue over the past few years because of the effects of the economic crisis and the transformation of the production system. In Spain, where this has coincided with an opening-up to more competitive markets, concern about productivity has been a feature of tripartite and general multi-industry agreements, which have introduced various provisions and undertakings aimed at increasing it. There has been a marked improvement in national productivity in Spain in recent years, though this is partly the result of the elimination of jobs and rising unemployment.

490. **PROFESION LIBERAL — PROFESSION:** Occupation, skill or trade exercised freely and independently without subjection to the orders or instructions of another person (and so sometimes called a "liberal profession"). See **professional body**.

491. **PROFESIONALIDAD — PROFESSIONAL COMPETENCE AND STATUS:** The sum total of a worker's occupational experience and ability; performance of a job or occupation with reliability and responsibility. Professional competence and status may be vouched for in several ways. Particular importance used to be attached to the testimony of the employer, documented in the "certificado de trabajo" (written testimonial or reference); to prevent discrimination, certain laws expressly stipulated that this testimonial should not include any comments on the worker's political or union views or activities. Nowadays, greater importance is attached to the written recommendations issued by employment services or by agencies specializing in the selection and appraisal of job applicants. Spanish law empowers **INEM** to certify workers' qualifications, authorizes **personnel selection agencies** to participate in the processes preceding **placement** and requires the employer to certify the training acquired by the worker only in the case of a **job-training contract**. See **occupational skills**.

492. **PROMOCION PROFESIONAL — CAREER PROGRESSION:** Advancement into a job with greater responsibility and better terms and conditions, particularly pay; **promotion** to a higher occupational category or level. Advancement within an enterprise is dependent on the **career path** opportunities offered by its internal structure and by the amount of external **recruitment**. Internal promotion of employees on the basis of seniority has always been the predominant practice in Spanish enterprises, but greater importance is now being attached to external recruitment and to the criteria of merit and ability (assessed through competitive selection or tests).

493. **PROPINAS — TIPS/GRATUITIES:** Sums of money which customers give to workers as a sign of their appreciation of the services performed. They do not form part of specified pay, but are usually included in calculations to assess the overall earnings associated with a job. In some jobs it is customary for tips to be pooled and then shared out proportionally between all the workers ("tronco de propinas").

494. **PROTECCION A LA FAMILIA — FAMILY BENEFITS:** Aspect of social policy whose aim is to cover part of the costs incurred by a family unit. In Spain, family benefits form part of the protection provided by the **social security** system. Collective agreements usually make provision for supplementing benefits and providing various other means of assistance (*e.g.* grants and loans).

495. **PROTECCIONISMO LABORAL — PROTECTION OF WORKERS' RIGHTS:** Doctrine which propounds the protection of workers' interests; all the measures adopted with this aim in view. This protectionism, which is also sometimes called "garantismo legislativo" (legislative guaranteeism), from the Italian, has largely inspired the drafting and application of labour law and is manifested in principles such as minimum guarantees and presumptions favouring workers' interests. It has guided the actions of governments under systems which favour the working class, but it has also guided the actions of authoritarian regimes, which have used it to try to counterbalance possible limitations on workers' collective rights and to gain the support of the Church. The past few years have seen some reaction against protection of workers' rights, which tends to be seen as a factor that limits the flexibility of industrial relations. In Spain, this recent current of opinion (which has coincided with the recognition of **freedom of association/trade union freedom** and the recasting of **employment policy**) has been one of the factors that have prompted the elimination of some of the guarantees which earlier legislation laid down in favour of the individual employee.

496. **PUESTO DE TRABAJO — POST/EMPLOYMENT POSITION/JOB:** Position or physical space in which the tasks assigned to an employee are performed; in a broader sense, all the activities or tasks involved in the work assigned to an employee. It is the main indicator of the employee's obligations and the **employer's managerial authority/managerial prerogative**. See **internal job transfer, labour mobility**.

497. PYME: Abbreviation used in Spanish to refer to small and medium-sized enterprises (SMEs) and the special organizations formed to defend their interests. See **Spanish Confederation of Small and Medium-sized Enterprises (CEPYME), small and medium-sized enterprises**.

R

498. READMISION — REINSTATEMENT: Employee's return to employment in the enterprise after a break in the contract of employment. Reinstatement is particularly controversial in the event of unfair or unjustified **dismissal**, where legal systems have either imposed compulsory or mandatory reinstatement (which is better for **job security**) or allowed the option of suitable compensation as an alternative. Spanish legislation permits in principle the option of compensation as an alternative to reinstatement, but in certain cases it obliges the employer to reinstate the worker because fundamental rights or rights with collective implications are at stake (for example, dismissal of **workers' representatives**). See **compensation for dismissal/severance pay**.

499. RECIBO DE SALARIOS — PAY STATEMENT: Document which indicates and certifies the settlement and **payment of wages**, as well as the period to which that payment relates; also called, incorrectly, "nómina de salarios" (pay list) or "hoja de salarios" (pay slip). A pay statement is required under Spanish law to itemize the various pay components, any pay deductions or deductions at source, and the amount actually received by the employee; itemized pay statements must be issued at least every month. They serve as documentary evidence in the event of a legal dispute or disagreement. See **"finiquito"**.

500. RECLUTAMIENTO DE PERSONAL — RECRUITMENT: All activities intended to attract candidates who are potentially qualified to fill vacancies in an enterprise. Internal recruitment (i.e. from among existing members of the workforce), which offers employees opportunities for **career progression** and self-development, has traditionally been the preferred method in Spanish enterprises. The past few years, however, have seen a growing trend towards the use of external recruitment, often through job advertisements in the press. Increasing use is also being made of employment offices, particularly for the recruitment of manual workers in certain sectors (construction, the car industry and the chemicals industry), and of **personnel selection agencies**.

501. RECONOCIMIENTO MEDICO — MEDICAL EXAMINA-TION: Spanish legislation requires enterprises to ensure that employees in jobs which imply a major health hazard undergo a medical examination before they are appointed to such jobs and at regular intervals thereafter. Medical examinations are also provided under the **social security** system and must be carried out before a worker can be declared to be suffering from **temporary incapacity for work** or **invalidity/disability**. See **verification of illness, occupational illness/industrial disease, health and safety**.

502. **RECONVERSION INDUSTRIAL — INDUSTRIAL RESTRUCTURING:** Planned process of reducing or adapting the production capacity of the industrial sector of the economy or of any of its components. Between the late 1970s and mid-1980s, somewhat later than in other countries, Spain's **structure of production** underwent extensive adaptation to the new market situation (rise in energy prices, opening-up to international competition, etc.); this had a significant impact on the level of employment (some 70,000 jobs were eliminated). The effects were felt particularly strongly in certain sectors (shipbuilding, iron and steel, special steels and white goods) and in certain geographical areas (the Basque Country and Galicia). To counter them, a range of special measures were adopted, called "medidas laborales de la reconversión industrial". These consist, on the one hand, of reinforcing the traditional forms of protection for the workers affected (allowances equivalent to retirement pensions, improved unemployment benefits and compensation for termination of the employment contract); and, on the other, of opening up new ways to assist the re-training and redeployment of the surplus manpower ("Fondos de Promoción de Empleo": Employment Promotion Funds) and to encourage investment and **job creation** in the areas most seriously affected ("Zonas de Urgente Reindustrialización": Priority Redevelopment Areas and "Zonas de Promoción Económica": Economic Development Areas). The trade unions and employers' associations have co-operated both in drawing up and in implementing the conversion plans for the various sectors concerned.

503. **RECORTE DE TIEMPOS — TIME-CUTTING:** Practice whereby the employer reduces the time considered standard for performing a certain set of tasks or for producing a certain quantity of product. It intensifies the **pace of work**.

504. **REDUCCION DE JORNADA — REDUCTION OF WORKING HOURS:** Reduction of the normal working time. The progressive reduction of **working hours** has been a long-standing goal on the part of employees, generally to increase leisure time but more recently also to assist **work-sharing**. In many instances enterprises resort to the reduction of working hours on a temporary basis because of economic difficulties, *force majeure* or decreased output, sometimes as an alternative to

collective dismissal/redundancy; this type of reduction of working hours is known as "jornada reducida" (short-time working), and under Spanish law it is subject to a formal procedure requiring the consent of the workers' representatives or permission from the **labour authorities**. Spanish law also provides for temporarily reduced working hours in particular circumstances (nursing an infant or caring for a child).

505. **REFERENDUM — BALLOT:** Procedure whereby employees vote secretly (using ballot-papers) to ratify or reject prior decisions affecting their interests; it generally takes place in the enterprise or workplace and is usually held directly after a **mass meeting** or by calling an election. Spanish legislation makes it obligatory only for the removal from office of workforce representatives, but it has become widespread practice in the Spanish industrial relations system, particularly for the ratification of collective agreements and for the approval of proposed industrial action.

506. **REGIMENES DE SEGURIDAD SOCIAL — SOCIAL SECURITY SCHEMES:** The various constituent sectors of the Spanish **social security** system, which correspond to the work or occupation of each of the groups concerned. The conditions governing membership, contributions and benefits vary from scheme to scheme. The Spanish system is essentially divided into the general scheme (which covers most employees in industry and the service sector) and special schemes (for certain groups of employees and some self-employed people).

507. **REGISTROS PERSONALES — PERSONAL SEARCHES (SECURITY CHECKS):** Term used to refer to action the employer is empowered to take to check on an employee's person or personal effects. Spanish law permits personal searches if they are necessary to protect the property of the enterprise or of other employees. Where possible, such searches must be conducted in the presence of a workers' representative or another employee.

508. **REGLAMENTO DE REGIMEN INTERIOR — COMPANY RULES:** Set of rules and instructions issued by the employer as regards work organization and working conditions in the enterprise. They were sometimes also called "reglamento de empresa" (works rules). Once a traditional feature of Spanish labour legislation, they are now tending to disappear since the Workers' Statute of 1980 abolished the regulations governing the procedure for their official approval. Employers are, however, still able to issue general orders and instructions on the basis of the **employer's managerial authority/managerial prerogative**.

509. **REGULACION DE EMPLEO — ADJUSTMENT OF EMPLOYMENT LEVELS:** Process whereby the workforce is adjusted to the changed circumstances of an enterprise or of the economic context in which it operates. The adjustment is generally a consequence of restructuring of the sector, reorganization of the enterprise, introduction of new technologies or replacement of labour by plant and equipment. The Spanish term is also used to refer to the procedures required by law for **collective dismissal/redundancy, suspension of the contract of employment** and **reduction of working hours** on economic grounds or due to *force majeure* ("expediente de regulación de empleo", *i.e.* **redundancy procedure**).

510. **RELACION DE TRABAJO — EMPLOYMENT RELATIONSHIP:** The relationship arising from the **contract of employment**, which binds the employee and the employer; also called "relación laboral". Spanish law distinguishes between the normal or ordinary employment relationship and **special employment relationships**, which apply in the case of the performance of work differing substantially from the norm. Collective agreements usually play the most important role in governing the employment relationship, since the law merely lays down minimum conditions and the regulatory function of the contract of employment is important only on very concrete matters (**probationary periods, duty of non-competition, minimum-stay clauses**) or when an individual employee has strong bargaining power.

511. **RELACIONES ESPECIALES DE TRABAJO — SPECIAL EMPLOYMENT RELATIONSHIPS:** Name given in Spanish legislation to employment relationships which are governed by legal provisions substantially different from those governing the normal or ordinary **employment relationship**, either because of the nature of the work involved or because of the place where it is performed. In many cases they have been the channel used to enable labour legislation to cover groups of employees or types of work previously excluded (**senior management, sales representatives/commercial representatives, domestic work, professional sportsmen and sportswomen**).

512. **RELACIONES HUMANAS — HUMAN RELATIONS:** Form or method of **personnel management** that gives consideration to aspects or factors which motivate the worker other than those of a strictly financial or mercenary nature. The school of human relations which emerged in the United States in the 1930s was a vast movement of social research and

experimentation constituting a reaction against the principles and techniques of Taylorism and scientific management. In Spain, given the late adoption of Taylorism, it is impossible to identify clearly the point at which employer practices began to follow the assumptions and principles of human relations.

513. **RELACIONES LABORALES — INDUSTRIAL RELATIONS/LABOUR RELATIONS:** Term used to refer both to the set of collective relations between employers and their associations, employees and their representative bodies and the state, and to the academic discipline concerned with studying and interpreting these relations. The Spanish industrial relations system has five fundamental features: a) the predominance of the legal context (labour legislation), which has a powerful ability to shape and control the human components of the system and their inter-relations (selection of social actors on the basis of representativeness, preference for generally applicable collective agreements, state intervention in the administration of agreements, etc.); b) the stratification of the system, largely caused by labour law itself, with some trade unions and employers' associations possessing "most representative" status and exerting strong influence; c) the central role of collective bargaining as the focal institution regulating individual and collective labour relations; d) forms of industrial action, particularly strikes, which are essentially bound up with collective bargaining; and e) external judicial means of settling labour disputes, with little use of autonomous channels such as conciliation, mediation and arbitration.

514. **RENDIMIENTO — PERFORMANCE:** Productive effort made by a worker, measured in relation to a time/output ratio which is considered as "standard" work effort based on standard calculations. See **piecework, payment by results, go-slow**.

515. **RENTA DE TRABAJO — EARNED INCOME:** Covers both **wage/pay** and the earnings of the self-employed. See **deductions from pay/deductions at source**.

516. **RENUNCIA DE DERECHOS — WAIVER OF RIGHTS:** Voluntary action to relinquish or forgo previously recognized rights. In contrast to civil law, Spanish labour legislation has from the outset prohibited or declared null and void any waiver of rights by employees, to prevent their weak contractual position from leading them to provide services in conditions which do not meet the minimum requirements laid down by law (principle of the inalienability of rights). Spanish law establishes the inviolability

of rights granted to employees whether arising out of legal provisions, collective agreements or court rulings, though it does not prohibit **conciliation** or mutual settlement as regards contentious or uncertain rights in exchange for appropriate compensation. Experience shows that waiver of rights is particularly likely to occur at the beginning or end of the **employment relationship**, when terms and conditions of employment are being agreed or when outstanding payments are being settled (**"finiquito"**).

517. **REPARTO DE TRABAJO — WORK-SHARING:** **Employment policy** schemes and measures whose aim is to redistribute jobs among the working population. In Spain, as in several other countries, they include reduction of **working time** (reducing working hours, banning overtime, increasing the length of annual holidays); reduction of the length of working life (raising the minimum working age or encouraging early retirement); and encouragement of **job-sharing** or the use of **part-time workers**. In the recent circumstances of low economic growth, work-sharing has acquired new significance as an alternative or complement to the creation of new jobs. It does, however, involve considerable difficulties as regards work organization, high wage costs, etc., and its usefulness as a way of reducing unemployment has been relatively limited up to now. Some of the regulations introduced in Spain over the past few years encourage work-sharing, either as a principal objective or as an additional one; these include reducing weekly working hours to 40 hours, increasing annual holidays to 30 days, making **overtime** more expensive for employers, authorizing **hand-over contracts** and **partial retirement**, etc.

518. **REPRESENTANTES DE COMERCIO — SALES REPRESENTATIVES/COMMERCIAL REPRESENTA-TIVES:** Persons who are paid to handle sales activities on behalf of an enterprise. Spanish law classes their provision of services as a **special employment relationship**, unless the work is performed on the enterprise's premises and in accordance with its usual working hours. Commercial law uses the term "auxiliares del comerciante" (sales staff) to refer to people who help an enterprise in distributing or selling to the public, acting in its name and on its behalf (agent) or undertaking the activities of retail selling (shop assistant of salesperson).

519. **REPRESENTANTES DE LOS TRABAJADORES — WORKERS' REPRESENTATIVES:** People elected to defend and promote employees' interests, particularly in dealings with

the employer. In the Spanish context, and in Spanish legislation, the term refers to a dual channel of representation: workforce representatives, who are elected by all the employees (irrespective of union membership) in an enterprise or workplace to represent their interests as a group (**workers' committees** and **workers' delegates** in the private sector, **staff councils** and **workers' delegates** in the public service); and trade union representatives, who are elected by and from among the members of a particular trade union within the enterprise or workplace concerned (**workplace branch** and **trade union delegates**). See **facilities for workers' representatives, guarantees for workers' representatives, workers' participation**.

520. **REPRESENTATIVIDAD SINDICAL — REPRESENTA-TIVENESS:** A method used by the law for assessing the practical power and influence of particular **trade unions** at the different levels at which they operate (*e.g.* regional or national), in order to identify which unions are appropriate social partners. The method was introduced in Spain after the recognition of **freedom of association/trade union freedom**, with a view to identifying the unions to be granted the right to negotiate **generally applicable collective agreements** and to have **representation on public bodies**. It was later extended to other trade union activities, such as calling **union elections**, representation within the enterprise, receiving funds distributed from the assets accumulated by the one-time Vertical Union (**union assets**), etc. In Spain, the representativeness of a trade union is assessed on the basis of its electoral strength or the results it achieves in union elections, which are used as a basis for distinguishing between **most representative trade unions** and other trade unions with lesser degrees of representativeness. The use of this method can lead to problems of consistency with trade union freedom, since it gives rise to unequal treatment of the various trade unions; in general terms, however, and provided that fair, objective criteria are used, it is considered compatible with this right.

521. **REQUISA DE TRABAJADORES — EMERGENCY CONSCRIPTION OF WORKERS:** The Government's power to take control of the workforce in enterprises to prevent any paralysing of essential public services, particularly in very serious situations; in a broader sense, the authorities' power to demand the compulsory provision of services in the event of grave risk, disaster or catastrophe. In other countries, this power is normally used in the event of **strikes**. Current Spanish legislation allows for such requisition of workers in a state of emergency, state of siege or exceptional circumstances. See **essential public services**.

157

522. **RESERVA DE EMPLEO — EMPLOYMENT QUOTA:** **Employment policy** measure aimed at facilitating the placement of certain groups of workers by allocating a minimum percentage of jobs to them. It is an exception to the principle of equality in access to employment which is justified by the weak position of these groups on the labour market. It is sometimes called "empleo selectivo" (selective employment). Spanish law provides for employment quotas for disabled workers (two per cent. of posts in enterprises with more than 50 employees), workers in rural areas (75 per cent. or 50 per cent. in work covered by the Rural Employment Plan) and unemployed people in general (75 per cent. or 50 per cent. in employment schemes funded by **INEM**). See **preferential employment, reservation of post.**

523. **RESERVA DE PUESTO DE TRABAJO — RESERVATION OF POST:** Arrangement whereby employees' jobs are reserved for them when they temporarily cease work. Spanish law grants this right to return to those employees who have to leave work temporarily as a result of incapacity for work, maternity, military service and unavoidable leave of absence, and in general to all employees who temporarily cease working because of **suspension of the contract of employment.** See **preferential employment, employment quota.**

524. **RETENCIONES DEL SALARIO — DEDUCTIONS FROM PAY/DEDUCTIONS AT SOURCE:** Sums which are deducted from gross pay before it is paid to the employee; the amount remaining after these deductions have been made constitutes the employee's net pay, known colloquially as "salario líquido" or "salario en mano" (take home pay). The deductions are essentially for **social security** contributions and income tax but may also be made for other considerations such as **trade union dues** or contributions to **social welfare** schemes. Spanish law declares null and void any negotiated agreement whereby the employer undertakes to pay an employee's tax and social security charges.

525. **RETIRO — PENSIONING-OFF/RETIREMENT:** Definitive cessation of a particular form of employment or occupational activity. In Spain it is to be distinguished from "jubilación" (**retirement**) since workers who are pensioned off are free to take up another occupation. It usually occurs for reasons of age, which is why the expression is often used to refer to welfare or insurance systems providing for this situation ("seguro de retiro" (pensioning-off insurance) or "pensiones de retiro" (service pensions)). It was used in early Spanish social welfare regulations

("Régimen de Retiro Obrero" (Workers' Pensioning-Off Scheme)) but has since been replaced by the terms "vejez" (old age) or "jubilación", except in the case of certain groups covered by the Clases Pasivas (Pensioners List) system (military personnel and the like).

526. RETORNO DE EMIGRANTES — RETURN MIGRATION: The return of migrant workers to their country of origin. The phenomenon has been widespread as a result of the economic crisis which began in the 1970s and led to a general increase in unemployment in the host countries. This return migration has markedly worsened labour market conditions in the countries to which emigrants have returned, obliging the authorities to devise special measures to provide assistance and protection. In Spain, where it has posed a particularly acute problem, the past few years have seen measures on vocational training, unemployment cover and health care specifically aimed at returning emigrants. See **emigration and internal migration, Employment Training and Integration Plan**.

527. REVISION DEL CONVENIO COLECTIVO — REVISION OF COLLECTIVE AGREEMENT: Partial alteration or renegotiation of a collective agreement, the basic aspects of which remain in force. The process usually concentrates on those aspects of the agreement which are most dependent on the economic environment or are less stable, particularly pay (**pay adjustment**). There is a distinction between the revision of an agreement and its administration, which concerns the application, management or monitoring of the agreed provisions.

528. REVISION SALARIAL — PAY ADJUSTMENT: Setting of new pay levels. In Spain, in the context of **collective bargaining** the revision of **wage/pay** is usually provided for under **pay adjustment** clauses in which pay increases are based on economic indices (retail-price index, inflation, etc.); discrepancy clauses may also be included to provide for pay increases if inflation overtakes the increase initially agreed. In the case of employees covered by the **national minimum wage**, the law provides for annual and six-monthly pay adjustments.

529. RITMO DE TRABAJO — PACE OF WORK: Speed or rhythm of work movements necessary to achieve the desired result. It may be determined by a very wide range of factors, such as the employer's instructions, the design of mechanical components, the method of production or the type of payment system. See **payment by results, production-line work**.

530. ROBOTIZACION — ROBOTIZATION: Introduction into the production process of devices or machines which perform automatically operations previously carried out by workers, as a more advanced stage of the processes of mechanization and automation. It usually implies a reduction in staffing levels.

531. ROMPEHUELGAS — STRIKEBREAKER: See **scab/blackleg.**

532. ROTACION DE PLANTILLA — LABOUR TURNOVER: Rate at which employees join and leave an enterprise expressed as a percentage of its average **staffing level/staff complement/workforce** over a given period. Low labour turnover is a feature of Spanish enterprises: in 1983, nearly a quarter of the employees of enterprises with a workforce of more than 250 had been working for the same enterprise for more than 19 years. Turnover has increased over the past few years as a result, in particular, of new forms of **temporary contracts/fixed-term contracts** and the spread of **early retirement** and **voluntary redundancy.**

533. ROTACION DE TAREAS — JOB ROTATION: Planned, periodic transfer of employees between different jobs, usually of the same level and involving similar tasks. In the Spanish context, job rotation or the alternating of tasks is usually most successful within **semi-autonomous work groups.**

S

534. **SABOTAJE — SABOTAGE:** The destruction or damaging of the enterprise's property (products, plant and equipment, etc.) to halt or restrict the production process. It is a form of industrial action, obviously illegal, sometimes used during **labour disputes/industrial disputes/trade disputes**.

535. **SALARIO — WAGE/PAY:** Compensation, recompense or return for work; also called "sueldo" (monthly salary) or "jornal" (day's wage). In a broad sense, it may be used to refer to the cost of the labour factor or the income received by workers, including **indirect pay**. In the narrower sense which is customarily used in Spanish law, however, the term refers solely to all the financial benefits that directly remunerate or compensate employees for their work; it is thus distinguished from the broader concept of **earned income**, which also includes the financial compensation for work performed in the context of **self-employment**, as well as other components or monies received unrelated to pay (**compensation for dismissal/severance pay, subsistence and travel allowance, expenses**). Pay may be calculated on the basis of time (time rate) or of results (**payment by results**); it may be paid in money or as **payment in kind**; and it usually consists of **basic pay** and **pay supplements**. Since it is the employee's main source of income, the law usually establishes certain guarantees to ensure that pay is sufficient to meet needs (**national minimum wage**) and that it is actually received by the employee (**payment of wages**). The trend in pay as a proportion of Spain's GDP has been variable: after rising from 53.2 per cent. in 1964 to a maximum of 64.5 per cent. in the period 1976-1977, the level gradually fell, with the period 1982-1986 seeing a fall (partly because of the policy of **pay restraint**) from 50.4 per cent. to 45.9 per cent., with a concomitant increase in the proportions represented by taxes and business profits. See **wage/pay structure, Wages Guarantee Fund**.

536. **SALARIO A LA PARTE — SHARE-OUT PAY:** Form of **payment in kind** in which the worker receives an agreed proportion of the physical product once costs have been deducted, for example in fishing and agriculture. It is usually accompanied by a fixed minimum wage. See **payment by results**.

537. **SALARIO A RENDIMIENTO — PAYMENT BY RESULTS (PBR):** Form of remuneration in which an element of pay is related to output and hence intended to reward effort. There are various systems of payment by results which, depending on the relationship between pay and **performance**, can be classified as

regressive, progressive or strictly proportional. Growing mechanization and group-based working are leading in Spain to the disappearance of individual forms of payment by results, which are being replaced by more up-to-date systems such as collective performance bonuses, similar to production bonuses. See **piecework, pay incentives, incentive bonus payments, job-and-finish**.

538. **SALARIO BASE — BASIC PAY:** That part of the employee's remuneration which relates solely to normal working time. It is usually the fixed component of pay and is used as the basis for calculating **pay supplements**. The term must not be confused in Spanish with the term "salario minimo" (**national minimum wage**).

539. **SALARIO DIFERENCIAL — PAY DIFFERENTIAL:** Difference between the pay of the various categories or classes of employees within a given enterprise or sphere; it expresses the **wage/pay structure** or pay hierarchy in that sphere.

540. **SALARIO DIFERIDO — DEFERRED PAY:** Financial compensation or benefits which are granted to employees but are not immediately available to them, normally from funds, institutions or services set up within the enterprise; these resources are accumulated from withdrawals from pay increases or from the enterprise's profits. At macro-economic level, contributory social security pensions are also classed as deferred pay.

541. **SALARIO EN ESPECIE — PAYMENT IN KIND:** Payment which takes the form of goods or services rather than money. It may take many different forms but usually includes food and accommodation. It is common in certain types of work (**domestic work**) and sectors (agriculture). Spanish legislation permits payment in kind but, to prevent fraud, it stipulates that it may represent not more than 30 per cent. of total pay (45 per cent. in the case of domestic work).

542. **SALARIO EN MANO — TAKE HOME PAY:** See **deductions from pay/deductions at source**.

543. **SALARIO GLOBAL — AGGREGATE PAY:** The adding or lumping together of the different components of pay to make its calculation simpler and easier to understand. Collective agreements and contracts of employment often contain an aggregate pay clause, which is deemed valid under Spanish case law provided the amount of the aggregate pay agreed is not less than the sum of its components.

544. SALARIO HORA — HOURLY PAY: Pay which is set at an hourly rate. It is typical of work contracted by the day or by the hour (agriculture, domestic work, etc.).

545. SALARIO INDIRECTO — INDIRECT PAY: Benefits, services or compensation of financial value, as distinct from the pay the employee receives from the enterprise (housing, shops run by the enterprise, assistance with children's school fees, medical treatment, etc.). It is in many cases similar to **payment in kind**. See **fringe benefits**.

546. SALARIO LIQUIDO — NET PAY: See **deductions from pay/deductions at source**.

547. SALARIO MINIMO INTERPROFESIONAL (SMI) — NATIONAL MINIMUM WAGE: The minimum wage set for all occupations, trades and economic sectors. Its main purpose is to ensure that pay is sufficient to meet needs. The national minimum wage was first set in Spain in 1963 and has since been adjusted at regular intervals, usually each year, although the law provides for half-yearly adjustment. It is set at a daily or monthly rate, always based on normal **working hours**, and distinguishes between minors and adults. It is set and adjusted in accordance with various economic indices (**productivity**, retail-price index, etc.), and is fully protected from seizure on behalf of creditors. Its amount (50,010 pesetas per month in 1990) is modest and is usually far below national average earnings, and it is therefore calculated that only some 400,000 workers are directly affected by the level of the minimum wage. However, its indirect repercussions are important since it serves as a point of reference for collective pay negotiations and for the setting of social security benefits and pensions.

548. SALARIO POR TAREA — JOB-AND-FINISH: System whereby pay is established on the basis of a set task to be completed within a set time; it may be referred to as mixed pay, since it relates both to **performance** and to **working time**. The time element distinguishes this system from **payment by results** and serves as an incentive for employees, since they are free to leave work once they have completed the set task.

549. SALARIO SOCIAL — SOCIAL WAGE: Name given in Spain to certain **social assistance** benefits granted by the authorities to remedy extreme situations of need. They are mainly paid to people who have retired but are not eligible to receive retirement pensions. At present this provision has been established in certain Autonomous Communities.

550. **SALARIOS DE TRAMITACION — BACK PAY AWARDED AFTER DISMISSAL APPEAL HEARINGS:** Amounts which, under Spanish law, are to be paid to employees in cases of **unfair dismissal** or **unjustified dismissal**, covering the duration of the legal proceedings or appeal. The state takes responsibility for part of these payments when they exceed a certain limit.

551. **SECCION SINDICAL DE EMPRESA — WORKPLACE BRANCH:** Group formed by the employees in an enterprise or workplace who are members of the same **trade union**; it is a channel of communication between the union and its members, and a means of representing these members and defending their interests in dealings with the employer. Under the **Trade Union Freedom Act (LOLS)** of 1985, any legally constituted trade union has the right to set up such branches and every branch has the right to hold meetings and distribute union information, provided it does not disrupt the normal functioning of the enterprise. In addition, branches of the most representative trade unions or of trade unions represented on the workforce representative body of the enterprise or workplace are entitled to have the use of a notice-board and of a suitable room in which to carry on their activities, and have the right to negotiate collective agreements; in certain circumstances they also have the right to appoint **trade union delegates**.

552. **SECRETO PROFESIONAL — PROFESSIONAL SECRECY:** Employees' obligation not to divulge any information relating to their employer's affairs which they may obtain as a result of their contract of employment. Under Spanish law, the obligation continues, though to a lesser extent, after termination of the contract of employment, and its non-observance can give rise to disciplinary sanctions, compensation for damages and, in serious cases, penal sanctions. It is to be distinguished from the **professional confidentiality** imposed by law on **workers' representatives**.

553. **SECTOR PUBLICO — PUBLIC SECTOR:** In the Spanish definition of the public sector, it includes the administrative branches and bodies (public administration) and enterprises controlled and managed directly by the state (*e.g.* RENFE: railways) or indirectly by state holdings (*e.g.* INI: industry). The number of people employed in the public sector in Spain has been

gradually increasing both in absolute terms (approximately 1.8 million in 1987 as against some 1.5 million in 1981) and in relative terms (approximately 23 per cent. of the working population in 1987 as against approximately 20 per cent. in 1981), probably because of the increase in the number of public servants caused by the creation of the Autonomous Communities and because the public sector has suffered less severely from the economic crisis. Public sector personnel can be divided into various groups, depending on the legal system under which they are contracted: **public servants** and similar personnel, who constitute the bulk of the public sector workforce and are covered by administrative law; employees, who constitute the majority of workers in public enterprises and are covered by labour legislation; and **personnel covered by special statutes**, characteristic of certain public services (health care), who are covered by public law statutes. In general terms, **job security** is greater in the public sector; but so too is the degree of public intervention (particularly in pay determination); and there are also tighter restrictions on exercise of the rights to trade union freedom and workers'participation or collective bargaining.

554. **SEGURIDAD E HIGIENE — HEALTH AND SAFETY:** Set of systems, measures and instruments directed at preventing and eliminating risks and factors which render work dangerous or unhealthy. Spanish health and safety legislation includes basic provisions in general laws (**Workers' Statute, General Social Security Act,** General Health Act), specific regulations (**General Ordinance on Health and Safety at Work**), sectoral and occupational regulations, plus the numerous provisions laid down by collective agreements and the regulations issued by the regions or Autonomous Communities. Spain's accession to the EEC also implies implementation of the many Community Directives on health and safety issued in the 1980s. The content of health and safety regulations is very varied: safety at work, industrial hygiene, occupational health and industrial medicine, training activities, etc. The obligations of employers, managerial staff and workers are also very diverse: they cover design and maintenance of work premises, use of machinery and tools, training in new work methods and new technologies and **medical examinations**. Similarly numerous are the research bodies (such as the National Institute of Health and Safety and other regional centres); the mechanisms of supervision and monitoring (some of which involve the participation of workers): **health and safety committee, safety officer**; and means of enforcement (liabilities and penal and administrative sanctions). Studies are in progress on far-reaching changes in the basic regulations to adjust them to modern

production systems and to bring them into line with EEC and ILO regulations. See **accident at work/industrial accident**.

555. **SEGURIDAD SOCIAL — SOCIAL SECURITY:** Public compulsory system of welfare and protection against social risks, particularly those arising from work. The Spanish social security system was established with the Basic Social Security Act of 1963, which systematized and restructured existing welfare mechanisms and laid the foundations of the new system of protection. This regulatory structure was later supplemented by various provisions (essentially the **General Social Security Act (LGSS)** of 1974), and its basic framework was confirmed by Article 41 of the 1978 Constitution, which opted for a public social security scheme for all citizens guaranteeing adequate social welfare benefits in times of need, without restricting the freedom to set up voluntary schemes to supplement it (**discretionary social benefits, mutual insurance societies, pension schemes**). The system covers virtually the entire working population (the number of people covered has varied between 10 and 11 million over the past few years); it provides cover for a wide range of situations and contingencies (accident, illness, **invalidity/disability, retirement**, widowhood, orphanhood, family benefits, **unemployment**) by means of health care and financial benefits, which are usually contributory; it is funded mainly by the payments or contributions made by workers and employers, although state funding has increased over the past few years (and now represents around 20 per cent.); it is administered by public bodies, sometimes in collaboration with private bodies and enterprises (particularly in the case of protection covering **accidents at work/industrial accidents** and provision of health care); and it tends to provide equal protection for all those covered by the system, although there are still differences between private sector employees and **public servants** and, within the first group, between the various **social security schemes**. The protection afforded by the system is supplemented by **social services** and **social assistance** mechanisms, which are also part of public provision. See **employers' mutual insurance societies, social welfare, family benefits, social security for migrant workers**.

556. **SEGURIDAD SOCIAL DE LOS TRABAJADORES MIGRANTES — SOCIAL SECURITY FOR MIGRANT WORKERS:** Body of rules drawn up by the EEC to co-ordinate different national social security regulations in order to facilitate **freedom of movement for workers**. The rules are contained essentially in EEC Regulations Nos. 1408/71 and 574/72, which apply to employees and the self-employed. The rules on social

security for migrant workers do not constitute a separate social security system but merely link the various national systems to ensure that migrant workers receive the same treatment as nationals and to prevent any loss of contributions or benefits as a result of movement from one country to another. Their basic provisions are the suppression of nationality and residence requirements as conditions of eligibility for benefits, the accumulation of qualifying periods credited in different Member States, the transfer from one country to another of benefits due, the *pro rata* payment of benefits by the various countries according to the contributions paid or credited in each one, and the coordination of the various administrative bodies.

557. **SEGUROS SOCIALES — SOCIAL INSURANCE:** Public measures providing protection against social risks which are based on insurance techniques. Historically, they represent the bridge between early forms of social protection (private savings, mutual benefit, charity) and modern **social security** systems. Social insurance schemes are characterized by the use of techniques borrowed from private insurance systems, by the fact that they are public and compulsory, by the fact that they cover concrete, clearly defined risks, and by the fact that they apply to previously defined groups. Social insurance first appeared in Spain in the early twentieth century, with the introduction of schemes for the retirement of manual workers, involuntary unemployment and maternity; it was greatly extended during the Second Republic (whose Constitution provided for a full system of social insurance) and reached its height in the 1940s and 1950s. It disappeared with the introduction of the modern social security system in 1963, though it strongly influenced the initial structuring and later development of that system. See **social welfare**.

558. **SELECCION DE PERSONAL — PERSONNEL SELECTION:** Process of assessing the suitability of candidates for a job by examining their skills, abilities, potential and interests. In Spain this process has been characterized (particularly in the case of the selection of senior management and technical personnel, middle management staff and non-manual workers) by its very formal structure and by the use made of consultancies and **personnel selection agencies**. The most commonly used selection method is the interview, since handwriting analyses are not common practice; and increasing use is being made of business "games" for the selection of managerial personnel. Formal qualifications and educational background are becoming progressively less important in the selection of personnel and are giving way to other means of assessing suitability such as skills

tests, **merit-based selection** and competitive examinations (as used in the public administration), usually devised with the collaboration of the **trade unions** and **workers' representatives**. Temporary employment and **probationary periods** in many cases serve as a trial stage in selection prior to the actual signing of a standard contract of employment.

559. **SERVICIO DOMESTICO — DOMESTIC WORK:** Work done in the home, whereby a person performs domestic chores in exchange for remuneration. Domestic workers sometimes live in, in which case food and accommodation form part of their pay. In Spain, domestic work was for a long time excluded from labour legislation, but since 1985 it has been covered as a **special employment relationship**. It is classed as such mainly because of where the work is performed and because of the special trust that is required between the worker and employer; it is reflected basically in the **placement** procedures, fixing of working hours, and grounds for termination of the contract of employment.

560. **SERVICIOS DE EMPLEO — EMPLOYMENT SERVICES:** Offices, agencies or departments responsible for matching labour supply and demand; also known as "agencias de colocación", "oficinas de colocación" and "oficinas de empleo". These services were first supplied by private agencies but, by the early decades of the twentieth century, international guidelines (laid down by ILO) were recommending the banning of private employment agencies (particularly profit-making ones) and their replacement by public agencies. Spanish legislation has long entrusted the tasks of placement and employment to public employment offices, which are currently organized and run by **INEM**; the main function of these services is to register offers of and applications for work, to issue certificates of **professional competence and status**, and to implement statutory provisions on **employment policy, vocational training** and **unemployment** protection. Their actual role in the **placement** of workers is relatively minor, a fact which is proved by the large number of offers of employment to named individuals, and placements, which are arranged before notification is sent to the public services. See **personnel selection agency, temporary employment agency**.

561. **SERVICIOS DE SEGURIDAD Y MANTENIMIENTO — SAFETY AND MAINTENANCE SERVICES:** Work that must be continued in the event of a **strike** in order to guarantee the safety of persons and property and to enable the normal resumption of work (premises, machinery, plant, raw materials,

etc.). Spanish law makes the provision of these services compulsory and stipulates that the decision regarding both the services and the workers required be made by agreement between the employer and the **strike committee**; in the event of disagreement, the decision is made by the labour courts.

562. **SERVICIOS ESENCIALES DE LA COMUNIDAD — ESSENTIAL PUBLIC SERVICES:** Activities and services considered to be of particular social significance. Spanish legislation requires that they be maintained in the event of **strikes** and **labour disputes/industrial disputes/trade disputes,** and to this end makes the authorities responsible for imposing **minimum services,** whose provision is compulsory. Although there is no prior definition, case law has regarded as essential services those which affect or fulfil constitutionally protected rights and interests. Up to now, the services declared to be essential have been, basically, transport (motorways, air transport, railways, underground rail networks, ports, trunk routes), communications (post and telecommunications, television, telephones), energy (fuel, petrol stations), health (hospitals and social security bodies), education (state education establishments, excluding universities), and culture (the Prado). See **self-regulation of strike action.**

563. **SERVICIOS MINIMOS — MINIMUM SERVICES:** Services that are to be provided in the event of a **strike** or **labour dispute/industrial dispute/trade dispute,** in order to maintain **essential public services.** The establishment of their level, and the maintenance of that level, are usually arranged either as part of **self-regulation of strike action** or through the imposition by the authorities of guaranteed minimum levels. Without excluding self-regulation, Spanish legislation has opted for intervention by the authorities (the Government or the Autonomous Communities), and this takes the form of "minimum service decrees". Because of their considerable impact on the effectiveness of strike action, these decrees frequently give rise to appeals before the courts, generally based on the fact that the levels imposed tend to involve a large number of workers and that little consideration is given to the offers and proposals on the matter made by the trade unions.

564. **SERVICIOS SOCIALES — SOCIAL SERVICES:** Adminstrative services whose aim is to provide assistance to certain population groups or those in need (the disabled, the elderly, marginalized groups, etc.) by providing non-cash benefits (training, rehabilitation, leisure and recreational activities). Many of these services (those run by **INSERSO**) are part of the **social security** system and serve as a complement to its protective measures.

565. **SERVICIOS SOCIALES EN LA EMPRESA — COMPANY WELFARE SERVICES:** Services set up and managed within an enterprise for the benefit of employees or their families (company discount stores, crèches, canteens, libraries, grants or subsidies, sports or cultural facilities, etc.). They are sometimes classed as forms of **indirect pay** or **payment in kind**. In Spain they are generally provided for in collective agreements. Workers' representatives are entitled to participate in their management.

566. **SIGILO PROFESIONAL — PROFESSIONAL CONFIDENTIALITY:** Obligation binding **workers' representatives** in an enterprise, both during and after their period of service as representatives, to treat as confidential any information provided by the enterprise under this condition and not to use certain documents outside the enterprise or for any purpose other than that for which they were handed over. It is to be distinguished from **professional secrecy**, which affects all employees. See **disclosure of information/rights to information**.

567. **SINDICALISMO — TRADE UNIONISM:** The trade union movement in Spain was relatively well established by the end of the nineteenth century (the **UGT** was set up in 1888) and grew rapidly during the early twentieth century, a period during which new organizations emerged (**CNT** in 1910, **ELA-STV** in 1911) and the Spanish trade unions had their record number of members (more than two million members during the Second Republic). **Freedom of association/trade union freedom** was suppressed during the Franco regime (1939-1975), but the original trade unions gradually re-emerged and new organizations (**CC.OO.**, **USO**) were formed, though they were clandestine or merely tolerated until trade union freedom was re-established in 1977. At present, the Spanish trade union scenario features two major national organizations and several confederations with wide influence in particular Autonomous Communities (**ELA-STV** in the Basque Country and **INTG** in Galicia) or in the public service (**CSIF**). Spanish trade unionism is marked by its low membership figures and lack of funds; its reformist character consisting in seeking social reforms on the one hand and aggressive collective bargaining with employers on the other; the fact that the unions are loosening their ties with their associated political parties; and its high degree of **centralization**. Most of the major Spanish trade union confederations are affiliated to **international trade union organizations**.

568. **SINDICALISMO DE CLASE — CLASS TRADE UNIONISM:** Trade unionism whose declared intention is to defend the interests of the worker as a member of a specific social class; it propounds the transformation of the political, economic and social system to make it more favourable to the working class, and is opposed to sectional unionism. It is a trade unionism which does not confine its activities to the economic sphere but also takes an active part in the political process, generally supporting political parties that claim to champion workers' interests. In Spain, the **UGT** and **CC.OO.** confederations tend to describe themselves as class trade unions.

569. **SINDICALISMO INDEPENDIENTE — AUTONOMOUS TRADE UNIONISM:** Term used in Spain to refer to **trade unions** which in their strategy and line of action claim to eschew political and ideological criteria, in contrast to **class trade unionism**. From this perspective, it has something in common with **free trade unionism** and **occupational trade unionism**. Autonomous trade unionism has relative **union strength** in the air transport, education, communications and construction sectors. The **USO** confederation also considers itself an autonomous trade union.

570. **SINDICALISMO LIBRE — FREE TRADE UNIONISM:** This term is used with two quite different meanings: firstly, trade unionism which emerges in response to **freedom of association/trade union freedom** and which is not controlled by the authorities; and secondly, a trade union movement that claims to be free of ideological or political influences, usually to distinguish itself from **class trade unionism**. This second meaning has, in its turn, been used for various purposes: sometimes by genuinely representative organizations (such as trade unionism based on Christian belief or **occupational trade unionism**), but also by **company unions/"yellow" unions**, which are usually set up with employer support as a means of obstructing or dividing class trade unionism (as happened in Spain in the early twentieth century).

571. **SINDICALISMO PROFESIONAL — OCCUPATIONAL TRADE UNIONISM:** Trade unionism which groups together workers in the same occupation or occupational category. In Spain as elsewhere it is to a certain extent the offspring of the craft unions, but differs from them in that it reflects a reaction against **class trade unionism** or industrial trade unions with the aim of more directly promoting the specific interests of particular groups of workers. Trade unions of this kind tend to be set up by

occupational groups with high skill levels, strong bargaining power or very specific occupational interests and characteristics, as is the case in Spain with doctors and health personnel, maritime and airline workers, senior public servants, teachers, etc. In order to draw a sharper distinction from class trade unionism, the unions formed by these professionals are sometimes called "asociaciones profesionales" (professional associations). Occasionally, the term "occupational trade unionism" alludes to the trade union strategy of not interfering in the political process rather than to the group of workers represented; in this sense, many general trade unions claim to practise occupational trade unionism (*e.g.* **ELA-STV, USO**). See **public service union, professional and managerial staff**.

572. **SINDICALISTA — TRADE UNIONIST:** Term indicating people who devote themselves to trade union activities or are known for their links with a particular **trade union**; sometimes called "activista sindical" or "militante sindical" (union activist). In Spain, the term "sindicalista" has in the past been applied to legal persons or bodies connected with syndicalist movements, particularly certain political parties, such as the Partido Sindicalista in the 1930s.

573. **SINDICALIZACION — UNIONIZATION/UNION DENSITY:** Membership of the various trade unions in a given sphere or period. Unionization can be measured in absolute terms, by calculating the total number of union members, or in relative terms, by comparing the number of members with the total working population ("tasa de sindicalización" or "tasa de afiliación", *i.e.* union density). This method makes it possible to assess real **union strength**, although the number of union members is not the sole indicator of a trade union's power, which can also be measured in terms of its **trade union influence** or ability to mobilize the workers. Union density in Spain seems to be stabilized at around 15 per cent. of the working population. This low level is due to various reasons: the existence of other channels of representation, the general applicability of collective agreements, the unions' lack of funds and consequent inability to provide many services for their members, the number of small enterprises, etc.

574. **SINDICATO — TRADE UNION:** Permanent organization whose purpose is to promote work-related interests. In Spain, unlike other countries, this term is usually reserved for organizations formed by employees (or public servants), although it is also used colloquially for organizations formed by the self-

employed and small entrepreneurs, mainly in agriculture. Historically, trade unions were born as resistance groups to fight against certain employer practices, in the form of spontaneous or transitory groupings called "coalitions" ("coalición" or "coligación"), or as mutual assistance and mutual protection bodies (friendly societies). Later, they took the shape of a kind of occupational association and, occasionally, occupational "corporation", depending on the legal context and the degree of government intervention in industrial relations. Nowadays, they are usually in the form of occupational associations characterized by the special nature of their aims (to promote social and economic interests) and their methods (**trade union activity**). The earliest type of trade union in the modern sense was the craft union based on the worker's occupation or craft; but this form of organization gradually lost its significance and was replaced by the industrial union, representing an entire industry or branch of activity, or by geographical criteria (district, provincial, regional unions, etc.). **Enterprise unions**, occupational unions, unions of **professional and managerial staff** and inter-occupational or general unions are also relatively common. Depending on their internal composition, a distinction is usually made between single unions and umbrella-type unions grouped together on the basis of geographical area (**territorial federations**), industry (**industrial federations**) or both (**trade union confederations** or central trade union bodies). The first unions appeared in Spain in the form of friendly societies; they were later covered by legislation governing associations in general (1887) and then by special legislation governing occupational associations (1931); following Spain's political transition and the recognition of **freedom of association/trade union freedom**, they were regulated in principle by the Trade Union Activity Act (LAS) of 1977 and subsequently by the **Trade Union Freedom Act (LOLS)** of 1985, which still governs the legal status of trade unions. Recognition of trade union freedom in Spain not only enables unions to be formed and operated, it also entitles them to a privileged position among associations of public and social significance, to public aid and subsidies and to some very strong legal guarantees. See **unionization/union density**.

575. SINDICATO AMARILLO — COMPANY UNION/ "YELLOW" UNION: The pejorative Spanish term traditionally used to refer to union organizations set up and supported by the employer or by management to hinder the representation and defence of employees' interests or to prevent the presence of more combative or demanding trade unions in the enterprise or workplace.

576. **SINDICATO DE EMPRESA — ENTERPRISE UNION:** A union which groups together the employees of a single enterprise or work/production unit. In Spain, enterprise unions are common in larger companies. They are sometimes branded as **company unions/"yellow" unions,** on the assumption that their formation has been encouraged by management to prevent the presence of class trade unions or more combative unions.

577. **SINDICATO DE FUNCIONARIOS — PUBLIC SERVICE UNION:** A union which organizes public servants. Public service trade unionism is a relatively new phenomenon, since it was until recently assumed that the public administration, governed by the principles of hierarchy and authority and accustomed to the unilateral regulation of working conditions, was closed to trade union activity. Over the past few years, however, public sector employees have shown an increasing tendency to organize for industrial relations purposes. In Spain, public service trade unionism has been little evident over the years, though it saw a marked upsurge as a result of recognition of trade union freedom. The promulgation of the **Representation of Public Servants Act (LORF)** led, in 1987, to the first public service **union elections,** which were dominated by the **CSIF** (24.9 per cent.), **CC.OO.** (24.2 per cent.) and **UGT** (23.1 per cent.). Trade unions have considerable influence in some sectors of the public service (e.g. education), although the proportion of public servants who are union members is still low. Some public service trade unions are specifically for members of police forces and security services.

578. **SINDICATO DE OFICIO — CRAFT UNION:** See **skilled worker/craft worker, trade (craft), trade union.**

579. **SINDICATO MAS REPRESENTATIVO — MOST REPRESENTATIVE UNION:** Term used to refer to **trade unions** accorded the status of possessing the highest level of **representativeness.** Under Spanish legislation such status is accorded to unions which achieve a minimum number of representatives in **union elections** (10 per cent. at national level and 15 per cent. at Autonomous Community level) and, by extension, to all the trade union organizations which are affiliated to them or federated or confederated with them. Most representative status confers the right to negotiate generally applicable collective agreements and to be represented on the appropriate public bodies; in all, it confers a special legal position within the industrial relations system and in relations with the

authorities. At present **CC.OO.**, **UGT** and **ELA-STV** have attained most representative status. Unions that achieve a certain level of support within a more restricted geographical area are known as "sindicatos suficientemente representativos" (sufficiently representative unions) and have the power to negotiate collective agreements within that area.

580. **SINDICATO SUFICIENTEMENTE REPRESENTATIVO — SUFFICIENTLY REPRESENTATIVE UNION:** See **most representative union**.

581. **SINDICATO VERTICAL — VERTICAL UNION:** In Spain this term is not used, as it is elsewhere, to refer to a trade union organized by industry or branch of activity, *i.e.* according to vertical criteria and thus as opposed to a horizontal union organized by craft or occupation. It was used, together with the names "Sindicato Nacional" and "Organización Sindical Española", to refer to the official union organization set up during the Franco regime.

582. **SMI:** See **national minimum wage** (salario mínimo interprofesional).

583. **SOCIEDAD ANONIMA LABORAL — WORKERS' LIMITED COMPANY:** Company whose share capital is held mainly by its workers. It is one form of access for workers to ownership of an enterprise. Over the past few years it has also been seen as an instrument of employment policy (**self-employment**) and a way of rescuing enterprises that are in economic difficulties. Spanish legislation encourages and offers financial support for the creation and maintenance of such companies, sometimes together with workers' co-operatives. See **workers' participation, profit-sharing**.

584. **SOLIDARIDAD DE TRABAJADORES VASCOS — BASQUE WORKERS' SOLIDARITY (ELA-STV):** Central trade union body formed in 1911 by Catholic union groups. It operates solely in the Autonomous Community of the Basque Country, where it dominates in terms of electoral strength. It is affiliated to the ICFTU, WCL and ETUC.

585. **SUBALTERNO — ANCILLARY EMPLOYEE:** Workers of a lower grade than other workers whom they assist by performing auxiliary or complementary tasks. Ancillary employees are usually categorized as a separate occupational group in industry-wide provisions.

586. SUBCONTRATACION — SUB-CONTRACTING: System of organizing business and economic activities characterized by the transfer by a principal enterprise of elements of its activity to auxiliary enterprises. Its use is common in activities which follow a complex cycle or which require the contribution of various special types of work (construction industry, shipyards, the iron and steel industry, etc.); it is also customary practice in the services which necessarily accompany production activities without being an integral part of them (*e.g.* cleaning, catering, accountancy, etc.). In addition to instances such as these (referred to in Spain as internal sub-contracting), sub-contracting may be used in any production activity in which it is possible to pass on part of the work to smaller enterprises, sometimes as an alternative to **homeworking/outwork** (referred to in Spain as external sub-contracting). Sub-contracting leads to the externalization of employment or decentralization of production, whereby the principal enterprise makes indirect use of the labour provided in the enterprises acting as contractors or sub-contractors (peripheral workers). For this reason, and also because sub-contracting has been relatively frequently used to conceal labour-only sub-contracting, Spanish legislation (like that of some neighbouring countries) has established certain precautions and guarantees for the employees of sub-contractors or auxiliary enterprises, such as the joint and several liability of the enterprises involved and, in certain cases, by means of industry-wide provisions, the worker's right to become a member of the **staffing level/staff complement/workforce** of the principal enterprise.

587. SUBSIDIO DE DESEMPLEO AGRICOLA — AGRICULTURAL UNEMPLOYMENT BENEFIT: Special system of unemployment protection for **casual workers** in agriculture. It has, together with the Rural Employment Plan (PER), replaced the former **community employment programme** formula, combining **employment policy** measures and social welfare benefits. The benefit is granted to workers who have paid contributions under the Agricultural Social Security Scheme and is equivalent to 75 per cent. of the **national minimum wage**, payable for a maximum period of 180 days. Because of the chronic lack of work in rural areas, it has been paid to virtually everyone registered in the agrarian census. In addition to this benefit, the Rural Employment Plan provides for the setting-up of schemes and services to create jobs in areas or periods of low employment.

588. SUELDO — MONTHLY SALARY: See **wage/pay**.

589. **SUPERVISOR:** Person responsible for performing control, supervisory or inspection functions in an enterprise or a particular section of an enterprise. Supervisors may, depending on the case, be classified as management or lower and middle management.

590. **SUPLIDOS — EXPENSES:** Sums which are paid to employees to reimburse them for any costs they may have to incur as a result of their work. They include **subsistence and travel allowances**.

591. **SUSPENSION DE EMPLEO Y SUELDO — SUSPENSION OF EMPLOYMENT AND PAY:** Disciplinary sanction, frequently provided for in **collective agreements**, which consists of an interruption of work and pay for a certain period. Its duration depends on the seriousness of the employee's offence or breach of rules. See **docking of pay/fine, employer's managerial authority/managerial prerogative, suspension of the contract of employment**.

592. **SUSPENSION DEL CONTRATO DE TRABAJO — SUSPENSION OF THE CONTRACT OF EMPLOYMENT:** Situation in which the employee and employer are temporarily released from their respective obligations to work and to remunerate work. It happens mainly with open-ended contracts of employment, though it may also apply to temporary contracts of employment. Under Spanish law, the contract of employment may be suspended, basically, as a result of mutual agreement of the parties, maternity, military service, **leave of absence**, economic or technological grounds or *force majeure*, **suspension of employment and pay, strike** or **lock-out**. Other contractual obligations remain in force during the period of suspension, particularly those relating to **good faith** (prohibition on disloyal competition, **professional secrecy**, etc.).

593. **SUSTITUCION DE HUELGUISTAS — REPLACEMENT OF STRIKERS:** Hiring of new workers to perform the work of striking employees. Spanish law prohibits this practice in principle; non-compliance may incur administrative and penal sanctions.

T

594. **TABLA SALARIAL — PAY SCALE TARIFF:** Tariffs listing all **wage/pay** levels and pay components in a given sphere (enterprise, sector, etc.); sometimes also called "tarifas salariales". Pay scale tariffs are usually included in collective agreements, generally in the form of annexes. They are fixed on a lump-sum basis or by the application of percentages or point ratings by group, category or job. They are one of the main issues covered by **collective bargaining**.

595. **TANTO ALZADO — LUMP SUM:** Basis used to fix **wage/pay, compensation** and **social security** benefits which are settled by a single payment, as opposed to periodic payments or payment by instalments. See **compensation for dismissal/ severance pay, compensation for termination of the employment contract**.

596. **TARIFAS SALARIALES — WAGE TARIFFS:** See **pay scale tariff**.

597. **TASA DE ACTIVIDAD — PARTICIPATION RATE/ ACTIVITY RATE:** Technically defined as the economically active population (those in work plus those actively seeking work) as a proportion of the total population of working age. In Spain, the Survey of the Working Population (EPA) calculates the participation rate by dividing the economically active population by the population over the age of 16. The rate has increased in recent years; it is higher for men than for women, though there has been a greater increase for women than for men; and it is concentrated in the 20-54 age group, followed by the 16-19 age group and then the over-55 age group. A supplementary concept is the employment rate, which is the number of people actually working or employed as a proportion of the economically active population. The employment rate in Spain has fallen in recent years, and is highest for men and the 25-54 age group. The unemployment rate is the number of people who are unemployed as a proportion of the economically active population. See **unemployment, stopping work/unemployment**.

598. **TASA DE AFILIACION — UNION DENSITY:** See **unionization/union density**.

599. **TASA DE SINDICALIZACION — UNION DENSITY:** See **unionization/union density**.

600. **TECNICO — TECHNICAL PERSONNEL:** Highly or specially skilled people who direct or perform tasks requiring

specialized training. Industry-wide provisions usually include them as an **occupational group** ranked above **workers, ancillary employees** and **office workers**, and divided into professionally qualified technical personnel and non-qualified technical personnel. They tend to form their own occupational trade unions or groups within class trade unions (federations of technical personnel and professional and managerial staff), and often seek to negotiate **occupational agreements**. Spanish law treats technical personnel and office staff as a single group for the election of workforce representatives.

601. **TELETRABAJO — TELEWORK:** Work in which use is made of telematics or telecommunications. It has given rise to new forms of **homeworking/outwork**, particularly those concerned with data processing. It is both a cause and a manifestation of the decentralization of production. It has a significant impact on the rights and obligations arising from the employment relationship.

602. **TIEMPO DE TRABAJO — WORKING TIME:** Time devoted to the performance of work. It is a generic concept in that it covers many different aspects of the employment relationship: **working hours, overtime, rest days, annual holiday** and **time off**. In general, the organization of working time is covered by collective bargaining and by the individual contract of employment, since Spanish law merely establishes some very general minimum rules. Working time may be calculated on a daily, weekly, monthly or annual basis; this last method (**annualized working hours**) has come to be widely used in recent years, since it allows work to be more effectively distributed to meet the enterprise's needs or fluctuations in demand during different seasons or periods. Working time can also serve as the basis for defining the duration of the employment contract (**temporary contract/fixed-term contract**) and classifying the type of contract (**part-time workers**).

603. **TRABAJADOR — EMPLOYEE:** Most widely used term for a person who works under the direction and control of another, *i.e.* under a contract of employment.

604. **TRABAJADORES A TIEMPO PARCIAL — PART-TIME WORKERS:** Workers who provide their services for a working day which is shorter than normal or for a number of days per week or per month which are fewer than normal. Part-time work is generally preferred by people who want to combine work with other activities (*e.g.* studies, family commitments), which is why it tends to be concentrated among particular groups of the working population, mainly young people and women. It

sometimes involves **job-sharing** by two or more people. In Spain, part-time work has been encouraged by new contractual formulas such as part-time contracts and **hand-over contracts**. Part-time workers enjoy the same rights as full-time workers; their pay and their social security rights and obligations are calculated on a *pro rata* basis.

605. **TRABAJADORES DE EDAD MADURA — OLDER WORKERS:** Term used to refer to workers who, because of their age, have special difficulties in finding work or in re-training; they are the group being worst affected by **adjustment of employment levels**. Various **job creation** and **vocational training** measures aimed at this group have been introduced since the 1970s. Current Spanish law makes provision for employment subsidies, assistance for employers towards social security contributions and training schemes for workers over the age of 45.

606. **TRABAJADORES ESTACIONALES — SEASONAL WORKERS:** See **seasonal work**.

607. **TRABAJADORES EXTRANJEROS — FOREIGN WORKERS:** Spanish legislation defines foreign workers as workers who are not of Spanish nationality and whose intention is to carry on gainful employment in Spain, either self-employed or as employees. This legislation distinguishes between EEC and other workers. But within the latter category Latin American workers are subject to less rigorous entry and residence requirements. As a general rule, foreign nationals wishing to work in Spain at present need a **work permit** (as well as a residence permit); once they are officially and legally employed, however, foreign workers have the same rights and obligations as Spanish nationals. There is nonetheless a high incidence of **undeclared employment** of foreigners and there are occasional cases of discrimination in employment. From 1992, EEC nationals will no longer be required to hold a work permit in order to work in Spain.

608. **TRABAJADORES EVENTUALES — CASUAL WORKERS:** Strictly, this term refers in Spanish to workers who are hired to meet short-term staffing requirements, respond to special market circumstances or deal with a build-up of work or orders; in a broader sense, it is used to refer to all those who provide their services on a temporary or occasional basis (temporary workers), in order to differentiate them from permanent employees or holders of an employment contract of indefinite duration. Their lack of job security, their lower skill levels and

the fact that they have greater difficulty in organizing themselves as a group mean that their terms and conditions of employment are usually worse than those of permanent employees and that they are in some cases not covered by collective agreements. Over the past few years, successive economic crises and the transformation of the production system have led to a significant drop in the number of permanent employees and a consequent increase in the number of casual workers, giving rise to destabilization of employment. It is calculated that around 20 per cent. of employment contracts in Spain are now temporary or casual contracts. Permanent employees include a special group of workers who provide their services on a seasonal or cyclic basis (intermittent permanent employees).

609. **TRABAJADORES INTERINOS — RELIEF WORKERS:** See **relief work**.

610. **TRABAJADORES MENORES — UNDER-AGE WORKERS/MINORS:** Term traditionally used in Spain to refer to employees who have not yet reached the age of majority (18). Labour legislation has from its beginnings laid down special rules for minors to remedy their incapacity in law to enter into a contract, to protect their health and well-being and to facilitate their basic and vocational training. Under current Spanish legislation, minors are required to have parental permission to enter into a contract of employment (except when they are married or living independently); are prohibited from performing night work, overtime and unhealthy or hazardous work; and are guaranteed a **national minimum wage** lower than that of adult workers.

611. **TRABAJADORES MINUSVALIDOS — DISABLED WORKERS:** Workers whose capacity for work is diminished as a result of physical, mental or sensory causes. Spanish legislation makes provisions for the treatment, rehabilitation and social and occupational integration of the disabled; these include employment quotas, employment subsidies and assistance for employers towards social security contributions, and special vocational training schemes.

612. **TRABAJADORES SUSTITUTOS — SUBSTITUTE WORKERS:** See **relief work**.

613. **TRABAJADORES TEMPOREROS — SEASONAL WORKERS:** See **seasonal work**.

614. **TRABAJO — WORK:** See **employment**.

615. **TRABAJO A DOMICILIO — HOMEWORKING/OUT-WORK:** Work which is performed at the place chosen by the workers, usually their own home. It has been a very traditional form of work, often performed by groups or families, and an effective method of providing services in certain economic sectors or of performing tasks which do not require any complex machinery or equipment or supervision by foremen or managers. Renewed interest has been shown in this form of work in recent years because electronics and telematics facilitate remote working (**telework**); it also opens up the labour market to people (essentially women workers) for whom conventional employment presents difficulties. Its decentralized, scattered nature and the isolation it implies can give rise to violation of workers' legal rights and even failure to declare employment (**undeclared employment**). To counteract this problem, labour law requires contracts for homeworking to be inspected by and deposited with the appropriate employment office.

616. **TRABAJO A REGLAMENTO — WORK-TO-RULE:** Synonym of **huelga de celo**.

617. **TRABAJO ASALARIADO — WORK UNDER AN EMPLOYMENT CONTRACT:** Work performed in exchange for **wage/pay** on another's account and in a position of subordination to and under the direction of another person; work as an employee. Most workers in industrialized societies are employees. In Spain, they represent some 75-80 per cent. of the employed population.

618. **TRABAJO ATIPICO — ATYPICAL WORK:** Work contracted or performed under conditions which differ from the norm in terms of the duration of the contract of employment (temporary or casual contract as opposed to an open-ended contract); working time (part-time work as opposed to full working hours); the place of work (homeworking, work outside the employer's premises, or telework); or the special nature of the employer (in sub-contracting or auxiliary enterprises, through temporary employment agencies, or nominal self-employment). The term is sometimes used incorrectly to refer to **undeclared employment** or work under irregular conditions. The number of atypical workers tends to increase during periods of high unemployment; these workers are essentially concentrated in certain sectors (agriculture, retailing, hotels and catering, light industry) and are mainly members of the most disadvantaged groups of the working population: young people, women and disabled or older workers.

619. TRABAJO AUTONOMO — SELF-EMPLOYMENT: Work performed independently and autonomously, without subjection to the orders or instructions of another person; it is usually on own account, though it may also be on another's account (doctors, lawyers, etc.). Those classed as self-employed include small traders, farmers, members of the liberal professions and, in general, anybody who works in their own business, with or without the assistance of employees. In Spain, self-employed persons (who represent some 20 per cent. of the employed population) are not covered by labour law. If they do not have any employees they are entitled to join a **trade union**, but not to form their own unions.

620. TRABAJO BENEVOLO — UNPAID WORK/VOLUNTARY WORK: Work which is performed for reasons of friendship, charity or good neighbourliness, without any pecuniary motive and without any of the usual contracts for the provision of services. It does not give rise to any legally enforceable rights or obligations, though in certain cases where it becomes habitual it may lead to expectations concerning reciprocal benefits. It is to be distinguished from what is called "intercambio de servicios" (reciprocal exchange of services), a formula sometimes used (eg in rural areas) as an alternative to employing labour. Unpaid work is not covered by labour legislation.

621. TRABAJO CLANDESTINO — CLANDESTINE EMPLOYMENT: See **undeclared employment**.

622. TRABAJO COMPARTIDO — JOB-SHARING: Form of part-time work in which two or more people share a single post and the pay and any other benefits attached to it. A form of job-sharing provided for by Spanish legislation to reduce unemployment among young people is one whereby a post is shared between an employee who is close to normal retirement age (who thus enters **partial retirement**) and a person (young person in their first job) being integrated into working life (under a **hand-over contract**). Job-sharing offers various advantages such as a reduction in absenteeism and training costs, easier cover for absent workers, etc.; its use is, however, accompanied by problems of organization and human resource management.

623. TRABAJO DE COLABORACION SOCIAL — COMMUNITY WORK: In general, work of a temporary nature intended to be of value to the local community. Under Spanish law, individuals in receipt of unemployment benefit and the administrative authorities can enter into a community work contract covering tasks which are of social value or to the benefit of the community, to be performed in exchange for a supplement (see **wage/pay**) to unemployment benefit. The aim is to obtain some kind of social return from unemployment benefit and to supplement the income of unemployed workers. Community work has never enjoyed much popularity and is being used less and less frequently.

624. **TRABAJO DE TEMPORADA — SEASONAL WORK:** Work that is typical of certain seasons of the year. Seasonal workers are usually called "trabajadores temporeros" or "trabajadores estacionales" in Spanish. In principle they are classed as temporary workers, but if they do the work habitually they acquire the status of "intermittent permanent employees" and have the right under Spanish law to be re-hired at the beginning of each season. Seasonal work is very common in certain sectors (agriculture, livestock production, hotel industry). See **casual workers**.

625. **TRABAJO EN CADENA — PRODUCTION-LINE WORK:** Work performed in a production system which, because it is fed or controlled mechanically, imposes a particular rhythm or pace on the worker's movements. See **assembly line, pace of work**.

626. **TRABAJO EN COMUN — JOINT WORK:** Form of work organization in which two or more workers undertake the joint or co-ordinated performance of a given task, sharing the total contractual pay proportionally. It is an outdated concept in Spanish labour legislation.

627. **TRABAJO FAMILIAR — WORK PERFORMED WITHIN THE FAMILY:** Work which is performed for family or kinship reasons. It is excluded from Spanish labour legislation, although the family member concerned must be registered with the **social security** system as self-employed. In Spain, this form of work (classified in official statistics as "family labour") is very widespread in certain independent activities (farming, retailing, etc.).

628. **TRABAJO FEMENINO — FEMALE EMPLOYMENT/ EMPLOYMENT OF WOMEN:** In Spain and in neighbouring countries, one of the oldest strands of labour law has included regulations on the employment of women (often linked with the employment of **under-age workers/minors**). The first provisions of this type merely restricted the length of the working day, established minimum rest periods and prohibited women from

performing certain types of work considered harmful to their health or moral well-being. Early legislation also recognized the right to suspend the contract of employment for childbirth and the right to have breaks to feed nursing infants. A more recent concern of the law is the equality of women, both as regards entering into a contract of employment and as regards terms and conditions of employment, by prohibiting unjustified or discriminatory distinctions and limiting special rules to situations in which the physiological peculiarities of women are of real relevance, such as maternity and the period preceding childbirth. Complementary to this concern is the adoption of **positive action** (vocational training, employment support, etc.) in favour of women to facilitate their insertion into the labour market and to give effect to the principle of equal opportunities. Recent years have also seen a change in society's attitude to the employment of women, and this, coupled with the transformation of the economic structure, has brought about an increase in the participation rate of the female population, and also in the number of female job-seekers (in percentage terms, they are more numerous than male job-seekers) and in the number of women registered as unemployed.

629. **TRABAJO INTERINO — RELIEF WORK:** Work whose purpose is to replace an employee who has temporarily ceased work, with **suspension of the contract of employment** and the right to have their job reserved for them (illness, **leave of absence**, military service, etc.). In principle it is temporary work, since it comes to an end when the employee being replaced returns, unless its continuation is implicitly or expressly agreed. People who act as reliefs are called "trabajadores interinos" or "trabajadores sustitutos" and are classed as temporary workers. In the public administration in Spain relief workers are often hired to fill temporarily the posts not occupied by **public servants**. See **temporary contracts/fixed-term contracts**.

630. **TRABAJO IRREGULAR — IRREGULAR EMPLOYMENT:** See **undeclared employment**.

631. **TRABAJO LENTO — SLOW-DOWN:** Form of industrial action by employees which consists in a deliberate, concerted reduction in work effort to below normal productivity levels (**go-slow**). When this reduction brings output to the level that would result from a strict, literal interpretation of work regulations and instructions, it is usually referred to as a **work-to-rule**. In Spain, this tactic tends to be used by office workers, particularly in the public service; it is in principle defined as illegal or improper practice.

632. TRABAJO NEGRO — UNDECLARED EMPLOYMENT: Work which is performed outside the legal framework or under irregular terms and conditions; in particular, employment which is not apparent to the authorities because it is not declared for tax and social security purposes. Also known in Spanish as "trabajo irregular" (irregular employment), "trabajo somergido" (hidden employment), "trabajo oculto" (concealed employment) or "trabajo clandestino" (clandestine employment). It is very common in **homeworking/outwork**, since it is difficult to monitor and control. Undeclared employment is usually subject to worse conditions than normal or declared employment and lies beyond the reach of trade union or collective instruments for the protection of workers' interests. It rises to particularly high levels during times of economic crisis and high **unemployment**. In Spain, as in other countries, it is concentrated in certain sectors (clothing industry and toymaking) and particularly affects disadvantaged groups of workers (young people, women and foreign workers). Although it is difficult to calculate its extent, it is thought to involve a sizeable percentage of the working population.

633. TRABAJO OCULTO — CONCEALED EMPLOYMENT: See **undeclared employment**.

634. TRABAJO SOMERGIDO — HIDDEN EMPLOYMENT: See **undeclared employment**.

635. TRAFICO DE MANO DE OBRA — ILLEGAL TRAFFIC IN LABOUR: Term used to refer to the practices of supplying or loaning workers and, in general, acting as intermediary in the contract of employment, when they occur habitually, involve groups of workers and are of a fraudulent or illegal nature; they are particularly common in operations involving migrant workers and in connection with **undeclared employment**. Spanish law prohibits these practices, and imposes sanctions. See **provision of labour, criminal labour offences, "prestamismo"**.

636. TRANSMISION DE LA EMPRESA — TRANSFER OF UNDERTAKING: Change in the ownership of an enterprise or transfer of the status of employer. It may occur as a result of the death, disappearance or incapacity of the previous employer, or as a result of the transfer of the enterprise or of a self-contained part of it by sale, leasing, merger, legally imposed sale by auction, etc., provided there is continuity of the enterprise's activity. The law has traditionally attempted to prevent any violation of employees' legal rights in such cases and to ensure their **job security**. Spanish legislation provides, as a general rule, for the employment relationship to be maintained and for the new employer to take over the obligations of the former employer. In the case of transfer *inter vivos* it also stipulates that the employer is obliged to consult the **workers' representatives**, and declares the new and former employers to be jointly and severally liable for any labour and **social security** debts. These provisions follow the general lines of EEC Directive No. 87/1977, which proposes not only the protection of labour rights, but also the harmonization of Member States' regulations. See **criminal labour offences**.

637. **TRASLADO — TRANSFER:** Movement of the employee to another job or workplace. Spanish law uses the term to refer solely to a change of workplace which lasts for more than a year and which requires a change in the employee's place of residence, as distinct from **temporary relocation**. An employer may decide to transfer an employee for technical, organizational or production reasons but must request the permission of the **labour authorities** to do so. The spouse of a transferred employee who works for the same enterprise is entitled to be transferred as well, provided there is a suitable vacancy at the new workplace.

638. **TRIBUNALES DE TRABAJO — LABOUR COURTS:** Judicial bodies responsible for passing and enforcing judgements on labour and social issues; they constitute a specialist branch of the judiciary. Spain's first labour courts were the industrial courts, some of whose functions were subsequently assumed by the "comités paritarios" (joint committees) and **joint councils**. The "Sala de lo Social del Tribunal Supremo" (Social Chamber of the Supreme Court) was set up in 1931 and later, from 1940 onwards, primary jurisdiction in this sphere was assigned to the "Magistraturas de Trabajo" (Provincial Labour Courts), with appeals referred to the "Tribunal Central de Trabajo" (Central Labour Court) and the aforementioned Social Chamber of the Supreme Court. After the 1978 Constitution and the Judicial Powers Act of 1985, the labour courts system was reorganized to bring it in line with the general judicial system; it now comprises "Juzgados de lo Social" (Social Courts), Social Chambers in the "Tribunales Superiores de Justicia" (Higher Courts of Justice) of the Autonomous Communities, a Social Chamber in the "Audiencia Nacional" (National High Court), and a Social Chamber in the Supreme Court. The distribution of cases between these bodies depends both on their nature and seriousness and on whether they involve first-instance proceedings or appeals. The Constitutional Court, the highest body responsible

for interpretation of the Constitution, has in its decisions created a significant corpus of material concerning fundamental labour rights, particularly **freedom of association/trade union freedom** and the right to **strike**. In comparative terms, the courts play a large part in Spain in the settlement of labour disputes, both individual and collective; voluntary procedures such as **arbitration, conciliation and mediation** are little used. The activities of the courts have therefore given rise to a considerable body of case law, a knowledge of which is essential to the understanding, interpretation and implementation of labour laws.

639. **TURNOS DE TRABAJO — SHIFTWORK:** Method of **work organization** whereby work and production activity is performed continuously by different teams of employees in succession. To cover absences and rest days, there are usually "correturnos" (relief shifts) or "equipos de apoyo" (back-up crews). Under Spanish law, the organization of shifts must provide for the rotation of all employees and ensure that, unless they wish to do so, no employee is obliged to work the night shift for more than two consecutive weeks. Rest days for shiftwork may be calculated over periods of up to four weeks. See **working time**.

U

640. UGT: See **General Workers' Confederation** (Unión General de Trabjadores).

641. UNIDAD DE NEGOCIACION — BARGAINING UNIT: Functional, geographical and occupational sphere in which **collective bargaining** is carried on; it determines the scope of application of a **collective agreement** and is one of the major features of the **collective bargaining structure**. Its demarcation corresponds in principle to the bargaining agents and the groups of workers they represent, but there are many influencing factors: tradition, the pattern of the production structure, the legal context, the needs and wishes of the representative bodies involved, etc.

642. UNIDAD SINDICAL — UNION UNITY: Strictly, a situation in which the representation of workers' interests is channelled through a single **trade union**; the opposite of **trade union pluralism**. In a broader sense, the term is also used to refer to the formation of a unitary body encompassing the various unions existing in a given sphere and at a given time, which is compatible with pluralism. In Spain, union unity has often featured among the aims of the trade union movement, but (except when membership of the single existing union was compulsory) has rarely been achieved in practice, even in limited areas or sectors, because of the effect of many different factors (occupational, ideological, territorial, political, denominational) that encourage trade union separatism. Only occasionally have all the major unions co-operated to take united action. Recent exceptions to this tendency have been the creation of the Union Co-ordinating Committee in 1976 and the signing of the Original Union Proposal in the late 1980s by the **UGT** and **CC.OO.** confederations. Also, recent years have witnessed, in certain sectors or on the part of groups of workers with very particular characteristics, a strong move towards union amalgamation, mainly with the aim of gaining the legal advantages conferred by **representativeness**.

643. UNION GENERAL DE TRABAJADORES (UGT) — GENERAL WORKERS' CONFEDERATION (UGT): Spanish central trade union body set up in 1888 by Socialist trade unions under the Associations Act of 1887. Its membership grew to one million during the Second Republic. After its proscription during the Franco regime, it gradually rebuilt itself to become one of the major **trade union confederations** in Spain, a position which it has maintained since the late 1970s. It claims to be a

189

revolutionary class trade union, but its union activities are restrained and markedly reformist. It is basically centred on collective bargaining, where it has played a major role, and, more recently, on providing services for its members. In general terms, it has been very cautious (except on certain occasions) about taking industrial action against enterprises and the authorities. It has from the very outset professed itself to be in favour of union-based representation within the enterprise, as opposed to the **CC.OO.**'s preference for unitary bodies representing the workforce as a whole, and this strategy is reflected in the content of the **Trade Union Freedom Act** and many other agreements which specifically promoted trade union structures within the enterprise. It has traditionally maintained close relations with the PSOE, a political party to which it is linked by historical and ideological ties and with which it has shared leaders and activists; however, since the late 1980s there has been a noticeable distancing between the two organizations, partly as a result of the united action adopted by the UGT and CC.OO. In 1983 its membership was estimated at around 661,000, or 37.4 per cent. of all trade union members. It is affiliated to the International Confederation of Free Trade Unions (ICFTU) and the European Trade Union Confederation (ETUC).

644. **UNION SINDICAL OBRERA (USO) — WORKERS' TRADE UNIONIST CONFEDERATION (USO):** Spanish central trade union body set up in 1960 by Catholic and Socialist sectors of the labour movement. It was at one stage the third most powerful trade union body in Spain but has over the past few years suffered from breakaways and lost much of its electoral strength, which has never exceeded 10 per cent. According to some sources, its membership in 1983 was some 100,000, or 5.6 per cent. of all trade union members. It is affiliated to the World Confederation of Labour (WCL).

645. **UNIONES TERRITORIALES — TERRITORIAL FEDERATIONS:** Aggregate trade union organizations set up on the basis of spatial or geographical criteria (town, province, region or sometimes Autonomous Community). They usually serve simultaneously as territorial representatives of the central trade union bodies and as umbrella organizations for trade unions in a given geographical area.

646. **USO:** See **Workers' Trade Unionist Confederation** (Unión Sindical Obrera).

V

647. **VACACIONES — ANNUAL HOLIDAY:** Nowadays, virtually all employees have an annual paid holiday entitlement, although a relatively large number, because they work on a temporary or casual basis or work in sectors or enterprises which form part of the **hidden economy**, still do not benefit from this entitlement, which is in some cases not even recognized. Provisions for annual holidays were first introduced in Spain in 1931; since then the period of annual holiday has been gradually extended to the 30 calendar days stipulated by current legislation. This may be further extended by collective agreements or individual contracts of employment, some of which already provide for a "fifth week". The timing of annual holidays must be fixed by mutual consent between the employer and the employee; it is usually established by collective agreement. The employer must make the holiday timetable available at least two months in advance, and holidays may either be organized on a rotation basis or involve a complete shutdown. Under Spanish law the annual holiday entitlement may not be waived, may not be replaced by financial remuneration (unless the contract of employment is terminated before employees have taken their annual holiday), and may not be withheld or shortened as a disciplinary measure. Employees retain the right to their pay during their annual holiday, usually calculated as an average of pay received throughout the year.

648. **VALORACION DE PERSONAL — STAFF APPRAISAL:** Assessment of the capabilities and performance of the employees of a given enterprise with a view to designing payment systems and training schemes and planning **career paths**.

649. **VALORACION DE PUESTOS DE TRABAJO — JOB EVALUATION:** Assessment of the relative importance of each job in an enterprise, based on the intrinsic requirements or demands of the job rather than the characteristics of its holder. Job evaluation is relatively widely used in Spanish enterprises, though subjective systems of occupational classification (into **occupational groups** and **categories**) and worker opposition (which seems to be diminishing) hinder its implementation.

650. **VERIFICACION DE ENFERMEDAD — VERIFICATION OF ILLNESS:** Confirmation of the real occurrence and seriousness of an illness or accident alleged by employees to justify their absence from work. To counter **absenteeism**, employers are entitled under Spanish law to seek such verification and, should an employee refuse to supply it, to suspend any financial

rights they may be under an obligation to honour (*e.g.* pay supplement for **temporary incapacity for work/sickness absence**). See **employer's managerial authority/managerial prerogative**.

651. **VIDA ACTIVA — WORKING LIFE:** The period of their life during which individuals are physically and mentally able to work. In a stricter sense, the period between the minimum age for entering employment (16 in Spain) and **retirement**. A worker's employment path may undergo interruptions (**suspension of the contract of employment, leave of absence, unemployment,** etc.) and changes of circumstance (change of job, employer, occupation, etc.).

652. **VIDA PRIVADA DEL TRABAJADOR — PRIVATE LIFE OF THE EMPLOYEE:** Concern for the employee's privacy and other personal interests is a feature of recent labour legislation, and to this end it is tending to ensure that people's rights as citizens are carried over into the world of work and to establish forms of protection against any violations of these rights originating in the employing organization or work environment. Spanish law upholds the right of employees to respect for their privacy, to due consideration of their dignity and, in particular, to protection against sexually aggressive or insulting behaviour (**sexual harassment at work**). Violation of these rights may incur disciplinary and even penal sanctions; and if it originates with the employer it can be used as grounds for **termination of the contract of employment** by the employee, who is then entitled to compensation. Protection of these personal rights is particularly important in the context of **personal searches (security checks)**.

653. **VIGILANTE DE SEGURIDAD — SAFETY OFFICER:** Person responsible for monitoring and providing assistance as regards **health and safety**. Under Spanish law, a safety officer must be appointed in enterprises whose small workforce exempts them from the obligation to set up a **health and safety committee** and which carry on harmful or hazardous production processes.

654. **VINCULACION A LA TOTALIDAD — "TOTALITY" CLAUSE:** Typical clause in **collective agreements** by which the parties make their compliance with the agreed provisions conditional on the continued force of these provisions in their entirety, so that any alteration implies reconsideration of the entire agreement. This type of clause is very common in Spain, largely owing to the traditional existence of a procedure for monitoring the legality of agreements carried out either by the **labour**

authorities (who up to 1980 exercised these controls through ''homologación'' (official approval) or by the courts (since the **Workers' Statute** of 1980).

655. **VOTO A MANO ALZADA — VOTE BY SHOW OF HANDS:** Voting system which differs from a written or secret vote (**ballot**) in that the individuals being consulted indicate their decision publicly by the physical gesture of raising their hand in the air. Spanish law makes no provisions on this form of voting but it is often used for the adoption of resolutions at **mass meetings** of employees and for the ratification of decisions made by workers' representatives.

Z

656. **ZONAS DE PROMOCION ECONOMICA — ECONOMIC DEVELOPMENT AREAS:** See job creation, industrial restructuring.

657. **ZONAS DE URGENTE REINDUSTRIALIZACION — PRIORITY REDEVELOPMENT AREAS:** See job creation, industrial restructuring.

TABLES

A. Employment (Tables 1-7)
B. Elections of workers' representatives (Tables 8-12)
C. Industrial conflict (Tables 13-19)
D. Court cases (Table 20)
E. Pay (Tables 21-24)

TABLE 1

ECONOMICALLY ACTIVE POPULATION, PARTICIPATION RATE, NUMBER IN EMPLOYMENT, NUMBER UNEMPLOYED AND UNEMPLOYMENT RATE

Year	Economically active population (millions)	Participation rate (%)	Number in employment (millions)	Number unemployed (millions)	Unemployment rate (%)
Total men + women					
1966	12.5	52.9	12.2	0.156	1.2
1971	12.8	51.6	12.3	0.213	1.6
1976	13.3	50.9	12.7	0.640	4.7
1981	13.0	48.1	11.1	1.873	14.4
1982	13.2	48.1	11.0	2.144	16.2
1983	13.3	48.0	10.9	2.369	17.7
1984	13.4	47.6	10.6	2.768	20.6
1985	13.5	47.4	10.5	2.970	21.9
1986	13.7	47.7	10.8	2.960	21.5
1987	14.2	48.8	11.3	2.942	20.6
1988	14.6	49.1	11.7	2.847	19.5
1989	14.8	49.1	12.2	2.560	17.3
Male population					
1966	9.54	85.7	—	—	—
1971	9.60	81.6	--	—	—
1976	9.59	77.4	—	—	—
1981	9.29	71.3	8.02	1.26	13.6
1982	9.33	70.8	7.92	1.41	15.1
1983	9.34	70.0	7.81	1.53	16.4
1984	9.40	69.3	7.57	1.82	19.4
1985	9.44	68.6	7.51	1.93	20.5
1986	9.53	68.5	7.65	1.87	19.7
1987	9.58	67.9	7.94	1.64	17.2
1988	9.62	66.9	8.15	1.46	15.2
1989	9.70	66.6	8.44	1.26	13.0
Female population					
1966	2.99	23.8	—	—	—
1971	3.25	24.7	—	—	
1976	3.78	27.2	—	—	—
1981	3.75	26.6	3.14	0.60	16.2
1982	3.87	27.1	3.14	0.73	18.9
1983	4.00	27.7	3.17	0.85	20.8
1984	4.03	27.6	3.09	0.94	23.4
1985	4.09	27.6	3.05	1.03	25.4
1986	4.25	28.3	3.16	1.08	25.6
1987	4.71	31.0	3.41	1.29	27.5
1988	4.99	32.5	3.61	1.38	27.6
1989	5.10	32.7	3.81	1.29	25.4

Sources: *Población, Activad y Ocupación en España* (Ministry of Economy and Finance) and *Boletín de Estadísticas Laborales* (Ministry of Labour)

197

Table 2

BREAKDOWN OF EMPLOYMENT BY SECTOR (%)

Year	Agriculture	Industry	Construction	Services
1976	21.39	27.56	9.82	41.23
1977	20.61	27.67	9.89	41.83
1978	20.20	27.66	9.72	42.42
1979	19.35	27.49	9.39	43.77
1980	18.63	27.36	9.03	44.98
1981	18.65	26.65	8.62	46.08
1982	18.24	26.28	8.50	46.98
1983	18.62	25.03	8.46	47.89
1984	18.41	25.13	7.58	48.88
1985	18.21	24.49	7.28	50.02
1986	16.08	24.32	7.64	51.96
1987	15.21	24.19	8.08	52.52
1988	14.39	23.81	9.63	53.12
1989	13.03	23.65	9.25	54.07

Source: *Boletín de Estadísticas Laborales* (Ministry of Labour) and author's own calculations

TABLE 3

BREAKDOWN OF EMPLOYMENT BY BRANCH OF ACTIVITY (%)

Branch of activity	1982	1983	1984	1985	1986
Agriculture and fisheries	18.29	18.46	18.24	18.00	15.90
Extraction industries	0.95	0.94	1.00	0.98	0.92
Electricity, water and gas	0.77	0.79	0.77	0.80	0.77
Processing of minerals & chemicals industry	3.84	3.80	3.74	3.55	3.53
Metalworking and precision engineering	7.39	7.40	7.51	7.19	7.18
Other manufacturing industries	12.57	12.18	12.18	12.07	12.00
Construction	8.62	8.48	7.60	7.29	7.65
Distributive trades, hotels and catering	17.97	17.76	18.14	18.34	19.03
Transport and communications	5.88	5.66	5.72	5.82	5.83
Financial and insurance institutions	3.82	3.95	3.96	4.21	4.54
Public administration and other collective and social services	13.47	14.09	14.62	15.47	16.41
Personal services	6.36	6.45	6.46	6.22	6.18
TOTAL	100	100	100	100	100

Source: *Mercado de Trabajo en España durante 1986 [Labour market in Spain in 1986].* Percentages calculated on the basis of Table II.9 on page 131.

TABLE 4

BREAKDOWN OF EMPLOYMENT BY
OCCUPATIONAL STATUS (%)

Year	Employers	Entrepreneurs without employees, and self-employed	Family labour	Public sector employees	Private sector employees	Others
1976	3.42	17.97	8.42	10.87	58.95	0.34
1977	3.27	17.90	8.21	11.01	59.37	0.24
1978	3.44	17.70	8.14	12.02	58.49	0.21
1979	3.39	18.07	8.01	12.50	57.82	0.21
1980	3.49	18.29	7.85	13.37	56.76	0.24
1981	3.37	18.66	8.02	14.03	55.63	0.29
1982	3.29	18.62	7.88	14.88	55.03	0.30
1983	3.20	19.25	7.76	15.98	53.52	0.29
1984	3.36	20.07	7.70	16.13	52.38	0.36
1985	3.21	20.01	7.27	16.92	52.22	0.37
1986	3.22	19.14	6.50	17.52	53.20	0.42
1987	3.41	19.48	6.59	16.00	54.17	0.35
1988	3.38	18.78	6.56	15.68	55.25	0.35
1989	3.49	17.84	5.99	16.31	56.12	0.25

Source: *Boletín de Estadísticas Laborales* (Ministry of Labour) and author's own calculations

TABLE 5

BREAKDOWN OF EMPLOYMENT BY TYPE OF OCCUPATION (%)

		1982	1983	1984	1985	1986
1	Professional, managerial and technical staff	7.10	7.95	8.25	8.34	8.90
2	Senior public servants and enterprise heads	1.54	1.50	1.58	1.62	1.70
3	Administrative and clerical personnel	10.79	10.87	10.96	11.13	11.57
4	Commercial and sales staff	10.31	10.24	10.41	10.53	10.95
5	Service workers	13.10	13.44	14.08	14.24	14.30
6	Agricultural and farm workers, fishermen and hunters and trappers	18.28	18.51	18.25	18.02	15.96
7	Non-agricultural labourers, machine operators and drivers of transport vehicles	37.82	36.61	35.60	35.16	35.66
8	Unclassified	0.00	0.00	0.00	0.00	0.00
9	Armed forces	1.02	0.83	0.82	0.91	0.92

Source: *Mercado de Trabajo en España durante el 86 [Labour Market in Spain in 1986].* Percentages calculated on the basis of Table II.14 on page 141.

TABLE 6

BREAKDOWN OF UNEMPLOYMENT BY THE
LENGTH OF TIME INDIVIDUALS HAVE BEEN
SEEKING WORK (%)

Year	Total	0-6 months	6-12 months	1-2 years	2 years
1981	100	35.4	24.5	24.5	15.6
1982	100	29.8	21.8	26.2	22.2
1983	100	27.0	20.2	24.5	28.3
1984	100	26.9	19.4	22.0	31.7
1985	100	25.1	18.2	22.3	34.4
1986	100	25.2	17.2	21.1	36.5
1987	100	24.2	13.7	18.5	43.4
1988	100	24.7	13.7	18.5	43.3
1989	100	26.9	14.1	17.6	40.2

Source: *Boletín de Estadísticas Laborales* (Ministry of Labour)

TABLE 7

UNEMPLOYMENT RATES BY AGE GROUP (%)

Year	Total	16-19	20-24	25-54	55+
1981	14.4	43.0	29.6	9.1	5.6
1982	16.2	47.6	33.5	10.4	6.4
1983	17.7	51.1	37.1	11.8	6.7
1984	20.6	55.6	42.1	14.2	9.2
1985	21.9	55.9	44.6	15.8	9.8
1986	21.5	52.3	44.2	15.3	10.7
1987	20.6	49.5	40.4	15.0	9.3
1988	19.5	45.6	37.3	21.4	8.3
1989	17.3	38.2	32.8	13.7	8.3

Source: *Boletín de Estadísticas Laborales* (Ministry of Labour)

TABLE 8

REPRESENTATIVES ELECTED AS MEMBERS OF WORKERS' COMMITTEES AND WORKERS' DELEGATES (% DISTRIBUTION)

	1978	1980	1982	1986
CC.OO.	34.50	30.87	33.40	34.54
UGT	21.70	29.28	36.71	40.92
USO	3.90	8.68	4.64	3.78
Non-members	18.20	14.60	12.09	6.67
ELA-STV	0.90	2.44	3.30	3.31
INTG	—	1.02	1.17	0.65
Miscellaneous	20.80	13.11	8.69	10.13

Source: Official results published in the *Boletín Oficial del Estado* of June 6, 1987

TABLE 9

REPRESENTATIVES ELECTED AS MEMBERS OF STAFF COUNCILS AND WORKERS' DELEGATES (PUBLIC SERVICE) IN 1987 (% DISTRIBUTION)

UGT	23.08
CC.OO.	24.22
CSIF	24.95
ANPE	2.55
UCSTE	1.21
CEMSATSE	8.24
SLCTCPA	0.94
ELA-STV	0.58
Others	14.15

Source: Official results published in the *Boletín Oficial del Estado* of March 30, 1988

TABLE 10

BREAKDOWN OF ELECTED REPRESENTATIVES IN 1986 BY CANDIDATURE AND ECONOMIC ACTIVITY

(% distribution; total per candidature = 100)

Economic activity	Total	UGT	CC.OO.	ELA-STV	Group of workers	Other unions	Not known
Total	100.0	100.0	100.0	100.0	100.0	100.0	100.0
Agriculture	2.5	2.4	2.9	4.4	1.0	2.2	—
Industry	45.8	43.1	49.7	55.8	55.0	37.4	42.0
Construction	6.0	6.9	6.5	3.6	3.4	3.8	5.6
Services	45.6	47.5	40.8	36.2	40.3	56.5	51.9
Agriculture, stock-rearing, hunting, fishing and forestry	2.5	2.4	2.9	4.4	1.0	2.2	—
Energy and water	3.2	3.0	3.1	1.9	2.3	4.8	3.1
Extraction & processing of non-energy-producing minerals, chemicals industry	11.0	8.6	10.3	39.0	14.9	11.2	3.7
Metalworking industry and precision engineering	10.8	10.5	13.1	1.9	12.5	7.0	17.9
Other manufacturing industries	20.8	21.0	23.2	13.0	25.3	14.3	17.3
Construction	6.0	6.9	6.5	3.6	3.4	3.8	5.6
Distributive trades, hotels and catering, repair services	17.6	21.3	15.9	10.7	13.4	14.8	16.0
Transport & communications	6.3	6.5	6.3	6.0	3.7	6.9	6.2
Financial institutions, insurance companies, business services, leasing companies	7.4	5.5	6.4	6.6	9.7	14.0	4.0
Other services	14.3	14.2	12.1	12.9	13.6	20.8	24.7

Source: *Elecciones Sindicales 1986* (Ministry of Labour and Social Security)

TABLE 11

BREAKDOWN OF ELECTED REPRESENTATIVES IN 1986 BY CANDIDATURE AND ECONOMIC ACTIVITY

(% distribution; total per economic activity = 100)

Economic activity	Total	UGT	CC.OO.	ELA-STV	Group of workers	Other unions	Not known
Total	100.0	40.9	34.5	3.3	6.7	14.5	0.1
Agriculture	100.0	39.0	39.8	5.8	2.8	12.7	–
Industry	100.0	38.6	37.5	4.0	8.0	11.8	0.1
Construction	100.0	47.2	37.7	2.0	3.8	9.2	0.1
Services	100.0	42.6	30.9	2.6	5.9	17.9	0.1
Agriculture, stock-rearing, hunting, fishing and forestry	100.0	39.0	39.8	5.8	2.8	12.7	–
Energy and water	100.0	38.1	33.1	2.0	4.8	21.9	0.1
Extraction & processing of non-energy-producing minerals, chemicals industry	100.0	32.1	32.4	11.7	9.0	14.8	0.0
Metalworking industry and precision engineering	100.0	40.0	42.1	0.6	7.8	9.4	0.2
Other manufacturing industries	100.0	41.4	38.5	2.1	8.1	9.9	0.1
Construction	100.0	47.2	37.7	2.0	3.8	9.2	0.1
Distributive trades, hotels and catering, repair services	100.0	49.5	31.2	2.0	5.1	12.1	0.1
Transport & communications	100.0	42.4	34.6	3.2	3.9	15.8	0.1
Financial institutions, insurance companies, business services, leasing companies	100.0	30.4	30.2	3.0	8.8	27.6	0.1
Other services	100.0	40.4	29.2	3.0	6.3	21.0	0.2

Source: *Elecciones Sindicales 1986* (Ministry of Labour and Social Security)

Table 12

BREAKDOWN OF ELECTED REPRESENTATIVES IN 1986 BY INSTITUTIONAL SECTOR AND CANDIDATURE

(% distribution; total per institutional sector = 100)
(excluding the Basque Country)

Institutional sector and candidature	Total	Private enterprise	Public enterprise	State administration	Social security administration	Autonomous administration	Local administration	Not known
All sectors								
Total	100.0	100.0	100.0	100.0	100.0	100.0	100.0	100.0
UGT	43.0	42.4	40.4	41.9	40.9	46.3	59.9	51.6
CC.OO.	36.3	36.7	35.6	26.0	39.4	37.3	29.3	35.8
ELA-STV	0.3	0.3	0.1	–	–	–	0.0	0.3
Group of workers	6.6	7.0	5.5	6.6	3.4	4.3	3.4	4.0
Other unions	13.7	13.6	18.3	25.3	16.4	11.9	7.2	8.2
Not known	0.1	0.1	0.2	0.3	–	0.3	0.2	0.1

Source: *Elecciones Sindicales 1986* (Ministry of Labour and Social Security)

206

TABLE 13

STRIKE TRENDS

Year	Number of strikes	Number of workers participating (in thousands)	Number of working days lost (in thousands)
1980	1,365	1,170.1	6,177.5
1981	1,307	1,126.3	5,153.8
1982	1,225	875.1	2,787.6
1983	1,451	1,483.6	4,416.7
1984	1,498	2,242.2	6,357.8
1985	1,092	1,511.2	3,223.5
1986	914	857.9	2,279.4
1987	1,497	1,881.2	5,025.0
1988	1,193	6,692.2	11,641.1
1988 (Jan-Oct)	1,192	1,894.5	6,843.4
1989 (Jan-June)	863	1,223.4	3,146.6

Source: *Boletín de Estadísticas Laborales* (Ministry of Labour)

TABLE 14

BREAKDOWN OF STRIKES BY ECONOMIC SECTOR

(number of workings days lost, in thousands)

Year	Total	Agri-culture	Industry	Con-struction	Services	General strikes
1980	4,712.5	211.8	2,278.6	1,049.1	1,145.0	28.0
1981	2,792.1	537.6	1,543.5	212.7	390.1	108.2
1982	1,988.6	9.0	1,268.6	367.5	262.7	80.9
1983	3,683.1	635.6	1,296.9	569.9	807.9	372.8
1984	4,229.0	130.5	1,428.1	1,385.4	435.0	850.0
1985	2,272.0	50.0	746.4	158.0	252.7	1,064.9
1986	2,279.4	114.8	872.5	64.5	1,162.2	65.4
1987	5,025.0	68.5	1,491.9	1,143.9	2,068.1	252.6
1988	11,641.1	118.4	1,487.0	2,004.1	3,176.0	4,855.5
1989 (Jan-June)	3,146.6	251.2	1,991.1	75.4	825.2	3.0

Source: *Boletín de Estadísticas Laborales* (Ministry of Labour)

TABLE 15

BREAKDOWN OF STRIKES BY DURATION AND EXTENT, 1986

(excluding the Basque Country)

TOTAL 914

Extent (number of workplaces participating)		Duration (in working days)	
1 workplace	703	Fewer than 6 days	643
2-20 workplaces	131	6-10 days	129
21-100 workplaces	45	11-20 days	71
More than 100 workplaces	35	More than 20 days	71

Source: *Anuario de Estadísticas Laborales* (Ministry of Labour)

TABLE 16

BREAKDOWN OF STRIKES BY CAUSE

	1987	1988
Total number of strikes	1,497	1,193
Disputes arising from the collective bargaining process	**588**	**459**
Pressure to prevent the negotiation of an agreement	174	192
Pressure to prevent the revision of an agreement	19	23
Pressure during the negotiation of an agreement	382	235
Interpretation of clauses of an existing agreement	13	9
Disputes not arising from the collective bargaining process	**823**	**668**
Industrial conversion	30	12
Adjustment of employment (excluding industrial conversion)	40	19
Work organization/work systems	84	132
Industrial accident; health and safety	34	45
Sanctions, dismissals and other disciplinary measures	43	36
Breaches of agreements or regulations	103	73
Non-payment of wages	178	102
Improvements independent of existing agreement	133	122
Collective improvements not based on an agreement	54	21
Other labour relations causes	124	106
Other disputes, not of a strictly labour relations nature	**86**	**66**
Disputes associated with trade union issues	8	7
Sympathy strikes	31	26
Disputes caused by the declaration or application of economic and social policy measures	18	10
Other causes	29	23

Source: *Anuario de Estadísticas Laborales* (Ministry of Labour)

TABLE 17

BREAKDOWN OF STRIKES ACCORDING TO THE AGENT RESPONSIBLE FOR CALLING THE STRIKE
(%)

	1987	1988
Group of workers	18.97	23.05
Workers' delegates or workers' committees	55.38	50.63
UGT	15.63	13.91
CC.OO.	21.78	22.38
ELA-STV	0.53	0.34
INTG	1.80	0.67
USO	1.54	2.01
CNT	0.60	0.67
Other trade unions	4.14	2.77
Other agents	1.80	1.09
Not known	0.07	0.08

Source: *Anuario de Estadísticas Laborales* (Ministry of Labour)

TABLE 18

BREAKDOWN OF STRIKES ACCORDING TO FORM
OF TERMINATION AND OUTCOME

	1987	1988
Total number of strikes	1,483	1,183
Form of termination		
End of period fixed in strike declaration	660	522
Workers' decision	598	550
Total call-off	385	305
Partial call-off	7	9
No call-off	206	236
Direct negotiation between the parties	104	62
Agreement between the parties as a result of		
mediation by third parties	64	25
Mediation by public institutions	63	24
Mediation by others	1	1
Other forms of termination	57	24
Lock-out	17	12
Unspecified	40	12
Outcome		
Agreement reached	652	377
Total acceptance of workers' demands	109	60
Acceptance of virtually all the workers' demands	227	148
Total maintenance of employer's position	8	3
Virtually total maintenance of employer's position	10	7
Compromise	298	159
No agreement reached	811	796
Lock-out	20	10

Source: *Anuario de Estadísticas Laborales* (Ministry of Labour)

212

TABLE 19

INSTANCES OF COLLECTIVE CONCILIATION AND MEDIATION

		Collective conciliation				Mediation
Year	Total	Settlement arranged	No settlement arranged	Failed attempts	Other	Total
1979	—	—	—	—	—	6
1980	—	—	—	—	—	104
1981	2,505	163	1,680	522	140	66
1982	2,247	103	1,418	639	87	64
1983	3,235	193	2,049	801	192	41
1984	2,266	114	1,373	632	147	46
1985	1,779	127	1,066	474	112	80
1986	1,488	130	959	241	158	63
1987	1,691	174	1,107	200	210	436
1988	1,871	197	1,257	206	211	448
1988 (Jan-Oct)	1,529	161	1,022	171	175	416
1989 (Jan-Oct)	1,611	176	1,091	158	186	208

Source: *Boletín de Estadísticas Laborales* (Ministry of Labour)

TABLE 20

PROVINCIAL LABOUR COURTS: TOTAL NUMBER OF CASES DECIDED

(broken down according to type of case and nature of decision)

Year	Type of case				Nature of decision					
	Total	Collective disputes	Individual disputes	Social security	Ruling in favour of the worker	Ruling partially in favour of worker	Ruling against the worker	Concili- ation	Suit abandoned	Other
1978	378,117	500	341,417	36,200	97,317	7,000	43,900	135,800	82,800	11,300
1979	419,783	1,300	384,783	33,700	105,483	10,600	39,200	170,200	82,900	11,400
1980	287,108	1,200	249,408	36,500	113,208	8,900	37,700	58,400	60,200	8,700
1981	268,689	1,200	228,289	39,200	125,089	9,000	39,200	37,600	46,300	11,500
1982	273,982	1,300	217,582	55,100	139,282	9,100	39,400	32,200	42,900	11,100
1983	296,092	1,655	223,330	71,107	148,819	9,459	48,891	27,864	48,377	12,682
1984	312,930	2,019	211,899	99,012	145,724	12,357	63,207	24,141	51,016	16,485
1985	293,077	1,394	190,723	100,960	126,254	11,842	69,112	23,181	48,188	14,500
1986	296,568	1,392	182,691	112,485	124,136	12,939	65,018	21,268	54,285	18,922
1987	293,791	1,439	183,883	108,469	122,797	12,956	64,032	19,983	54,075	19,948
1988	297,964	1,680	206,230	90,054	119,832	16,664	68,565	19,771	53,802	19,330
1988 (Jan-June)	160,905	894	110,115	49,896	66,006	8,349	36,099	10,983	30,774	8,694
1989 (Jan-June)	146,545	856	102,528	43,161	58,802	8,418	35,938	10,697	22,716	9,974

Source: *Boletín de Estadísticas Laborales* (Ministry of Labour)

TABLE 21

RISE OF NATIONAL MINIMUM WAGE

Law	Date of entry into force	For workers aged 18 and over		
		Pesetas		Increase over previous wage (%)
		per day	per month	
Decree 55/1963	1.1.1963	60	1,800	—
Decree 2419/1966	1.10.1966	84	2,520	40.0
Decree 2342/1967	1.10.1967	96	2,880	14.3
Decree 2187/1968	1.1.1969	102	3,060	6.3
Decree 720/1970	1.4.1970	120	3,600	17.7
Decree 496/1971	1.4.1971	136	4,080	13.3
Decree 622/1972	1.4.1972	156	4,680	14.7
Decree 527/1973	1.4.1973	186	5,580	19.2
Decree 797/1974	1.4.1974	225	6,750	21.0
Decree 547/1975	1.4.1975	280	8,400	24.4
Decree 619/1976	1.4.1976	345	10,350	23.2
Royal Decree 2325/1976	1.10.1976	380	11,400	10.1
Royal Decree 458/1977	1.4.1977	440	13,200	15.8
Royal Decree 2499/1977	1.10.1977	500	15,000	13.6
Royal Decree 614/1978	1.4.1978	548	16,440	9.6
Royal Decree 2458/1978	1.10.1978	600	18,000	9.5
Royal Decree 888/1979	1.4.1979	640	19,200	6.7
Royal Decree 2343/1979	1.10.1979	692	20,660	7.6
Royal Decree 1257/1980	1.6.1980	759	22,770	10.2
Royal Decree 1326/1981	1.4.1981	854	25,620	12.5
Royal Decree 124/1982	1.1.1982	948	28,440	11.0
Royal Decree 100/1983	1.1.1983	1,072	32,160	13.1
Royal Decree 3238/1983	1.1.1984	1,158	34,740	8.0
Royal Decree 2299/1984	1.1.1985	1,239	37,170	7.0
Royal Decree 2474/1985	1.1.1986	1,338	40,140	8.0
Royal Decree 2642/1986	1.1.1987	1,405	42,150	5.0
Royal Decree 1681/1987	1.1.1988	1,468	44,040	4.5
Royal Decree 23/1989	1.1.1989	1,556	46,680	6.0

Source: *Anuario de Estadísticas Laborales* (Ministry of Labour)

215

TABLE 22

PAY INCREASES (%) AGREED BY COLLECTIVE AGREEMENT

(Broken down by sector, year of financial effect and registration period. Cumulative data. All agreements.)

Year of financial effect	Total	Agricultural	Non-agricultural			
			Total	Industry	Construction	Services
1981[1]	13.06	11.78	13.19	13.02	13.27	13.38
1982[1]	12.02	10.80	12.17	12.01	12.60	12.27
1983	11.44	10.02	11.56	11.38	11.30	11.81
1984	7.81	7.38	7.85	7.85	7.72	7.89
1985[2]	7.90	7.74	7.91	7.95	6.98	6.03
1986[3]	8.11	7.71	8.16	8.23	8.12	8.09
1987	6.51	6.60	6.50	6.32	6.39	6.70
1988	6.20	6.31	6.19	6.07	6.03	6.35

[1] Excluding Catalonia as regards company agreements, provincial agreements and agreements at a lower level

[2] Introduction of "safeguard clause" pay adjustments as provided for in the Economic and Social Agreement

[3] Provisional figures

Source: *Boletín de Estadísticas Laborales* (Ministry of Labour)

TABLE 23

AVERAGE EARNINGS PER PERSON PER MONTH

(thousands of pesetas)

Year	Total	Industry					Construction	Services			
	All activities	Total	Energy & water	Extraction & processing of non-energy-producing minerals, chemicals industry	Metal-working industry	Other manufacturing industries	Total	Total	Distributive trades, hotels & catering	Road transport	Financial institutions & insurance companies
1983	92.75	93.66	133.99	105.72	99.19	77.40	82.30	95.20	76.98	77.15	142.00
1984	101.35	101.56	141.68	112.13	107.49	85.85	90.82	104.70	84.94	86.57	154.35
1985	111.07	112.77	157.58	125.10	119.48	94.97	95.00	112.84	91.70	93.95	164.61
1986	123.67	126.28	176.71	136.82	133.58	107.06	105.47	124.84	102.59	100.85	178.85
1987	132.45	136.02	185.98	148.44	145.11	114.70	110.65	132.88	108.42	110.35	192.40

Source: Banco de España, *Boletín Estadístico*

TABLE 24

AVERAGE HOURLY PAY

1987 (monthly average)

AVERAGE HOURLY PAY IN PESETAS

ACTIVITY	NON-MANUAL WORKERS						
	Senior management	Middle management	Heads of department	Technical personnel	Administrative staff	Clerical staff	Ancillary & service personnel
All activities	1,832	1,337	1,282	980	856	583	661
Extraction, preparation and briquetting of solid fuels, and coking plants	1,810	1,423	1,122	1,350	889	724	774
Extraction of oil & natural gas. Oil refining. Extraction & processing of radioactive materials	2,435	1,866	1,700	1,319	1,171	994	934
Production, transportation & distribution of electricity & gas	2,421	1,606	1,438	1,223	1,116	931	978
Extraction & preparation of metalliferous ores	1,847	1,319	1,133	979	832	695	691
Production and preliminary processing of metals	2,025	1,289	1,285	1,025	931	720	842
Extraction and processing of non-metalliferous minerals	2,125	1,403	1,238	971	806	549	750
Chemicals industry	2,112	1,544	1,513	1,119	894	671	729
Manufacture of metal products, construction of machinery, mechanical equipment and precision instruments (excluding transport equipment)	1,997	1,369	1,435	1,086	889	606	710
Manufacture of office machinery, computers (including installation) & electrical & electronic machinery & equipment	1,716	1,345	1,275	1,009	876	568	711

Source: *Anuario Estadístico* (National Institute of Employment)

TABLE 24 *(continued)*

AVERAGE HOURLY PAY

1987 (monthly average)

ACTIVITY	AVERAGE HOURLY PAY IN PESETAS						
	NON-MANUAL WORKERS						
	Senior management	Middle management	Heads of department	Technical personnel	Administrative staff	Clerical staff	Ancillary & service personnel
Manufacture of motor vehicles & parts.							
Construction & maintenance of ships.							
Construction of other means of transport	1,880	1,492	1,311	1,205	963	696	885
Food, drink & tobacco industries	1,727	1,297	1,322	961	851	558	669
Textiles industry	1,483	1,229	1,039	783	723	467	537
Leather, footwear & clothing industries & manufacture of other textile goods	1,235	1,119	1,063	910	678	487	558
Timber, cork & wooden furniture industries	1,163	999	906	710	682	465	541
Paper industry & manufacture of paper products	1,920	1,551	1,235	1,060	938	583	728
Printing & publishing	1,749	1,228	1,164	1,041	794	550	653
Rubber & plastics industries & other manufacturing industries	1,870	1,379	1,247	1,117	938	553	775
Construction industry	1,587	1,220	1,046	864	749	534	600
Wholesale & retail distribution, dealers and agents, recovery & recycling of products & repairs	1,437	1,126	1,133	809	684	487	568
Hotels and catering	1,118	915	672	654	576	523	469
Road transport	1,198	770	1,038	720	621	508	511
Financial institutions	2,207	1,875	1,437	1,109	1,077	820	842
Insurance companies	2,031	1,007	1,241	740	906	628	698

Source: *Anuario Estadístico* (National Institute of Employment)

TABLE 24 *(continued)*

AVERAGE HOURLY PAY

1987 (monthly average)

AVERAGE HOURLY PAY IN PESETAS

ACTIVITY	MANUAL WORKERS					Average pay per activity	Average number of workers
	Foremen & supervisors	Grade 1 & 2 skilled workers	Grade 3 skilled workers & semi-skilled workers	Unskilled workers	Apprentices & labourers		
All activities	940	707	647	492	319	795	2,885,799
Extraction, preparation and briquetting of solid fuels, and coking plants	865	1,100	871	637	479	1,022	45,863
Extraction of oil & natural gas. Oil refining. Extraction & processing of radioactive materials	1,399	1,165	941	672	–	1,415	13,865
Production, transportation & distribution of electricity & gas	1,269	1,043	940	716	343	1,226	60,814
Extraction & preparation of metalliferous ores	944	855	744	720	–	909	9,693
Production and preliminary processing of metals	1,062	845	810	607	322	916	89,436
Extraction and processing of non-metalliferous minerals	830	699	631	505	363	739	112,120
Chemicals industry	1,079	840	844	613	–	1,022	142,269
Manufacture of metal products, construction of machinery, mechanical equipment and precision instruments (excluding transport equipment)	993	766	680	516	320	843	281,583
Manufacture of office machinery, computers (including installation) & electrical & electronic machinery & equipment	959	753	683	494	231	839	108,099

Source: *Anuario Estadístico* (National Institute of Employment)

TABLE 24 *(continued)*

AVERAGE HOURLY PAY

1987 (monthly average)

ACTIVITY	AVERAGE HOURLY PAY IN PESETAS						
	MANUAL WORKERS					Average pay per activity	Average number of workers
	Foremen & supervisors	Grade 1 & 2 skilled workers	Grade 3 skilled workers & semi-skilled workers	Unskilled workers	Apprentices & labourers		
Manufacture of motor vehicles & parts.							
Construction & maintenance of ships.							
Construction of other means of transport	1,155	906	800	546	273	929	193,686
Food, drink & tobacco industries	918	768	655	518	275	772	214,599
Textiles industry	921	576	475	429	286	592	128,357
Leather, footwear & clothing industries & manufacture of other textile goods	756	541	434	388	222	531	115,883
Timber, cork & wooden furniture industries	801	531	512	443	265	553	80,094
Paper industry & manufacture of paper products	1,024	821	669	579	421	852	36,445
Printing & publishing	993	731	576	473	333	782	57,804
Rubber & plastics industries & other manufacturing industries	984	728	733	476	288	832	64,090
Construction industry	787	597	548	469	281	659	287,274
Wholesale & retail distribution, dealers and agents, recovery & recycling of products & repairs	981	679	575	494	312	685	409,463
Hotels and catering	757	518	447	435	354	524	119,928
Road transport	592	665	543	493	437	632	62,928
Financial institutions	1,362	986	943	729	400	1,188	218,227
Insurance companies	945	869	656	604	—	1,035	33,278

Source: *Anuario Estadístico* (National Institute of Employment)

BIBLIOGRAPHY

BIBLIOGRAPHY

Economic and social context

For information on the economic and social context of industrial relations in Spain, various basic works can be consulted. An account of the developments undergone by Spain's economic system can be found in the study by J.B. DONGES, *La industrialización en España [Industrialization in Spain]* (Barcelona, 1976) and, with reference to the last few decades, in the collective works *Economía Española: 1960-1980 [The Spanish economy: 1960-1980]* Madrid, 1982, and *La industria española en la crisis: 1978-1984 [Spanish industry in crisis: 1978-1984]* (Madrid, 1989) edited by J. SEGURA. An exhaustive analysis of the present situation of the Spanish economy is given in the collective work *España. Economía [Spain. The economy]* (Madrid, 1988), edited by J.L. GARCIA DELGADO. Specific details on the labour market, pay and incomes policy are provided by the studies entitled *El mercado de trabajo en España [The labour market in Spain]* published annually by the Ministry of Labour; the report compiled in the same Ministry on *El paro: magnitud, causas, remedios [Unemployment: its scale, causes and remedies]* (Madrid, 1988); and the collective works *El trabajo en España: empleo y salarios [Labour in Spain: employment and pay]* (Madrid, 1985) and *Estudios de economía del trabajo en España: salarios y política de rentas [Studies on labour economics in Spain: pay and incomes policy]* (Madrid, 1987). From a more multidisciplinary perspective, there is *Reparto de trabajo y crisis social [Work-sharing and social crisis]* (Madrid, 1986), VARIOUS AUTHORS. For information on living and working conditions, the following can usefully be consulted: *Informe sociológico sobre el cambio social en España (1975-1983) [Sociological report on social changes in Spain (1975-1983)]* (Madrid, 1983), prepared by the Fundación Foessa; the Banco de Bilbao's periodic reports on *Renta Nacional de España [Spain's national income]*, the most recent of which was published in 1987; the study by the Centro de Investigaciones Sociológicas on *Condiciones de vida y trabajo en España [Living and working conditions in Spain]* (Madrid, 1986); and, lastly, the study by the Ministry of Economy and Finance entitled *Análisis de las condiciones de vida y trabajo en España [Analysis of living and working conditions in Spain]* (Madrid, 1988). These topics are also examined in the recent report prepared by the UGT on *Condiciones de vida y trabajo en España [Living and working conditions in Spain]* (1989). The studies by the Ministry of Economy and Finance on *El sector público empresarial [The public enterprise sector]* (1987) and *El Plan de Desarrollo Regional 1989-1993 [The Regional Development Plan 1989-1993]* (1989) are also relevant.

Legal framework

There are numerous studies dealing with the legal framework of industrial relations in Spain, most of them by experts in labour law.

The historical development of this legal system is described in MARTIN VALVERDE's study on *La formación del Derecho del Trabajo en España [The shaping of labour law in Spain]*, published in the collective work *La legislación histórica en la historia de España. De la Revolución Liberal a 1936 [Historic legislation in Spain's history. From the Liberal Revolution to 1936]* (Madrid, 1987). A valuable overall analysis of recent developments and the present situation is provided by the Spanish contribution (written by ALONSO OLEA and RODRIGUEZ-SAÑUDO) to the *International Encyclopaedia for Labour Law and Industrial Relations* edited by BLANPAIN (Volume 8, Deventer, 1988). The present situation in labour and trade union law is also covered in the numerous general books on labour law (including the monographs by ALONSO OLEA and CASAS BAAMONDE, *Derecho del Trabajo [Labour law]* (Madrid, 1988), and MONTOYA MELGAR, *Derecho del Trabajo [Labour law]* (Madrid, 1988); on trade union law (such as the monographs by OJEDA AVILES, *Derecho Sindical [Trade union law]* (Madrid, 1987) and PALOMEQUE LOPEZ, *Derecho Sindical Español [Spanish trade union law]* (Madrid, 1987); and on social security (such as the monographs by ALONSO OLEA and TORTUERO PLAZA, *Instituciones de Seguridad Social [Social security institutions]* (Madrid, 1988) and ALARCON and GONZALEZ ORTEGA, *Compendio de Seguridad Social [Compendium of social security]* (Madrid, 1987). An exhaustive analysis of these regulations from the perspective of labour flexibility can be found in the study by DURAN, MONTOYA and SALA on *El ordenamiento laboral español y los límites a la autonomía de las partes y a las facultades del empresario [Spanish labour law and the limits to the parties' autonomy and to the employer's powers]* (Madrid, 1987).

Industrial relations system
Information on the industrial relations system itself and, in particular, the employees' and employers' representative bodies can be found in the collective work *Empresarios, sindicatos y marco institucional [Employers, trade unions and the institutional framework]* published in Papeles de Economía Española, No. 22, Madrid, 1985, which is compiled from a multidisciplinary perspective. A more legalistic approach is adopted in the studies by GARCIA MURCIA, *Organizaciones sindicales y empresariales más representativas. Posición jurídica y dimensión política [Most representative trade unions and employers' associations. The legal position and political dimension]* (Madrid, 1987) and by ESCUDERO RODRIQUEZ, *Los sujetos de los convenios colectivos de empresa: representación unitaria y representación sindical [The parties to company agreements: workforce-based representation and union-based representation]* (Madrid, 1985), the latter of which is confined to representation at company level. A specific treatment of the public service is given in the study by REY GUANTER, *Estado, sindicatos y relaciones colectivas en la función publica [The state, the unions and collective relations in the public service]* (Madrid, 1987), and a useful source in the Spanish literature dealing specifically with collective bargaining in small and

medium-sized enterprises is the study by VALDES DAL-RE *et al.*, *La negociación colectiva en las pequeñas y medianas empresas [Collective bargaining in small and medium-sized enterprises]* (Madrid, 1982). For a general view of collective bargaining in Spain, with emphasis on the scope, duration and content of collective agreements, it is also helpful to consult the publications of the Ministry of Economy and Finance on *La negociación colectiva en las grandes empresas [Collective bargaining in large enterprises]* (published annually), and of the Ministry of Labour on *Estructura y contenidos básicos de la negociación colectiva en España [Structure and basic content of collective bargaining in Spain]* (Madrid, 1988). A useful compilation of material on collective bargaining experience in Spain, with special emphasis on tripartite and general multi-industry agreements, is given by VILLA GIL, *Los grandes pactos colectivos a partir de la transición democrática [Major collective agreements since the transition to democracy]* (Madrid, 1985). The same subject is dealt with, although from a perspective closer to industrial sociology, political sociology or the theories of human resource management, in the studies by PEREZ DIAZ, *Clase obrera, partidos y sindicatos [The working class, the parties and the trade unions]* (Madrid, 1979); CASTILLO PRIETO, *Condiciones de trabajo. Un enfoque renovador de la Sociología del Trabajo [Working conditions. A fresh industrial-sociology approach]* (Madrid, 1982); ALCAIDE CASTRO, *Las nuevas formas de organización del trabajo [New forms of work organization]* (Madrid, 1983); and GINER and PEREZ YRUELA (eds.), *El corporatismo en España [Corporatism in Spain]* (Madrid, 1988). An overall view of the Spanish industrial relations system, paying particular attention to developments over the last few decades, can be found in the reports entitled *La situación laboral y sindical en España [The labour relations and trade union situation in Spain]* and *Situación sindical y relaciones laborales en España [The trade union situation and industrial relations in Spain]* which were compiled and published by the ILO in 1969 and 1985 respectively. There are studies by the Ministry of Labour and the Ministry of Public Administration dealing, respectively, with *Las Elecciones Sindicales de 1986 [The 1986 union elections]* (Madrid, 1987) and with *Las Elecciones a órganos de representación del personal al servicio de las Administraciones públicas de 1987 [The 1987 elections to representative bodies of employees of the administrative authorities]* (Madrid, 1989). A specific analysis of the characteristics of workforce representatives elected on the UGT slate is given in the study compiled by this major trade union confederation on *Perfil, actitudes y demandas del delegado y afiliado a UGT [The main characteristics, attitudes and demands of UGT delegates and members]* (Madrid, 1989).

Periodicals
Spanish periodicals which cover industrial relations, with varying degrees of specialization, are relatively numerous. For information on the legal framework, problems of its interpretation and implementation and changes in the law, the most important periodicals are *Revista Española*

227

de Derecho del Trabajo (published by Civitas), which appears quarterly and is edited by Prof. ALONSO OLEA; *Relaciones Laborales* (published by La Ley), which appears fortnightly and is edited by Prof. RODRIGUEZ-PIÑERO; and *Actualidad Laboral* (published by Editora General de Derecho), which appears weekly and is edited by Prof. BORRAJO DACRUZ. These last two also incorporate a useful corpus of case law, and the first of them contains, in addition, other types of material such as reports and studies relating in general to the industrial relations system. Details of current legal provisions and case law can also be obtained from the *Boletín del Ministerio de Trabajo y Seguridad Social*, which the Ministry of Labour and Social Security publishes monthly. Statistics on employment, the labour market, collective bargaining, strikes and disputes, legal actions, industrial accidents, social security benefits and, in general, on national economic trends can be found in the *Boletín de Estadísticas Laborales del Ministerio de Trabajo* and *Coyuntura Laboral*, both published monthly by the Ministry of Labour, although the latter is confined more to employment and labour market topics and contains information which is more up to date and, consequently, less processed. These publications are supplemented by the *Anuario de Estadísticas Laborales*, which the Ministry publishes at the end of every year. The review *Economía y Sociología del Trabajo*, which is published quarterly by the Ministry of Labour (edited by J.A. GRIÑAN MARTINEZ), covers labour economics and industrial sociology. Lastly, the review *Estudios de Historia Social* (edited by Prof. ELORZA), which is published quarterly by the Ministry of Labour, contains studies and research on the history of the labour movement, of the industrial relations system and of Spanish labour law. In addition, the *Anuario Estadístico* published annually by the National Institute of Employment, and the *Avances*, the Institute's periodic statements, provide statistics and information relevant to the Spanish industrial relations system. Events and issues in labour relations are usually dealt with periodically in the numerous publications of the trade unions and employers' associations.

ENGLISH INDEX

References are to entry numbers. This index is to be used in conjunction with the list of main entries at the front of this volume.

230

Human Resource Management *see*
  Human Resource Planning
Human Resource Planning 463

Illegal Traffic in Labour *see* **Labour
  Offences**
ILO Conventions 160
Incapacity *see* **Invalidity**
Incomes Policy 474
Index-Linking *see* **Indexation**
Indexation 326
  pay scale 255
Industrial Accident 9
  see also **Health and Safety**
  employers' mutual insurance societies
    397
  social security 555
Industrial Action 381
  see also **Industrial Dispute; Strike;
    Trade Union**
  blacking *see* boycott 69
  blockading of goods 68
  boycott 69
  go-slow 220
  lock-out 93
  occupation *see* sit-in 404
  protest 464
  sabotage 534
  sit in 404
  slow-down 631
  traffic blockade 164
Industrial Democracy 182
Industrial Disease *see* **Occupational
  Illness**
Industrial Dispute 136
  see also **Industrial Action; Strike;
    Trade Union**
  special legal procedure for industrial
    disputes 487
Industrial Federations 271
  see also **Union Structure**
Industrial Peace 443
Industrial Relations 513
Industrial Restructuring 502
  dismissal 201
  economic development areas 502
  employment promotion funds 502
  enterprise plan 460
  priority redevelopment areas 502
  redundancy 202
Informal Economy *see* **Hidden
  Economy**
Information *see* **Rights to Information**
Institute of Social Reform 334
International Division of Labour 221
**International Trade Union
  Organizations** 419

Invalidity 342
  see also **Pensions**
  medical examination 501
  sickness absence *see* temporary
    incapacity for work 322
  temporary incapacity for work 322
Irregular Economy *see* **Hidden
  Economy**

Job 496
  see also **Job Creation**
  description 193
  enlargement 32
  enrichment 250
  evaluation 649
  moonlighting *see* multiple jobholding
    470
  multiple jobholding 470
  occupational job profile 450
  quitting 2
  rotation 533
  security *see* **Job Security**
  -sharing *see* **Job-Sharing**
Job -and-finish 548
"Job Club" 288
Job Creation 277
  economic development areas 277
  industrial restructuring 502
  local employment schemes 329
  older workers 605
  priority redevelopment areas 277
  wage support 39
Job Security 258
Job-Sharing 622
  hand-over contract 147
  part-time workers 604
  partial retirement 354
Joint Work 626

Labour
  international division of 221
  provision of 91
  unit cost 165
Labour Administration 25
  Commission for Social Reform 110
  extension of collective agreements
    268
  Institute of Social Reform 334
  labour authorities 57
  Labour Inspectorate 332
  Ministry of Labour and Social
    Security 387
Labour Charter 291
Labour Code 105
Labour Dispute *see* **Industrial Dispute**
Labour Flexibility 275
  multi-skilling 475

232

234

professional and managerial 171
staffing complement *see* staffing level
465
staffing level 465
Strike 306
see also **Industrial Action**
"abandono de servicio" 1
committee 116
compulsory arbitration 42
declaration 176
essential public services 562
fund 72
general 312
go-slow 220
industrial conflict (level of) 135
intermittent 313
lock-out 93
minimum services 563
notice of 479
picket 458
political 315
replacement of strikers 593
right to 188
rotating 316
safety and maintenance services 561
selective 311
self-regulation of strike action 58
sit-down 308
slow-down 631
stopping work 429
suspension of the contract of
employment 592
sympathy 310
token *see* intermittent 313
wildcat 317
work-to-rule 309
Strikebreaker *see* **Scab**
Sub-Contracting 586
Substitute Workers *see* **Relief Work**
Supervisor 589
**Supreme Council of the Public
Service** 143
Survey of the Working Population 247
Suspension of Employment and Pay
591
fine *see* docking of pay 395
**Suspension of the Contract of
Employment** 592
leave of absence 265
lock-out 592
reservation of post 523
strike 592
suspension of employment and pay
591

Technical Personnel 600
Telework 601

Temporary Incapacity for Work 322
Temporary Relocation 206
subsistence and travel allowances 213
**Termination of the Contract of
Employment** 269
see also **Dismissal**
compensation for 325
end-of-service pro rata entitlements
434
finiquito 274
notice 478
Time Off 453
Tips 493
Trade (Craft) 410
Trade Dispute *see* **Industrial Dispute**
Trade Union 574
see also **Industrial Action; Trade
Unionism; Union Structure**
activity 14
anti-union activity *see* anti-union
behaviour 128
anti-union behaviour 128
assets 439
company *see* "yellow" union 575
craft *see* **Trade (Craft)**
enterprise union 576
freedom *see* freedom of association
368
freedom of association 368
general congress *see* **Union Structure**
general meeting *see* **Union Structure**
influence 52
most representative union 579
pluralism 468
public service union 577
representativeness 520
strength 320
sufficiently representative *see* most
representative union 579
territorial federations *see* **Union
Structure**
union density *see* unionization 573
union unity 642
unionization 573
vertical *see* **Vertical Union**
"yellow" union 575
Trade Union Freedom Act 365
Trade Unionism 567
anarcho-syndicalism 35
autonomous 569
class 568
free 570
national syndicalism 398
occupational 571
Training *see* **Vocational Training**
Transfer 637
internal job transfer 75

236

of undertaking 636
temporary *see* **Temporary Relocation**

Undeclared Employment 632
Under-Age Workers *see* **Minors**
Unemployment 195, 429
  agricultural unemployment benefit
    587
  Community Employment Programme
    235
  cover 104
  long-term 197
  recorded 196
  suitable offer of employment 405
Union *see* **Trade Union**
Union Structure 262
  see also **Trade Union**
  activist *see* trade unionist 572
  ballot 505
  centralization of trade unions 84
  check-off system *see* trade union dues
    173
  executive commission 262
  executive committee 262
  executive council 262
  general meeting 262
  membership or affiliation 28
  multi-plant workers' committee 119
  rank and file 64
  territorial federations 645
  trade union confederations 134
  trade union delegates 179
  trade union dues 173
  union activist *see* trade unionist 572
  union democracy 183
  union discipline 216
  union elections 230
  union official 78
  union rule-book 260
  vote by show of hands 655
  workers' delegates 178
  workers' representatives 519
  workplace branch 551
Unit Labour Cost 165
Unpaid Work *see* **Voluntary Work**
Unskilled Worker 447
  unskilled labour 449

Verification of Illness 650
Vertical Union 581
  infiltration strategy 252
Vocational Training 285
  continuing 282
  Economic and Social Agreement 285
  Employment Training and
    Integration Plan 459
  grant 66

job-training contract 150
occupational 283
occupational job profile *see*
  professional profile 450
professional profile 450
sandwich courses 286
vocational education 287
work experience 476
Voluntary Work 620

Wage 535
  see also **Pay**
  advance 37
  bill 378
  drift 199
  national minimum 547
  occupational category 82
  payment of 428
  social 549
  spread 3
  structure 264
  support 39
  tariffs *see* pay scale tariff 594
Wages Guarantee Fund 279
Women
  employment of 628
  positive action 11
  sexual harassment at work 13
Work 614
  see also **Employment**
  pace of *see* **Pace of Work**
  performed within the family 627
  sexual harassment at 13
  -to-rule *see* **Industrial Action**
  under an employment contract 617
Work Environment 33
  quality of 74
Work Experience 476
  contract 149
Work Organization 416
Work Permit 452
  foreign workers 607
Work-Sharing 517
Worker 403
  performance 514
  professional profile 450
  transfer of *see* **Transfer**
Workers' Control 152
Workers' Limited Company 583
Workers' Participation 437
  see also **Workers' Representatives**
  board of directors 140
  co-determination 106
  consultation 144
  employee share ownership 12
  in public enterprises agreement 22
  workers' limited company 583

SPANISH INDEX

References are to entry numbers. This index is to be used in conjunction with the list of main entries at the front of this volume.

241

244

245